MOSBY

The War Years

By
C.W. Whitehair

∞ INFINITY
PUBLISHING

All rights reserved. No part of this book shall be reproduced or transmitted in any form or by any means, electronic, mechanical, magnetic, photographic including photocopying, recording or by any information storage and retrieval system, without prior written permission of the publisher. No patent liability is assumed with respect to the use of the information contained herein. Although every precaution has been taken in the preparation of this book, the publisher and author assume no responsibility for errors or omissions. Neither is any liability assumed for damages resulting from the use of the information contained herein.

Copyright © 2013 by C.W. Whitehair

ISBN 978-0-7414-8438-3

Printed in the United States of America

Published May 2013

INFINITY PUBLISHING
1094 New DeHaven Street, Suite 100
West Conshohocken, PA 19428-2713
Toll-free (877) BUY BOOK
Local Phone (610) 941-9999
Fax (610) 941-9959
Info@buybooksontheweb.com
www.buybooksontheweb.com

TABLE OF CONTENTS

Reflections and Acknowledgements ....

Early Life 1

The Skills of a Soldier 9

My First Campaign 16

The Beginning of a Friendship 21

Worthy of Promotion 27

A Scout Around McClellan's Army 32

Fear and Respect 41

Virginia and Maryland Campaigns 48

I Never Returned 55

My Command 61

Partisan Operations 70

Capture of a Yankee General 79

April Fool's Day 91

Railroad Raids 103

The Gettysburg Campaign 114

After Gettysburg 125

A Battle in the Snow 136

Anker's Shop 144

Stuart's Death and the Calico Raid 152

Point of Rocks and Mt. Zion Church 160

The 1864 Shenandoah Valley Campaign 170

Retaliation 180

...ds Raids II	193
...aliation II	206
Old Blaze	223
Fiery Trails	230
The Final Days	242
Is It True	250
Mosby References	263

REFLECTIONS AND ACKNOWLEDGEMENTS

One autumn day in mid October 1959, during the 100th Centennial Celebration of John Brown's Raid on Harpers Ferry, I had the privilege of meeting a little lady who lived near the community park in Harpers Ferry. Her name was, Mary Barker. She was over 100 years of age, small and very frail, with long gray hair. But do not be fooled - her memory was very sharp. She remembered in great detail all that her father, mother, and uncle had shared with her about their experiences while living in Harpers Ferry and serving in the Confederate army during the Civil War. Mary had lived in the town all her life. Several times a week, I sat in the little living room of her Gingerbread cottage and listened to her reminisce about her father's experiences while serving in the 2nd Virginia Infantry under General "Stonewall" Jackson, and her uncle's adventures of serving under the "Gray Ghost," Colonel John S. Mosby. Even though I was at a young age, I was already enthusiastic about John Brown's Raid on Harpers Ferry and the Civil War. Her stories, often told with the greatest emotion, moved me to greater enthusiasm. Since those early days of my youth, I have always been interested in studying about America's most costly war.

Over the years, I have written numerous articles for Civil War publications, I have written seven books and one best selling short story for Amazon, entitled, *"The Struggle for Harpers Ferry."* I have had the privilege of speaking at various historical societies, civic organizations, Civil War reenactments, and many other venues over the past seven years. I have had the pleasure of signing books and speaking in many different locations across our great land, always striving to teach others about the war and the mistakes of past societies, that we not tread in that direction again. The greatest honor was speaking to the Midshipmen at the United States Naval Academy in Annapolis, Maryland about the escape of 1,500 federal cavalrymen from Harpers Ferry during the "1862 Maryland Campaign."

Mosby: The War Years is my latest project. I have always been enthusiastic about the experiences and the adventures of Colonel John S. Mosby. What has always intrigued me about Colonel John S. Mosby is that how, with such a small number of men, he could disrupt, confuse, and outwit his adversaries. Mosby was very bold, aggressive, and even undertook risky challenges, such as riding among Yankee soldiers with his prisoners while they were escorting their wagon trains. Mosby's greatest military influence came from the Revolutionary War hero, Francis Marion, the "Swamp Fox." Like Marion, Mosby had no formal military training and never fought his battles in a military manner, but instead used irregular or guerrilla tactics that, some would insinuate, was fighting unfairly by discarding all the rules of war. Mosby's tactics were hit and run, fighting at close range, and laying in ambush for the enemy and then pouncing on them. John Mosby was extremely focused on his objective, very disciplined, and very loyal to the men who served in his command. Mosby and his men lived among the inhabitants of what was known as "Mosby's Confederacy" It is said of Mosby and his men that "they had for us all the glamour of Robin Hood and his merry men, the courage and bravery of ancient crusaders, the unexpectedness of benevolent pirates and the secrecy of Indians." When Mosby loss a man in a fight, it was not only the family's loss, but also his loss as well.

In *Mosby: The War Years*, Colonel John S. Mosby narrates his own adventures and experiences while leading the Forty-Third Battalion Virginia Cavalry during the war. In the book, I have written in Mosby's own words in detail about some of the smaller, but more risky adventurous experiences that he personally encountered. I have relied on the following publications by Colonel John S. Mosby to put together this work. They are *Mosby's Memoirs, War Reminiscences and Stuart's Cavalry Campaigns,* and *Stuart's Cavalry in the Gettysburg Campaign.* I used publications Mosby had written for newspapers, his personal letters, and magazines. I used other resources written by men who served under Mosby and had personal conversations with him. They are: *Reminiscences of a Mosby Guerrilla,* by John Munson; *Mosby and His Men* by J. Marshall Crawford; *Partisan Life With John S. Mosby* by John Scott; *Mosby's Men* by John Alexander and *Mosby's Rangers: Forty-Third Battalion Virginia Cavalry* by James J. Williamson. I also used the *Official Records of the Union and Confederate Armies, Southern Historical Society Papers,* and journals that were recorded by civilians who interacted with Mosby and knew him personally.

Mosby: The War Years includes 17 period sketches and photographs. I would like to thank the Library of Congress, Stars & Bars, Find a Grave, and West Virginia in the Civil War for the use of their sketches and photographs. I would especially like to thank the following individuals for the use of their photographs. Bernie Becker for the use of the photograph of his great-great-great grandfather, Fount Beattie. From the beginning of the war until its conclusion, Fount Beattie was one of Mosby's most trusted friends. I would like to thank Carol Underwood Sharpe for the use of her family's photographs of Samuel and Bushrod Underwood. I would like to also thank Forrest R. Martin for the photograph of Mosby posing with his men.

Finally, no literary work can be published without an excellent editor to dot all of the I's and cross all of the T's. I would like to thank Arlene Pombo for reading, correcting, and giving her input on *Mosby: The War Years*. And I would like to thank Colonel Mosby Whitehair, my six-pound poodle for staying by my side and not raiding everything in the house on long days and evenings while I was working on this project.

Chapter One

Early Life

My name is John Singleton Mosby. I was born on December 6, 1833 at my grandfather's home, Edgemont, in Powhatan, Virginia. My parents were Alfred Daniel Mosby and Virginia Jackson (McLaurine) Mosby. I came from a fairly large family of eight girls and two boys. My siblings were Victoria, Eliza, Lelia, Lucy, Florence, Ada, Isabella, Cornelia, and a brother William. William, or as we called him, Willie was my adjutant, serving in my Command during the war. Unfortunately, two of my sisters, Isabella and Cornelia, died in their youth. It was a very sad time for my family.

When I was in my youth, I was frail and sickly. I was very delicate and often heard from physicians that I would never live to be a grown man. The physicians said I had a tendency to consumption. The prophets were wrong because I have outlived nearly all the contemporaries of my youth. Her concern for my sickly condition sometimes caused my mother to send one of the young servants to escort me to and from school. I could have allowed this condition to overcome me, but I fought back and learned to overcome my sicknesses and my weaknesses. As a man I grew to five foot eight inches tall and weighed one hundred and twenty-eight pounds. I was considered small in stature.

I could have allowed my poor health and my status in society to hinder me, and draw me into shyness and lost esteem, but that did not happen. Instead, I fought back with my good family up-bringing to develop a spirit of confidence, strong courage, a good character, a deep sense of justice, and honesty. I have my mother to thank for my good virtues. She played an important part in my life while rearing me and I will always love her for all that she did for me.

When I was six years old, my father purchased a farm on the Old Lynchburg Road in Albemarle County, four miles south of Charlottesville. Our farm which we called Tudor Grove, was almost four hundred acres. My father was a slave holder, and I still cherish a strong affection for the slaves who nursed me and played with me in my childhood. That was the prevailing sentiment in the South, not one peculiar to myself, but one prevailing in all the South toward an institution which we now thank Abe Lincoln for abolishing. Tudor Grove was prosperous because the land my father purchased was fertile. We grew corn, wheat, oats and raised hogs, cattle, and sheep. We prospered so greatly that my father paid off the debt on the land in a short period of time.

We lived a short distance from Monticello, once the home of Thomas Jefferson, the third President of the United States. I recall standing on a high ridge, out in the peach orchard with my father one clear quiet evening, gazing at the lights in the old mansion's windows. My father told me about some of the history of the man who wrote the Declaration of Independence. While living on my father's farm, I learned how to shoot and became very skillful in the use of a weapon. I found it to be a challenge and sport to hunt game, and made it a point to do so every week. On Saturday mornings, well before daylight, while everyone else in the house was sleeping, I would be awake and dressed to go hunting. One of the servants would already be up and have my coffee prepared for me to drink before leaving the house. I spent long hours hunting game before I would return home. Other than hunting game, I loved to ride horses. Early in life, I learned quite a lot of useful things from my father. The most important of these was learning to ride and handle a horse, and knowing the animal's manner. I learned from my father about a horse's temperament and how to handle them proficiently even in difficult situations. The good use of a weapon and handling a horse would all play into the abilities that I needed when the War of Northern Aggression commenced.

While attending school, I was not a good student when it came to my studies. I was really only interested in history and Greek literature. I enrolled at the University of Virginia in Charlottesville and studied Greek language and literature under Doctor Harrison. While there, I joined the Washington Society, a literary organization, and finished my Greek literature studies with honors.

While at school, some individuals thought of me as a troublemaker because I rode my horse at a fast gallop through the streets of Charlottesville, breaking the city's ordinance. This was not the only episode. On more then one occasion I did get into trouble. During my first year at the University of Virginia, I took part in what was known as a "calathump." A "calathump" was the symbol of great resistance to any kind of authority. During a "calathump" students don a mask and parade along the streets blowing horns and whistles. One night we were in front of the town's courthouse causing such a ruckus. George Slaughter, one of the town's police officers, grabbed one of my friends, threw him to the ground and began beating him. I believed that the brutality against my friend was unjust so I jumped into the fight and began to beat the officer with my fist before finally striking him with his gunstock. For the clash with the police officer, I was arrested and paid a fine of ten dollars.

Another and more serious incident took place in my life on March 29, 1853, while at the University of Virginia. All my life I had to put up with the bullying of kids or as it would be later in life, men much larger than I. Like when I became involved in an episode with George Turpin, a medical student at the University of Virginia. George was athletic and much more muscular than I and he had the reputation of being a bully. The episode began when I invited some friends to a party at my parent's home. John Spooner a violinist, and another musician were hired to play for my party. Those same musicians were also asked to perform for a party at the Turpin's home on the same Saturday evening. When Spooner declined the Turpin's offer, George became angry and threatened that he would eat me "blood raw," on sight. In the past, George had seriously injured Frank Mannoni with a knife and had severely beaten Fred Wills with a rock. It did not appear that Fred would recover, but he did. I took George's threats seriously. I decided I must meet him, settle the matter, and defend my honor as a true Southerner.

One day after morning classes at school, I returned to my boardinghouse for a meal. George had been invited to the meal by a friend who was also boarding at the house. After the meal, I knew matters would be settled. After borrowing a pepper-box pistol, which is a revolver with multiple barrels that when fired, the barrels revolve like a pepper shaker, I waited with two of my friends at the top of the steps outside of my room. I had my hand on the pistol, which was concealed inside of my coat. When George was finished with his meal, he came looking for me. After George ascended the stairway, I said to him, I understand that you have been making some assertions against me? Without a word or warning, George charged me. In what I believed was self defense, I shot him in the neck and was arrested. George lived and I was convicted for shooting him. Even with my friends testifying that it was self defense, I received the more severe penalty of a long imprisonment.

Immediately, physicians, my friends, and family feared that I would not survive a jail sentence of long duration because of my health. It was through their intervention I finally received a pardon from Governor Johnson. Even though I was granted my freedom, the episode greatly affected me and was something that troubled me the rest of my life.

While I was in jail serving out my sentence, I began the study of law. One day, William Robertson, the commonwealth attorney for Albemarle County who prosecuted my case, paid me a visit. He felt that I should try writing to pass the time, but I surprised him with my determination to study law. He agreed and allowed me the use of his library. William became my close friend, spending many hours teaching me the law. After the War of Northern Aggression, he came to my home in Warrenton to help in some of the cases that I was involved in defending. I came to have a great respect and passion for the law. In 1855 I was admitted to the Bar and made it my profession in life.

When I first began practicing law, I went to Howardsville, about thirty miles south of Charlottesville. While there, I met Miss Mariah Pauline Clark of Franklin, Kentucky. To me, she was just Pauline. She was very charming, deeply religious, well educated, and displayed all of the social graces of the time, and was a good conversationalist. Her spirit of confidence was just as strong as mine. Pauline came from an aristocratic family. Her father was an attorney and a gentleman of many accomplishments. He had served as a state legislator, congressman, and candidate for governor. I was very fond of Pauline, so much so that on December 30, 1857, I married her at the City Hotel in Nashville, Tennessee.

Pauline and I both loved literature. We spent countless evening hours by the fireside reading to each other. The only thing that Pauline and I did not have in common was her religious beliefs. She was raised and practiced the Catholic religion. I rarely attended church, but when I did, it was with Pauline at a Catholic place of worship.

Seventeen months after our marriage, we became the parents of a beautiful baby girl, who we named May Virginia. At the time of May Virginia's birth, Pauline and I had moved to Bristol where I continued to practice law. The town of Bristol was divided by two states, Virginia and Tennessee. Pauline and I rented a home and office on the Virginia side. Bristol was a community that held promise for a young couple. The Virginia and Tennessee Railroad, which ran east and the East Tennessee and Virginia Railroad, which ran west caused the town's economy to thrive. Our second daughter, Beverly was born in Bristol on October 1, 1860. Our life as a family was peaceful and content.

After the insurrection of John Brown and his followers at Harpers Ferry, a number of militia companies were organized in both the North and South. It was a time of great anxiety for all of us. The public mind was already strained to a high pitch of excitement, and it required only a spark to produce an explosion. The previous summer I had allowed my name to be added to the muster rolls of the Washington Mounted Rifles. Joining a militia company was considered a civic duty such as one that is asked to serve on a jury. The Washington Mounted Infantry company's captain was William Jones. William Jones would soon be known as "Grumble Jones." By the third year of the war, he was promoted in the Confederate service as a general. General Jones was killed in the Shenandoah Valley at the battle of Piedmont on June 5, 1864.

As the election of 1860 approached, there were four candidates to choose from for President of the United States. Abraham Lincoln represented the Republican Party, John Bell the Constitutional Union Party, and because of a split in the Democrat Party there were two candidates, Stephen Douglas and Vice President John Breckinridge. Senator Douglas represented the Northern view that slavery must not be expanded into the territories and Vice President Breckinridge represented the Southern view of allowing slavery to be expanded into the territories. I voted for Senator Douglas and believe that I was the only citizen to do so in Bristol. As the election turned out, Stephen Douglas did not become the sixteenth president, but instead Abraham Lincoln. Concerning the question of secession, nobody cared whether it was a constitutional right they were exercising or a revolution. Immediately, South Carolina seceded from the Union. Over the winter months of 1861, Georgia, Florida, Alabama, Mississippi, Louisiana, and Texas followed. Virginia still remained in the Union, taking a wait and see attitude.

I was opposed to secession when Fort Sumter was bombarded the following spring in April 1861, by secessionist troops. This act of war dramatically changed things for all of us Virginians. It happened when my state was forced to make a choice because of President Lincoln's call for seventy-five thousand volunteers to put down the rebellion. Virginia refused to meet her call of volunteers placed by the U. S. Government. The indignation aroused by the President's proclamation spread like a wild fire on a prairie, and the laws became silent in the midst of arms. People of every age, sex, and condition were borne away on the tide of excited feelings that swept over the land. All of the pride and affection that Virginians had felt in the traditions of the government, which their ancestors had made, and the great inheritance, which they had bequeathed, were lost in the overpowering sentiment with the people, who were threatened with invasion, the Deep South. It was not until Virginia passed the Ordinance of Secession five days after Fort Sumter was bombarded that I changed my mind concerning my loyalties to the old flag. I considered it my duty to serve my state where I was born and had lived all of my life.

Pauline Clark Mosby
Source: *Courtesy of Find A Grave*

Chapter Two

The Skills of a Soldier

With the commencement of war, Captain Jones called the company together. The men went into camp in a half-finished building of the Martha Washington College in the suburbs of Abingdon. Captain Jones allowed me to remain in Bristol for some time to close up the business I had in hand for clients and provide for my family. For a few weeks, the company drilled in Abingdon and then it was time to depart for Richmond. When I said my farewells to Pauline and the children, it was there that I fought my hardest battle of the war.

It was drizzling rain on May 30, the morning we left Abingdon. I don't think a man was missing. The men were boiling with enthusiasm and afraid the war would be over before they got to the firing line. When we rode through Abingdon, I was very impressed as well as the rest of the company over the town's population filling the street with one continuous ovation. I recall one man who was conspicuous on the march. He rode at the head of the column and got the bouquets the ladies threw at us; but in our first battle, he was conspicuous for his absence and stayed with the wagons. I was riding within listening distance of Lieutenant William Blackford. I recall him saying, "every delicacy the country could afford was spread before us, and we imagined ourselves heroes."

Our company, one hundred strong, spent the next eighteen days heading for Richmond. I had been considered by some in my company to be a slouchy rider, indifferent, and that I took little interest in military drill. That soon changed. On the way from Abingdon, the grief of parting from home and friends soon wore away, and we all were as gay as if we were going to a wedding or a picnic. Gloom was succeeded by mirth and songs of gladness, and if Abraham Lincoln could have been sung out of the South as James II was of England, our company would have done it and saved the country all of the fighting.

We arrived in Richmond on June 17, 1861. At Richmond, and through a friend, Tim Rives, an orator and a gentleman who I had campaigned with for Stephen Douglas, I was offered a commission as a lieutenant by Governor John Letcher. I did not know the rudiments of drill and discipline and therefore, I turned down the promotion. That was not the only reason. I also wanted to serve under Captain Jones. I decided that if I had to remain a private to do so, then I was willing to make the sacrifice of higher rank.

Captain Jones was well respected by those in authority at Richmond. Because of the respect he enjoyed, Captain Jones received some Sharp's carbines. The carbine was a breech-loading weapon that fired three times faster than the muzzle-loaders. I was given one of them, but it also meant that I would be required to take on additional challenging duties. Having the carbine was considered a great compliment to me.

After a few days in Richmond at the fair grounds, the company proceeded north to the camp of instruction for the cavalry at the little community of Ashland. While at the camp of instruction near Ashland, my company drilled with the saber. I really didn't care for the weapon, although, I carried it around for about a year. I found that the thing was only good for cooking, such as holding a piece of meat over a fire. Other than that, sabers were of no use to me against guns. When I received my command, I discarded the weapon and only used pistols.

While at Ashland, my parents visited me and brought me food, which I greatly cherished and was thankful for. Although I had begun to learn to adjust to military life and liked the experience, the food was a different thing. Also, my parents brought a slave by the name of Aaron to serve as my body servant. Aaron cooked, took care of my horse, and attended to my personal needs. He performed these tasks for me throughout the war.

The private soldier usually makes friends with another private soldier or as we called them, messmates. I met a gentleman by the name of Fountain Beattie. I quickly came to appreciate and cherish his friendship. We spent evenings around a campfire reminiscing about home and family and the past that we shared with them. Later in the war when I got my command, Fount as I called him, served under me as a lieutenant in Northern Virginia. We became close friends and cherished our relationship for many years.

Another good friend of mine was Captain Jones. He was a profane, strict-disciplinarian with a competent proficiency in the skill of soldiering and as a commanding officer. Captain Jones possessed a rugged manner, a very impracticable temper, but his heart beat with warm impulses. He had been a professional soldier, graduating from the United States Military Academy. I can still recall sitting many late hours of the evening in his tent talking to him. From Captain Jones, I learned the value of vigilance, enforcement of fair discipline, and exhibiting good management over soldiers. For some reason, he favored me. Why, I do not know, unless it was because I was the smallest and frailest man in the company. Maybe we had both been through a lot before the war. Then too, maybe it was because our greatest strength was in fighting.

* * * *

On July 9, 1861, near sunset, my company arrived in the Shenandoah Valley at a place called Bunker Hill in Berkeley County. The camp was in a little valley. I was impressed with all that I noticed. A business kind of atmosphere prevailed in the camp. It was much different than the military camps around Richmond, where they were very lax in military standards. The tents were in neat and organized rows and the camps were kept clean. Horses were haltered to a picket rope. Headquarters was on a hill overlooking the camp with its flag flying in the breeze.

As we approached headquarters, there were about forty-five men drawn up for inspection. They were going out for the evening on picket duty. A young officer stood in front of the company giving them detail instructions in a clear voice. The officer was dressed in a United States Army uniform. He was Lieutenant-Colonel James Ewell Brown Stuart or as we called him during the war, Jeb Stuart.

Colonel Stuart greatly impressed me. He was above average height, muscular, auburn red hair, blue eyes, ruddy complexion, a full beard, and was the same age as myself. Colonel Stuart graduated from the United States Military Academy in 1854. He possessed distinguishing traits of character, dash, great strength of will, and indomitable energy. That first night in camp, I learned from Private Thomas Colley of my company that Colonel Stuart had already fought Cheyenne Indians at Solomon's River in Kansas.

Private Colley continued speaking of Colonel Stuart. He said that just a few days ago near Falling Waters in Berkeley County, Colonel Stuart used a ruse to capture a company of Yankees of the Fifteenth Pennsylvania Infantry. The Fifteenth Pennsylvania was a regiment of General Robert Patterson's army who had crossed the Potomac River on July 2. Since he was still wearing his blue United States uniform with shoulder straps indicating his rank, he easily deceived the Yankees, ordering them to dismantle a fence to allow his cavalry to pass. When the Pennsylvanians complied with the order then he demanded their surrender. They were quickly surrounded by Colonel Stuart's cavalry and taken prisoner. What was different about Colonel Stuart above many of the other officers that I had come to know, was that he appeared very confident and comfortable in his role as a commanding officer. He displayed sound judgment, quick intelligences to penetrate the designs of an enemy, mingled with brilliant courage. As I observed him on that particular day when we first arrived at the camp of the First Virginia Cavalry, little did I know that I would rise from the ranks to a very close relationship with him.

Colonel Stuart understood the tactics and strategy of modern warfare. The chief function of the cavalry was to learn the designs and to watch and report the movements of the enemy. I believed then as well as now that he never had an equal in such service.

* * * *

Two days later, I participated in my first scouting expedition with Captain Jones. Captain Jones led fifty men from our camp north along what was known as the Valley Turnpike toward the Yankees' camp near Martinsburg, Virginia. On the way at Snodgrass Springs, we came across a small forging party of Yankee cavalry. Immediately upon recognizing who we were, the Yankees fled from the road into a cornfield. Captain Jones chose a squad of five men to chase and capture them. I was one of the five men chosen for the task. Meanwhile, Captain Jones continued to lead the rest of the men toward Martinsburg. The squad I was chosen to be a part of galloped through a wooded area to capture the fleeing Yankees. After a short pursuit, we caught up with two of the scoundrels. A few shots were fired, which injured no one. I must admit, I was scared, but we forced the

Yankees to surrender. Out of all of the prisoners I captured during the war, those first two gave me the greatest joy.

We sent the prisoners back to camp with one of our men and caught up with the rest of our company. The company under Captain Jones came to the Yankees' camp near Martinsburg. The men of my company scoured around in the woods and fields for a full two hours in plain view of the Yankees, and for whatever reason they chose not to attack us. I was disappointed now that I had experienced my first taste of battle. We departed without a fight or the capture of anymore Yankees. On this scouting expedition and the one that I would take the following day, I learned the value and benefits of the local civilian population. They were very detailed in their observations of our enemy and could be relied on for the purpose of spying. They would serve a great purpose to the Confederate Cause.

General William "Grumble" Jones
Source: *Author's Collection*

Chapter Three

My First Campaign

General Patterson's army departed from Martinsburg and advanced to Bunker Hill, which was between Winchester and Martinsburg. For four days we waited for a fight, which did not happen. General Patterson became so fearful concerning his supply line being in jeopardy, that on July 17 he withdrew his forces toward Charlestown, Virginia. Most of us knew that a great many of General Patterson's soldiers were ninety-day men and were about to be mustered out of the service. I felt then as now that General Patterson did his best to avoid a collision with our army.

At 1:00 o'clock in the morning on July 18, General Johnston received a telegram from Adjutant-General Samuel Cooper at the Confederate War Department in Richmond. The telegram informed General Johnston that Brigadier-General Irvin McDowell with an army of thirty-five thousand men was marching from Washington City on our men under General P. G. T. Beauregard at Manassas, Virginia. General Beauregard had a force of twenty-two thousand men along a stream named Bull Run. While our infantry and artillery were heading toward Manassas, we were ordered to protect General Johnston's forces from penetration by General Patterson's infantry and cavalry. In order to properly achieve this purpose, Colonel Stuart placed our men as far in advance of the Confederate infantry brigades and artillery as possible. Our pickets and scouts were so close that we would be able to know if and when

General Patterson and his force would move against us. We believed at the time that General Patterson and his Yankee army would attempt to move between our forces and those at Manassas, hindering the merger of both Confederate forces, but that did not happen.

On the early morning of July 19, most of the First Virginia departed and headed toward Manassas, using the same road that General Johnston's forces had used, which would take us across the Shenandoah River and through Ashby's Gap to Piedmont Station. When we caught up with the infantry and artillery on the way between Millwood to Piedmont Station, we found the road clogged with wagons, limbers, caissons, and cannons. I noticed along the way weary foot soldiers had left the road and were sitting along fence rows to rest or sleep. We had to be conscious enough not to trample any of them and cause injury. To avoid delays and injury to the infantrymen, Colonel Stuart led us through fields that paralleled the roads where we could travel at a quicker gait.

Colonel Stuart had ordered our supply wagons to meet us on the march, but because of the heavy congestion and confusion of the marching Confederate army, they fell far behind us. All of us were very hungry. My good friend and Colonel Stuart's new adjutant, Lieutenant Blackford, was so hungry that he ate a bullfrog a farmer had caught in a creek. Lieutenant Blackford built a fire, cooked the frog and ate all of it. He became very ill and had to fall out of the ranks. It wasn't until the next day that he joined us. But for the rest of us, that first day of march, we went hungry.

That night, we kept moving without stopping to bivouac. Along our way, we had some delays to open fences and cross ditches. We had to be especially conscious not to trample and injure any of the soldiers that had left the road to sleep in the fields. The pace we maintained was not only difficult on the riders, but also the horses. After we arrived at Piedmont

Station along the Manassas Gap Railroad, the cavalry column moved at a greater speed toward Manassas.

When the First Virginia arrived at Manassas on the evening of July 20, Colonel Stuart reported to General Johnston's headquarters. General Johnston had already arrived ahead of us. We were ordered by General Johnston to bivouac along the southern bank of Bull Run Creek, about one mile from a stone bridge where the Warrenton Pike crossed. My company camped at a place called Ball's Ford. All of the horses and soldiers were exhausted and very hungry. Rations were issued, quickly cooked and eaten.

After eating, I settled down for the evening in some broom sedge under a pine tree. Nearby was my messmate, Fount Beattie. As I looked up at the stars in the heavens, I said to Fount that this, perhaps would be our last night on earth. We both knew a great battle would be fought in the morning because several days before, July 18, there had already been a spirited fight at Blackburn's Ford along Bull Run Creek.

* * *

The next morning, Fount and I were awakened to the sound of musketry. We both knew the fight had begun. After a quick breakfast, General Stuart ordered Captain Jones and our company on a reconnaissance across Bull Run Creek. When we counted off, I was number one in the first set of fours, which meant that I would ride at the head of the squadron. This gave me the greatest satisfaction and something I would remember the rest of my life.

A few days before the fighting along Bull Run, Captain Jones had received six Colt pistols. I was one of the six that received one of the weapons. Why, I do not know. Captain Jones informed the six of us that we would be called on for the most dangerous duty. He was not long in fulfilling his promise.

That morning after crossing Bull Run Creek, we came upon a wooded area. Captain Jones called for the six of us that had the Colt pistols. We quickly responded. Captain Jones ordered us to search a wooded area, but there were no Yankees to be found, so we returned to Captain Jones and the rest of the company, re-crossing Bull Run Creek. As the battle continued, I noticed Colonel Wade Hampton's South Carolina Legion was in full retreat. We begged the men to return to their post and do their duty to God and country. They refused and could not be rallied. I thought the Southern Cause was lost. Just then, General Beauregard rode along the lines, assuring the men that the day will be ours. This lifted the spirits of the fighting men.

On June 17, Colonel Jackson was promoted to brigadier-general in the Confederate army. His First Virginia Brigade was in a defensive position on a hill, which took its name from the Henry family. General Jackson was concerned about his right flank and requested cavalry support from Colonel Stuart. Around noon, my company and the Amelia Light Dragoons were placed under Major Swan's command and held in reserve on General Jackson's right flank. For two hours, we sat there on our horses exposed to a perfect storm of grapeshot and balls. The cannonballs burst over our heads, pass under our horses, yet no one in the company was killed or wounded. As the shells continued to burst and explode, I thought of Pauline and May. I removed May's daguerreotype from my pocket. For a moment, her prattling innocence almost unfitted me for the stern duties of a soldier. To keep my mind occupied and off of my family, I rode my horse backward and forward watching the enemy that they did not attempt to outflank our position.

Late in the day, the Yankees gave way and appeared to be in a panic. Captain Jones' company joined the pursuit of the fleeing Yankees, along with the rest of Colonel Stuart's cavalry. Our infantrymen and artillerymen gave shouts of victory as we raced by them in pursuit of the enemy. We chased the Yankees for about six to eight miles until darkness made it impossible to continue the pursuit. The Yankees left everything imaginable behind in their hasty retreat. We took enough arms and accoutrements to equip our army.

As I observed the dead and the wounded on the battlefield, I realized that war loses a great deal of its romance after a soldier has seen his first battle. It is a classic maxim. It is sweet and becoming to die for one's country, but whoever has seen the horrors of a battlefield feels that it is far sweeter to live for it.

That evening, Captain Jones complimented the company and said that we fought like veterans. When I had time after the battle, I knew that this would only be the beginning of a long and trying conflict that would affect every home in both the North and South. That night, the First Virginia camped at Sudley's farm. I slept in a fence corner in a drenching rain.

Over the next couple of days, I wrote Pauline about the details of my first taste of battle. I also informed her that I was uninjured and safe.

Lieutenant Fount Beattie
Source: *Courtesy of Bernie Becker*

Chapter Four

The Beginning of a Friendship

After the first battle at Manassas, Brigadier-General McDowell was relieved of his command and replaced by Major-General George McClellan. In June of 1861, General McClellan had been successful in winning victories at Philippi and Rich Mountain in western Virginia and had thus far been the most successful Yankee general in this short conflict. When General McClellan came to Washington City, he began to organize and train his new force. He called his soldiers the "Army of the Potomac," a name which would become infamous for the rest of the war. When he was ready, General McClellan moved several divisions from his army across the Potomac River into Virginia. Some of those soldiers we soon confronted at Lewinsville.

On September 11, 1861, Colonel Isaac Stevens led an eighteen-hundred-man Yankee reconnaissance force toward Lewinsville, about four miles from the Chain Bridge. It was their intention to examine the grounds in front of Lewinsville with a view of permanent occupancy. We countered with a much smaller force of about three hundred men under Colonel Stuart. When we arrived along their right flank, the Yankees were already retiring. I was thrilled to make contact with them. I immediately took aim at their Colonel Stevens, who was dressed in a fancy uniform and riding a beautiful horse. Colonel Stuart noticed what I was about to do and ordered me not to fire. He made the excuse the officer might be one of ours. I must admit, I never regretted anything more in my life than the opportunity to shoot him.

On September 24, 1861, Colonel Stuart was promoted to brigadier-general and placed over all of the cavalry regiments in our army. Captain Jones of my company took General Stuart's place and was promoted to colonel of the First Virginia. My friend William Blackford was elected as captain of my company. Under the reorganization, we were known as Company D, First Virginia Cavalry.

By middle of October, General Johnston moved his headquarters to Centreville while Colonel Stuart's cavalry moved to within fifteen miles of the Potomac River at Fairfax Court House. At first I thought we were going to attack Alexandria, which was on the Southern shore of the Potomac River, opposite of Washington City, but that did not happen. Instead, the First Virginia served on picket duty at Fairfax Court House. I came to prefer picket duty over the routine and irksome camp life. Picket, or outpost duty as we called it, was where cavalrymen would be placed at strategic locations such as fording areas, road junctions, and roads of importance. The pickets or sentinels would be the first soldiers to sound the alarm of an advancing or attacking enemy force. When our company was on picket duty, we watched the enemy over a twenty-four hour period and then were relieved by another company of cavalry.

Four to six men would be placed in a particular area on picket duty. It could be very dangerous. I can still recall at nights while on such duty from midnight to daybreak, listening to the owls and nighthawks. It could be a lonely place to be. While on outpost duty, Captain Jones preferred we not build a fire for warmth, but some of the men did so anyway. In the mornings, I ate breakfast with the local civilians, becoming more and more acquainted with them. They knew the area roads, paths through wooded areas, the surrounding landscape, and streams. They could also get Northern newspapers. I began to realize the utmost importance that they would serve during the war once I received my command.

At times while not on picket duty, I rode closer to Washington City, which was against the rules of war. One time I was close enough to the Yankees and the capitol that I could hear their drummer boys beating the long roll, and see their fortifications with the stars and stripes floating over it. While taking in my observations of the capitol, I could not help but to feel some regret that it was no longer the capitol of my country, but that of a foreign foe.

During this time on picket duty, I learned many important skills that I would later use during the war when I received my command, like how to ambush the enemy, and when ambushed by the enemy, to shoot low. I remember one such incident that took place. Ten men from my company came onto one hundred and fifty of the enemy's cavalry. We fired on them and retreated before such superior numbers. Then we hid behind some bushes, trees, or anything that gave us good cover and reloaded our weapons. When the Yankees arrived in their pursuit of us, we fired on them again. This happened more than once, but most of the time they would give up the chase.

I learned something very early during the war. Strange events could take place, and without any warning. One day we would be fighting and trying to harm each other and the next, we would have a truce. During those first days of the war while we were close to Washington City on picket duty, I recall one incident. Some Yankees came to my post under a flag of truce. We had supper together and then they asked and stayed all night. We treated each other with as much courtesy as possible. We spoke of wives, sweethearts, children, family, and good times before the war. It was almost as if we had always known each other, but that all changed. The next morning they departed and the war continued.

The cavalry did not have an opportunity to do much fighting the first year of the war. They learned to perform the duties and endure the privations of a soldier's life. My experiences in this school were of great advantage to me in the after years when I became a commander. There was a thirst for adventure among the men in the cavalry, and a positive pleasure to get an occasional shot at a Yankee.

On February 12, 1862, we were relieved of picket duty and on our way back to Centreville. General Stuart joined us. I noticed that an empty carriage was with his escort, but I did not know the reason. We continued on until we arrived at Fairfax Court House, where the mystery of the empty carriage was made known to us. General Stuart asked Captain Blackford to detail a man to go with the carriage to escort two young ladies through our lines to Frying Pan. I was chosen for the detail because I knew the father of one of the ladies and had been previously at his home. Even though it was just starting to snow, I did as requested. After escorting the ladies to their destination, I returned to General Stuart's headquarters at the Grigsby farm. It was dark, several inches of snow had fallen and the wind was still blowing. I informed General Stuart that his orders were completed as requested and that I needed a pass to get by the sentinels so that I could rejoin my company camped along Bull Run Creek.

Instead of issuing the pass, General Stuart said the weather was too bad and I should spend the night. I did not feel the weather was any worse outside than if I had been on picket duty, but I obeyed his orders. I don't know why General Stuart invited me to spend the night at his headquarters. There was nothing special about me in my general appearance that he would make an exception for me. I was as roughly dressed as most any other soldier in the Confederate army.

I took a seat in front of the fireside with Generals Stuart, Gustavus W. Smith, and the commanding officer of the army, General Johnston. I was astonished, I felt insignificant and out of place. I kept quiet, and continued to gaze at the blazing fire. I never uttered a word while the generals spoke in conversation. I would have felt better at trudging back through the snow to camp.

After some time had passed, supper was announced. The generals rose and headed for the supper room. General Stuart invited me to join them, but even though I was very hungry, I remained seated in front of the fire. Again after noticing that I had not joined them, General Stuart sent for me. Only this time I obeyed his request. The generals chatted freely, but I remained silent and did not raise my eyes from my plate. It was an oppressing feeling for me to be in the presence of such high ranking officers, although there was nothing in their manner to produce it. After supper, General Stuart had some blankets spread on the floor for me and I was soon asleep.

The next morning when I rose from a good night's sleep, I was again invited by General Stuart to have breakfast with him and Generals Smith and Johnston. I stayed behind, but he again called for me and this time I complied with his request. This time, I freely committed to conversation with General Johnston. All of the generals spoke freely in front of me about Secretary of War Judah Benjamin and General Jackson. Why I was so privileged and shown such favor by General Stuart on that evening has always remained a mystery to me. It was the beginning of a friendship that would last until his death in 1864.

After breakfast, General Stuart loaned me a horse and sent a courier with me back to my camp. When I arrived back at camp around the middle of the morning, Colonel Jones sent a telegram for me to come immediately to his tent. When I went to his headquarters tent, he promoted me to first lieutenant and made me the adjutant of the First Virginia Cavalry. I was surprised. I had no expectations of receiving such an honor. Along with scouting, which I preferred, I served my regiment in this capacity until April 23, 1862.

General Jeb Stuart
Source: *Courtesy of the Library of Congress*

Chapter Five

Worthy of Promotion

In early March, General Johnston moved his army from Centreville, south to the Rappahannock River. During the movement, my regiment was the rear guard of the army. On the way, we destroyed bridges and trestles. The regiment continued to scout and do picket duty, acting as the eyes and ears of the army.

On March 26, a considerable Yankee force was marching along the Orange and Alexandria Railroad near Warrenton Junction, about seven miles from General Johnston's defensive position along the Rappahannock. I was on a nearby hill and observed the Yankees' advance. When they were near our picket post along Cedar Run, their cavalry came close to the men from my old company. There was a brief skirmish. My old company held them off with their carbines. The Yankees fled in the wildest confusion. I observed one Yankee soldier thrown from his horse into the water. The water was over his head. He scrambled out of the water and left his horse. Another horse fell, rose, and fell again, burying his rider with him under the water. We ceased firing, we rejoiced, we tossed our caps into the air and indulged in the most boisterous laughter. As for the Yankee infantry that followed, it was the most magnificent sight I had ever seen. I watched them move into battle line formation in a large open field and make a great display. They began shelling our position with their artillery and we withdrew. This left the way open for the Yankees to cross

Cedar Run and head toward Warrenton Junction. That night my regiment camped near Bealeton Station.

The next morning, I rode over and spoke with General Stuart. The general and I had become friendlier since that snowy, cold night when I had supper at his headquarters. Since that time, he had been frequently using me for scouting duties. When I saw General Stuart, he appeared puzzled. He earnestly said to me, "General Johnston wants to know if McClellan's army is following us, or if this is only a feint he is making."

This was an opportunity I had longed for. I answered, "I will find out for you if you will give me a guide." General Stuart gave me the guide I requested and two other soldiers to go with me on the mission. As the Yankees marched south toward the Rappahannock River, my scouting party rode along their flank and then we headed north, gaining the rear of their force. It did not take long before I discovered that the Yankees were not part of a large army, but instead were completely isolated. I was glad to make the discovery. It was clear the Yankee column was a diversion. The corps of Yankees who had been before us was under the command of General Edwin Sumner. General Sumner commanded the Second Corps of the Army of the Potomac.

When I returned to our lines, I found General Stuart. He was with General Richard Ewell. General Ewell had already drawn his division up in line of battle along the Rappahannock River ready to receive battle from General Sumner's Yankees. I informed General Stuart the Yankees did not have a supporting force and they were falling back, leaving only some cavalry behind. General Stuart gladly received the news. General Stuart ordered our regiment in pursuit of the Yankee cavalry. We captured thirty of the scoundrels and sixteen of their horses.

General Stuart later wrote in his report to General Johnston that I had "volunteered to perform the most hazardous service, and accomplished it in the most satisfactory and creditable manner." He also added that I was "worthy of promotion."

* * * *

On April 2, General Stuart learned from a civilian that General McClellan's forces were departing on transports from Alexandria along the Potomac River. Three days later, the advance regiments of General McClellan's forces disembarked at Fortress Monroe located at the tip of the Virginia Peninsula. General Johnston was sure then that General McClellan was going to take the back door to try and capture Richmond with his one hundred thousand man army. Our army was on the move to defend the capital of the Confederacy.

On our way to the Virginia Peninsula, the First Virginia Cavalry marched through Richmond. Captain Blackford of my old company was excited to see the great numbers of people who had assembled on the streets of Richmond to see General Stuart and his now famous cavalry pass through their city. The windows, doors, and sidewalks were crowded with ladies waving their handkerchiefs.

Once through Richmond, we camped for the night and then the next day moved to within five miles of Yorktown, the place where General Washington received the surrender of the British army under Lord Cornwallis to end the American Revolution against England.

The Confederate Congress had passed a law where officers below the rank of general could be elected by the men of the regiment. So while my regiment was at Yorktown, the First Virginia reorganized by electing new officers. In the vote, Colonel Jones lost his position commanding the First Virginia. He left for Richmond, expecting to be promoted to brigadier-general, but instead was transferred to the Seventh Virginia Cavalry. Lieutenant-

Colonel Fitz Lee, General Lee's nephew, was promoted to colonel of my regiment.

Within an hour after the election of officers, I handed in my resignation to Colonel Lee. I did not feel that Colonel Lee thought too highly of me. At one time, he had threatened to have me arrested because I called a bugle a horn. If I was not going to be his first choice then I would give up my commission. When I look back on this episode in my life, had I not resigned my commission as lieutenant on the spot where Lord Cornwallis surrendered his sword, I might have never had a command.

After I resigned my commission, I was now a private. I immediately went to General Stuart's headquarters, where I found favor with him. General Stuart assigned me to his personal staff as a scout and courier. This was only the beginning of becoming a partisan. On April 21, the Confederate Congress passed the Partisan Ranger Act, which authorized the organization of units to conduct guerrilla style military operations behind enemy lines. The new organizations would be part of the army, operating under the same regulations, given the same rations, and pay. Only the partisans would be allowed to keep and split all that they captured from the enemy.

The Confederate army gave up Yorktown without a fight because General Johnston believed that it was a death trap to his army. On our retreat toward Richmond, rains caused muddy roads and slowed our army down considerably, but it would also slow General McClellan's army in their advance. We moved up the peninsula and along with General Longstreet's division fought a bloody rear guard fight at Williamsburg on May 5.

Neither General Johnston nor President Jefferson Davis wanted a siege of Richmond by General McClellan's approaching army. Our army needed the opportunity to strike General McClellan's army. That chance came at the battle of Seven Pines, which was fought on May 31 until June 1. Two

Yankee corps under Brigadier-Generals Erasmus Keyes and Samuel Heintzelman had been isolated on the south side of the Chickahominy River from the rest of General McClellan's army by heavy rains that caused the river to flood. We had our chance and took it by attacking the Yankees. Our assaults on the Yankees were not too well coordinated. Both sides continued to bring up reinforcements for the struggle, but the two-day fight ended without a decisive victory for either side. During the fighting at Seven Pines the cavalry was of little use. The reason was that the terrain was so wooded that it did not allow for us to maneuver. At the battle of Seven Pines there were over six thousand casualties from our army. One of those casualties was General Johnston. He had been wounded by a shell fragment in the chest. The next day, President Davis gave General Lee command of our army.

Chapter Six

A Scout Around McClellan's Army

In early June 1862, General McClellan and the Army of the Potomac were still close to Richmond. General McClellan's forces were on each side of the Chickahominy River. The right flank of the Army of the Potomac rested on the Pamunkey River although there was a several mile gap between General McClellan's left and the James River. The two armies were so close that our cavalry could not operate; therefore, our cavalry was inactive and kept behind the main Confederate line of defense. At the time, we were positioned along the Richmond and York River Railroad about two miles behind our main army and about the same distance from Richmond.

During the early morning hours of June 9, General Stuart sent for me to have breakfast with him. I arrived at his headquarters, a farmhouse just north of Richmond. When I arrived and was seated, General Stuart dismissed his staff. During our breakfast of bacon and cornbread, General Stuart informed me that General Lee was considering an offensive on the north side of the Chickahominy River. General Stuart asked me to find out if General McClellan's forces were fortifying along the Totopotomy, a creek that empties into the Pamunkey River. I was glad for the assignment because it was the very thing that I wanted to do.

General Stuart gave me three men from my old company for the assignment. On the road that we chose, we found a flag of truce between our side and the Yankees so we had to take another direction, a wide detour, moving further north toward Hanover Court House. I did not want to go back to General Stuart without doing something. The scouting party never did get to scout along Totopotomy Creek, but we did get to scout on the south side of the Pamunkey River. I ask questions of civilians living in the area and was told that the supply line on the Richmond and York Railroad was thinly guarded by Yankee cavalry. The information that I discovered was worth more than if had I been able to proceed in the direction of Totopotomy Creek. We were able to penetrate General McClellan's lines and discover that for six to eight miles, he only had cavalry pickets guarding his lines of communications with his supply depot at White House along the Pamunkey River. There was no Yankee infantry. It was just as the local civilians had told us. It seemed to me that there was an opportunity to strike General McClellan a blow. He apparently had not anticipated a strike by our forces in this area of his flank because he had not made provisions for defending it. With the information and discovery, I hastened back to General Stuart's headquarters.

It was a very hot day when I returned to General Stuart's headquarters. He was sitting in a chair in the front yard under some trees. I was tired from the journey and lay down on the grass. I used my finger as a pencil to sketch roads and landmarks on the ground concerning the discoveries of my scouting mission. I also told him all of the information that I had learned from the local civilians. General Stuart listened with interest to my story and told me to go to the adjutant's tent and write it all down. I complied with his request. When I returned with my report, General Stuart went off at a gallop to General Lee's headquarters at the Dabbs' farm.

Generals Lee and Stuart came to an understanding and a plan was formulated. The plan called for a force of cavalry to head north and then east to determine for certain General McClellan's troop disposition and strength north of the Chickahominy River. We were also to disrupt and if possible destroy General McClellan's communication and supply line south of Pamunkey River. General Stuart selected twelve hundred men who were well equipped and had good horses. They came from the First and Ninth Virginia regiments along with several squadrons from the Fourth Virginia regiment. Also joining the force was the Jeff Davis Cavalry Legion from Mississippi and an artillery section from the Stuart Horse Artillery.

* * * *

    Early on the morning of June 12, I was at headquarters when General Stuart was about to leave. An officer asked him when he would return. General Stuart replied, "It may be for years, it may be forever." His spirits were high.
    General Stuart placed Colonel Fitz Lee in command of one-half of the cavalry column and Colonel W. H. F. Lee was in command of the other half of the cavalry column. Colonel Fitz Lee was General Lee's nephew and Colonel W. H. F. Lee or as he was known to us, Rooney, was the son of General Lee.
    General Stuart and the cavalry column began an adventure that would make his name famous. In days to come, he would be hailed as a hero.
    General Stuart wanted to give the impression to the many Northern spies in Richmond and to even our own loyal Southerners that his cavalry force was heading to the Shenandoah Valley to reinforce General Jackson. Once we departed Richmond, we marched north along the Brook Turnpike toward Ashland. I rode with my old company. I knew where we were going, but said nothing to any of my comrades. After about a twenty-two miles march from Richmond, our cavalry halted and camped for the night on the Winston's farm near Taylorsville.
    On June 13, the march resumed on the Old Church Road. I was ordered by General Stuart to scout ahead of the main

cavalry column. I was filled with enthusiasm to be selected for such duty and to know that I had General Stuart's full confidence in my ability. I rode with a few men across the same road that I had used four days before.

When we came into sight of Hanover Court House, I observed about one hundred and fifty Yankee cavalrymen near the village. We halted, but did not run away from them. I sent one of the men assigned to me back to General Stuart to report to him about the Yankee cavalry's presences. When the Yankees sighted us, they turned and departed from the village. I was sure they believed that our main column was not far behind. I found out later that same day that General Stuart had sent Fitz Lee with my old regiment on a round about way in the attempt to cut-off the Yankees and capture them, but Fitz Lee's efforts came to naught when he and his men got caught up in a swamp.

No serious resistance by the Yankee cavalry regiment was offered until they reached Totopotomy Creek where the ground had greater advantages for them to fight. The road that we were on passed through a deep ravine whose banks were fringed with laurels and pine. The road was narrow and only allowed us to attack the Yankees in columns of four. There were many of us and our forces outflanked the Yankees, causing them to give up the advantageous position and fall back to a junction of the road which leads by Bethesda Church to Mechanicsville. Again, the Yankees prepared to fight. General Stuart ordered a charge. Captain Latane was in command of one of the squadrons, the Essex Dragoons of the Ninth Virginia. They were leading General Stuart's cavalry column. Captain Latane ordered his squadron to charge. Captain Latane was shot and killed while leading his squadron. After a brief struggle, the Yankee cavalry retreated.

We found out through some captured Yankee prisoners that their regiment was camped not too far away. When we arrived at the Yankee regiment's camp, we found it deserted.

The Yankees left in haste because their tents, camping utensils, and commissary stores had been left behind. We knew that we had broken through General McClellan's cavalry screen.

While our men were plundering the Yankees' camp, General Stuart spoke with Colonels Fitz Lee and Rooney Lee. I was sitting on my horse, buckling on a newly captured pistol near General Stuart and the two Lee's. I could hear their conversation. General Stuart wanted to urgently press on to Tunstall's Station, along the railroad, which was nine miles ahead. Only Colonel Rooney Lee agreed with the idea.

General Stuart's decision to press on proved to be a wise one. He was a brave and gallant officer, willing to take certain risk. Before General Stuart gave the order to march, he turned to me and said, "I want you to ride on some distance ahead."

"All right, but I must have a guide; I don't know the roads," said I.

General Stuart gave me two cavalrymen who were familiar with the roads. My horse that I had been riding was so broken down that I had to borrow another horse which happened to be slow. We had not gone far when General Stuart sent a staff officer with the order to increase the distance between us and the main cavalry column. The reason for his request was that he did not want to run into an ambuscade.

It was important for us to reach the railroad depot before dark and before any Yankee infantry or cavalry arrived. On the way, my men and I came upon a sutler's wagon. Sutlers were civilian merchants who traveled with the Yankee army and sold soldiers all kinds of tempting delicacies, which the army did not supply. The sutler who we came across had things that I had not seen in two years. While we exercised our right to search the sutler's wagon, I noticed not more than a mile away two schooners at anchor in the Pamunkey River unloading supplies to a wagon train for General

McClellan's army. I immediately sent one of my men back to inform General Stuart of the prize that I believed awaited our capture.

Tunstall's Station was still two to three miles ahead. I left my other comrade in charge of the captured sutler's wagon and dashed ahead alone to Tunstall's Station. When I turned a bend in the road near Tunstall's Station, I noticed a cavalryman around another sutler's wagon a few yards away. The cavalryman was dismounted. I approached and ordered the cavalryman and the sutler to surrender. They complied with my demand. Suddenly, I heard a bugle and then a company of Yankee cavalry appeared a few hundred yards off. My horse was pretty well rigged out. I was in a predicament as to what I should do. I thought there would be more danger in trying to escape the Yankee cavalrymen than to stay where I was, so I concluded to play a game of bluff. I immediately drew my saber, turned around, and beckoned with it to imaginary followers. I cried out in a loud voice, here they are Jeb and come on boys, come on. Just as I did, Lieutenant Robins, commanding General Stuart's advance guard arrived at a fast trot. The Yankee cavalry before me, which I have since discovered was the Eleventh Pennsylvania, retreated without firing a shot.

As General Stuart and the rest of the cavalry arrived, a train of loaded cars came into sight with Yankee infantry on board. We quickly placed logs on the track to stop the locomotive. The engineer discovered the danger and quickly began to press his locomotive at full speed. Our men began to pour fire into the train from both sides of the track. Some of the Yankees jumped from the train and were captured.

White House was the large supply depot for General McClellan's army. White House was four miles away from Tunstall Station. It was tempting to make the attempt to destroy General McClellan's supply depot, but it was guarded by gunboats, and their infantry was not too far away. So, at Tunstall's Station we rested for a brief period of time and cut the telegraph wires. This also gave our cavalry column time to close ranks before moving on.

We pressed on from Tunstall's Station. We found large encampments of army and sutler wagons. I must say that many of those sutlers were ruined that night. With sad hearts, they were made to fall in line with our prisoners and witnessed their wagons and contents vanishing in flames. The expedition was a carnival of fun. Nobody thought of danger or of sleep, when champagne bottles were bursting and Rhine wine was flowing in abundant streams.

At dusk, our cavalry column moved through New Kent. We crossed the Chickahominy River where we had already crossed once, but knew that by dawn we would have to cross it again. When we reached the Chickahominy River around daylight, the river was un-fordable. General Stuart was not disappointed or discouraged and did not appear to be the least amount anxious. He was just as full of hope and joy as when we left the Yankees' captured camp near Hanover Court House. General Stuart had two guides with him by the name of Christian and Frayser, who knew all of the roads and crossings along the Chickahominy River. One of the guides knew of a bridge downstream about a mile. We headed in that direction only to discover the bridge was also destroyed by the flooding water. Luck was with General Stuart on this expedition. There were several men in the ranks who knew how to build bridges. One of them was an older gentleman by the name of Redmond Burke. He was a canal stonecutter from Harpers Ferry, Virginia, who served as a scout such as I was with General Stuart. Nearby we discovered the remains of an old warehouse, which we tore down. Redmond Burke and his men used the wood to build a new bridge across the river. It was not the best bridge, but it served our purpose.

While the bridge was being constructed, General Stuart was lying along the bank of the river in the gayest humor that I had ever seen him in. He did not display any concern or oppression. During the night, I had foraged among the sutlers and brought off a lot of their stores. I spread a feast for us to enjoy. Our fare included beef, candy, fruit, cakes, and Rhine wine. It was a carnival of fun that I will never forget. The enemy did not appear during this time. When the bridge was finished, we crossed and then destroyed it so the Yankees could not have the benefit of using it.

About the time that we fired the bridge, the first Yankee cavalry arrived, but it was too late for them to interfere with us in anyway. Our cavalry column moved on, but we were not out of danger. We were still thirty-five miles from Richmond and had to pass through a swamp. I can still recall how the horses sunk to their saddle girths. Then after leaving the swamp, we had to ride a good ways within view of the Yankee gunboats. When we reached Charles City Court House, our cavalry column was halted, ordered to rest, and feed our horses. We knew the road to Richmond was open. General Stuart left Colonel Fitz Lee in charge of the cavalry and rode on to Richmond to report to General Lee. The cavalry column moved again at moonlight and arrived back in Richmond by daylight. I rode in front the whole time.

The cavalry column was gone four days on this raid. This raid was unique, and distinguished from all others on either side on account of the narrow limits in which it was performed. From the time when we broke through General McClellan's lines until we had passed entirely around him, we were enclosed by three un-fordable rivers, without bridges, one of which it was necessary for us to cross.

General Stuart allowed me to keep the horses and equipment that I had captured, which were worth three hundred and fifty dollars in Yankee money. I also captured a carpet from a Yankee officer's tent, which I sent to Pauline. When the *Richmond Times Dispatch* newspaper reported my part in the expedition, they said that I was "a gallant lieutenant." I was still only a private. After the raid, General Stuart recommended to Secretary of War George Randolph that I should receive a commission as captain of a company of sharpshooters.

As soon as I could, I wrote Pauline and told her a great many things I had done on the raid. I wrote the raid was something that I helped to execute, and was the first to conceive and demonstrate that it was practical. Our hometown newspaper in Abingdon wrote about me after the scout and raid. The newspaper said, "Mosby is evidently of the same stuff Morgan and Ashby and such men are made of." I believed that partisan warfare was the only way for me to contribute effectively to the Southern cause.

CHAPTER SEVEN

Fear and Respect

From June 25 until July 2, 1862, our army under General Lee fought a string of battles against General McClellan's Army of the Potomac. On June 25, Major-General Ambrose P. Hill's division fought valiantly against the Yankees under Major-General Fitz John Porter's Fifth Corps at Beaver Creek Dam near Mechanicsville. General Jackson and his army from the Shenandoah Valley were supposed to support the attack on the Yankee's flank, but General Jackson failed to accomplish his part in the assault. We were unable to defeat General Porter's men and suffered great loss in the endeavor.

The next morning when General Hill renewed the attack, the Yankees were gone. They had retreated to Gaines' Mill. Our men followed. Again our force attacked the Yankees at Gaines' Mill. After a very costly struggle, our army drove the Yankees back. The battle was the turning point in the campaign for General Lee and the Army of Northern Virginia. General McClellan's army began to retreat toward Harrison's Landing along the James River. While General McClellan's army was heading toward Harrison's Landing, three more battles took place before General McClellan took a final stand and held our army at Malvern Hill. Malvern Hill was a costly battle for us because we did not gain one single inch of land from the Yankees. They held a hill that was impregnable against our disjointed attacks. Not only did they hold the high ground, but their gunboats on the James River added to the slaughter of our forces.

By July 7, our army fell back closer to Richmond and away from the Yankee gunboats. This move allowed for us to be closer to our supplies.

After the Virginia Peninsula Campaign, another great threat was poised against Richmond. While General McClellan's Army of the Potomac was inactive against our army and still camped around Harrison's Landing under the protection of their gunboats, General John Pope's new Army of Virginia was advancing toward Richmond by way of Culpepper County. General Pope had been successful in the western theater of the war. General Pope liked to boast about his accomplishments, such as his capture of New Madrid, Missouri and Island Number Ten. These victories were the reason that Abraham Lincoln brought him east.

I was at headquarters in Hanover County, north of Richmond when I heard of General Pope's declaration. General Pope proclaimed, "In the West he had seen only the backs of his enemies, and that he would only look to his front and let his rear take care of itself." I saw the opportunity for which I desired. General Pope had opened a promising field for partisan warfare, and had invited anybody to take advantage of it. When I was a young lad in school, I was always interested in the Revolutionary War hero, Francis Marion. Francis Marion was called the "Swamp Fox." His method of warfare was irregular. He attacked British regulars quickly with a small force of men and then just as quickly withdrew from the field of battle. With a small force of twelve men, I wanted to make the harvest where the laborers were few, and do for General Pope what he would not do for himself, take care of his rear and communications.

My partisan operations would be in areas of Northern Virginia that I was familiar with like Fairfax, Loudoun, and

Fauquier Counties. I had knowledge of these areas since serving there the first year of the war.

When I made my request to General Stuart for the chance at partisan warfare, he refused to grant it. I was surprised. General Stuart said he needed all of his men for the upcoming campaign against General Pope's army. I was greatly disappointed because I saw the opportunity to do something effective for our Cause. Instead, General Stuart gave me a letter to General Jackson, who liked the partisan idea. General Stuart believed that General Jackson would furnish me with men from his command and allow me to carry out my operations.

On July 19, I accepted General Stuart's letter of introduction. General Stuart said of me in his letter that I was bold, daring, and discreet, and the information that I would be able to obtain for General Jackson would be valuable. General Stuart also sent a courier with me by the name of Mortimer Weaver. Mortimer Weaver was from Company H, Fourth Virginia Cavalry of Fauquier County. But before reporting to General Jackson at Gordonsville, I decided that I wanted to visit my parents for a few days. Pauline was there and it would also give me some time to spend with her.

When Mortimer Weaver and I left General Stuart's camp, we rode almost to Beaver Dam Station. There, we had supper and spent the night with a farmer. The next morning, Weaver departed from the railroad depot with my horse and headed for General Jackson's camp. I wanted to look my best for Pauline and the family, so I wore my best uniform with a plume in my hat. When I arrived at the depot, I laid my two Colt pistols and haversack with General Stuart's letter of introduction to General Jackson in the depot storage room. Suddenly someone shouted, "Here they are."

I stood and looked off in the distance. A Yankee cavalry regiment was about one hundred yards away, coming toward me at a trot. Without hesitation, I took off running, but did not get too far before they captured me. The Yankees were a detachment under Lieutenant-Colonel Judson Kilpatrick of the Second New York Cavalry. The Yankees confiscated my pistols, haversack, and letter from General Stuart to General Jackson. They did however allow me to keep Napoleon's Maxims, which was a present from General Stuart to General Jackson. This was the first time that I met Lieutenant-Colonel Judson Kilpatrick. Later during the war, he became a brigadier-general in the cavalry. I informed him that a train loaded with Confederate infantry and artillery was due to arrive at the depot any minute. The Yankees did not hesitate, but left in a hurry, taking me with them as their prisoner.

    I was taken to Fredericksburg where I was interviewed by General Rufus King. I must say I was treated with the utmost courtesy by the Yankees and allowed to write Pauline a letter. General King had my letter to Pauline passed through the lines.

    At the time of my capture, I was wearing a uniform with the rank of captain. Since General Stuart had recommended me for promotion after our raid around General McClellan's army, I believed it was going to happen. Maybe, this is why I was sent to Washington City and imprisoned at the Old Capitol Prison. I was there for ten days, keeping up my habit of scouting and spying before being exchanged.

    The transport that I was on, along with hundreds of other prisoners who had been exchanged began the journey down the Chesapeake Bay to Hampton Roads. While arriving at Hampton Roads, none of the prisoners were allowed on deck, so I observed through a port hole as much as I could concerning any Yankee army or naval operations. I soon learned the other transports at Hampton Roads were carrying Yankee soldiers under Major-General Ambrose Burnside. They were soldiers of the Ninth Corps. I reasoned that if these transports were carrying Yankee troops up the James River then they would be used to reinforce General McClellan and the Army of the Potomac. This meant General McClellan would attempt to undertake once more operations against General Lee and the Army of Northern Virginia. If the transports with the Yankee troops moved up the Chesapeake Bay then this meant they were going to be used to reinforce General Pope and his Army of Virginia. If the Yankee troops on the transports did indeed move up the Chesapeake Bay this would also mean General McClellan would no longer pose a threat to Richmond: that his offensive operations were finished.

There were several officers of high rank on my ship. I did not confide my thoughts to them, but I was surprised that they did not take greater notice of the transports carrying Yankee soldiers than what they indicated. I had made good use of my time since leaving imprisonment. During our journey down the Chesapeake Bay from Washington City, I became good friends with the captain of our transport. I found out that he was a Southern sympathizer from Baltimore. When we arrived at anchor, the captain went ashore to learn his orders. I used my friendship with the captain to my advantage. I gave him five dollars in Yankee greenbacks and asked him to purchase a dozen lemons for me. I also asked him to find out where the transports were heading with the Yankee troops. Later, when he returned to the ship, he whispered, "Aquia Creek, on the Potomac."

I was so anxious with the news I had learned from the captain that I could not sleep that night. The next day, my transport headed up the James River to the point of prisoner exchange at Aiken's Landing. When we arrived at the landing around 10:00 o'clock in the morning, I was the first to leave the ship. I approached one of the Confederate Exchange Commissioners, Judge Culd, and informed him that I was carrying important news for General Lee. The commissioner allowed me to be exchanged first.

It was about twelve miles and over the dustiest road that I ever traveled to General Lee's headquarters, which was still located at the Dabbs' house near Richmond. It was a very difficult journey. At one point, it was very hot and humid. I was very exhausted and footsore and had to lie down along the road. I would not have made it to General Lee's headquarters if it were not for a cavalryman from the Hampton South Carolina Legion. The cavalryman, whose name I do not know, seeing my dilemma, placed me on his horse and took me to his camp, which was about one-half mile away. I was very anxious to get the information I had obtained to General Lee's headquarters. I did not rest at the cavalryman's camp. As quickly as possible, I obtained another horse. The cavalryman who helped me rode the rest of the way to General Lee's headquarters with me.

When I arrived at General Lee's headquarters, I told a staff officer who was seated on the porch that I had valuable information for General Lee and requested to see him immediately. My request was denied. My appearance was rough-looking because I was covered with dust and in shirtsleeves. I thought the officer believed that I was just trying to obtain a furlough. I turned and began to walk away when another officer sitting on the porch and overhearing the conversation intervened on my behalf. The officer soon returned and I was invited to speak with General Lee.

When escorted into the room by an officer, General Lee was sitting alone at a table studying a map. He was looking over General Pope's position. He appeared frustrated. I informed him of all that I had learned while at Hampton Roads concerning General Burnside's Yankee force. I did not know if General Lee would put any dependence in me so I told him my name and that I had scouted for General Stuart on many occasions. I also called to General Lee's remembrance the part I had played in General Stuart's raid around General McClellan's army several months ago. General Lee remembered me and immediately called for an aide to have a courier nearby to carry orders to General Jackson. General Lee was using a system of relay messengers for communication with General Jackson.

Before departing from General Lee, I offered him the lemons that I was carrying in my haversack. He declined to accept them, but instead he suggested to me that they be sent to the hospital for the sick and wounded.

This was my first meeting with General Lee. I was greatly impressed with his grace and manner. I never forgot the fear and respect of that first meeting.

CHAPTER EIGHT

Virginia and Maryland Campaigns

After leaving the meeting with General Lee, I immediately took a packet boat up the James River Canal to Lynchburg to visit with Pauline and the family. I was gone from the army for the next ten days. During that time, the battle of Cedar Mountain was waged. The battle was fought by General Jackson and General Banks' Corps of General Pope's army. General Jackson was victorious. The battle of Cedar Mountain was the first struggle of the Second Bull Run Campaign.

On August 17, 1862, I was on my way to report to General Jackson with a comrade, who I had been with in prison. His name was Gibson. Both Gibson and I had the intentions of rejoining General Jackson and the Army of Northern Virginia when Gibson and I came across General Stuart. He had just come from a meeting at Orange Court House with General Lee and was on his way to Clark Mountain to observe General Pope's army. General Stuart invited me to join them. I accepted and so did Gibson. General Stuart told me that in his meeting with General Lee, the commanding general had ordered him to conduct a raid on General Pope's lines of communication.

When we arrived at Clark Mountain, I rode with General Stuart to the crest to get a good view. While on the crest, we could see General Pope's army off to the northwest. We all agreed General Pope's army was moving back to the Rappahannock River.

The plan called for General Stuart to meet up with Fitz Lee, who had also just recently been promoted to brigadier-general. General Fitz Lee was commanding the cavalry in General Stuart's absence and was to meet us at Verdiersville with the main column. When General Stuart and our little party arrived at Verdiersville later that evening, the village was deserted of its residents. Also, General Fitz Lee and the cavalry had not yet arrived from Hanover Court House. General Stuart was anxious and disappointed. He sent Major Fitzhugh of his staff in search of our missing cavalry. After Major Fitzhugh departed, I tied my horse and lay down on the front porch and fell asleep.

The next morning around sunrise, I was awakened by Gibson. He said he heard the muffled sound of horses coming down the Plank Road. He thought that it might be General Fitz Lee and the cavalry or possibly Yankee cavalry. He was not sure. We were near the Rapidan River and I thought we were still within General Longstreet's picket lines. But I had to be sure because I did not want to get captured a second time and sent back to prison.

I immediately roused General Stuart from his sleep and told him what Gibson had heard. I assured him Gibson and I would ride down the road and see what was there. General Stuart agreed.

Once we departed from General Stuart, we did not ride too far before we discovered a body of cavalry at a farmhouse. It was foggy and difficult to distinguish friend from foe. Suddenly, two cavalrymen noticed us and rode in our direction. When they got within pistol range, they began to fire on us. That settled the issue. They were Yankee cavalrymen. Neither Gibson nor I had pistols and weapons of any kind, so we had to wheel our horses around and race back and warn General Stuart and the rest of his staff so they could escape capture.

General Stuart had already heard the gunshots and knew something had gone wrong. When Gibson and I came near headquarters, racing our horses at a full gallop, General Stuart was already mounting his horse, Skylark for the escape. Chriswell Dabney, an aide, and Heros Von Borcke, a tall Prussian soldier, who was serving the Confederacy were also mounting their horses. A lady, who owned the house, opened a gate and allowed Von Borcke and Dabney to pass, but General Stuart and his horse jumped the fence.

After about a mile, the Yankee cavalry could not catch up with us and abandoned their chase. It was a narrow escape for all of us. Our haste was so great that General Stuart left behind his plume hat, a nice leather haversack I had given him, his sash, cloth, and gloves. General Stuart always dressed well with top boots and accoutrements polished, and cocked felt hat with a long black plume. We eventually found each other in a wooded area, but we also counted our blessings that we were not captured. What was more costly was something I later discovered after a prisoner exchange, involving Major Fitzhugh. The previous evening, Major Norman Fitzhugh and the courier, who were sent to find General Fitz Lee and our cavalry, were captured by the same Yankee cavalry who had chased us. What was most important about this capture was that Major Fitzhugh was carrying a copy of General Lee's orders describing his plan to trap General Pope and his Army of Virginia.

A few days later, General Stuart began to carry out General Lee's orders of raiding General Pope's supply trains, which were located about ten to twelve miles behind his main army. After we crossed Waterloo Bridge with about fifteen hundred men and two pieces of artillery, we reached Warrenton, Virginia. It was early in the afternoon as General Stuart and his staff were riding at the head of the cavalry column down the streets of Warrenton. The inhabitants of the village received us with great joy. The ladies came out to greet us with tears of joy streaming from their eyes. General Stuart exchanged greetings with them and received a great amount of information concerning the enemy's movements.

The ladies were always valuable for obtaining important information for us.

While in Warrenton, we were informed that we were going to attack Catlett's Station. Catlett's Station was General Pope's supply depot. It was not until sometime during the afternoon before we got started toward our destination. I can still recall how the sky became dark and the rain fell in torrents. Flashes of lighting illuminated the scene, and peals of thunder seemed to roll from pole to pole, but we continued on.

It was well after dark when we arrived near Catlett's Station. By a stroke of luck, we came across a black man, who General Stuart had previously known at Berkeley. The black man agreed to act as a guide for General Stuart and the cavalry. He was very useful. He revealed the location to General Stuart where many of the Yankee army's supplies were located and where an infantry regiment was quartered that had been assigned to guard them. The black man was placed under guard to insure his trustworthiness. We continued on in the darkness. It was so difficult to see that it would be hard to tell friend from foe when we came across the enemy.

Soon, we arrived at our chosen area and were placed in formation for the attack. General Stuart galloped by me and said, "I am going after my hat." I laughed, knowing he intended to keep his promise. General Stuart then inspected the ranks and instructed us to give the wildest Rebel Yell when we charged the Yankees. At General Stuart's order, the bugler sounded charge and we attacked. The Yankee infantry regiment, the buck tails from Pennsylvania, were surprised. We set fire to the railroad depot, the Yankees' tents, and anything else of military importance. In the brief fight, we defeated the Yankees and captured three hundred prisoners, five hundred thousand dollars in Yankee greenbacks, and twenty thousand dollars in gold. Most of the stores we had to destroy because we could not carry them off. I captured a good pair of Colt revolvers to replace the ones that I had lost at Beaver Dam Station. On the more humorous side, we captured General Pope's dispatch book and other important papers, his personal baggage, and one of his horses. General Pope's uniform was sent to Richmond. For many days after the raid on Catlett's Station, the uniform was placed on display at a dry goods store on Main Street. General Stuart took great joy in the prize capture of General Pope's uniform.

During the Second Manassas battle, I remained with General Stuart. About dark on August 30, we halted along the pike to bivouac for the night. Discharges of musketry were heard about one-half mile to our front. General Stuart asked my friend Captain Blackford to ride in that direction and to find out what it was all about. When Captain Blackford returned to General Stuart, he reported, "General Pope had, it seemed, taken up the impression that General Jackson was retreating and had sent a brigade up the pike in pursuit which ran head foremost into General Wilcox's division which was deployed in line of battle across the pike near Groveton. Being on the paved pike their approach was heard in the dark and General Wilcox, after allowing the brigade to come quite close, poured a murderous fire which routed them instantly."

During the fighting at Manassas, our cavalry was protecting the army's left flank at Sudley Springs and our right flank at Dorkins Branch. We advanced with General Longstreet's men and found the Yankee cavalry ready to resist our advance. They put up a spirited effort, but our men prevailed over them.

Later, I wrote to Pauline concerning my welfare and the events of the fighting at Manassas. I wrote Pauline that I had a bullet pass through the top of my hat, slightly grazing my head, and my horse was wounded in the shoulder. With the help of one other cavalryman, during the battle we captured seven Yankee cavarlymen and two infantrymen. The fight at

Second Manassas was a glorious victory for our Cause. We almost destroyed General Pope's army. It was the best chance we had during the war to destroy a Yankee army.

On September 5, 1862, our army crossed the Potomac River near Leesburg, Virginia into Frederick County, Maryland. At Frederick City, General Lee did not relish the idea that three thousand Yankee soldiers at Martinsburg and eleven thousand Yankee soldiers at Harpers Ferry could threaten our lines of communications and hinder our operations in Maryland. To deal with the Yankee army's threat, General Lee divided our army, sending six divisions, about twenty-three thousand men under General Jackson back to Harpers Ferry and Martinsburg to deal with the enemy. Martinsburg was evacuated and after a brief siege, Harpers Ferry surrendered on the morning of September 15. We captured over twelve thousand Yankee soldiers, and much needed artillery and supplies. The greatest disappointment to General Jackson was the escape of one thousand five hundred of their cavalrymen on Sunday evening, September 14.

Once we had re-crossed the Potomac River at Shepherdstown, Virginia, I had the chance to speak with my friend William Blackford about the fighting at Harpers Ferry. He said General Jackson sadly expressed his disappointment about the escape of the Yankee cavalry, "I would have rather have had them, than everything else in the place."

Captain Blackford continued by speaking his feelings about the Yankee cavalry's escape from Harpers Ferry: "To think of all the fine horses they carried off, the saddles, revolvers, and carbines of the best kind, and the spurs, all of which would have fallen to our share, and the very things we so much needed, was enough to vex a saint. The party not only got off, but pitched into and captured one of our wagon trains and then made good their escape."

On September 17, 1862, General McClellan battled General Lee at Sharpsburg, or as the Yankees called the fight, Antietam. During the day, I served as a courier for General Stuart. Our cavalry was on the extreme left flank of our army between the Hagerstown Road and the Potomac River. We did not see the kind of fighting that the infantry was engaged in, instead our cavalry supported some of our batteries. The fight was severe and costly. Never had I witnessed such reckless destruction of life. The killed and wounded were strewn on the ground. They were like leaves of the forest when autumn has blown. I had to be careful guiding my horse because I did not want to ride over them. Many of these men were dead in ranks after being struck down by volleys of musketry. Hundreds of men lay nearby. My attention was drawn to a wounded Yankee officer, who appeared in great agony. I dismounted and made him as comfortable as possible before getting the canteen of water from the body of a dead soldier lying nearby. As I passed, another wounded Yankee soldier was about to give him a drink. He refused, asking me to give it to his colonel, which I did. I asked the colonel his name. He replied that he was Colonel Isaac Witsar of the Seventy First Pennsylvania Infantry.

Colonel Witsar recovered from the wounds he suffered along Antietam Creek. Some years after the war in 1869, while visiting Philadelphia, a friend took me to the Pennsylvania Canal Company where I had the honor of visiting him. It was an enjoyable visit.

General Lee's army re-crossed the Potomac River at Pack Horse Ford just below Shepherdstown, Virginia. On September 19, the Yankees tried to cross the river, but Major-General A. P. Hill's division repelled their efforts. Our army moved up the Shenandoah Valley to Winchester. The Yankees were content to stay along Antietam Creek.

CHAPTER NINE

I Never Returned

After the campaign in Maryland, my horse had become unserviceable. Since it was a cavalryman's responsibility to supply his own horse or serve in the infantry, I returned to my parent's home to obtain a fresh mount. While there, I had the opportunity to visit with Pauline and the children before returning to the army. Our time together was such a blessing because I had missed them more than words could be expressed. When my time with them had ended, it was difficult to leave them and return once more to the army.

On November 5, 1862, while General Longstreet's troops were withdrawing from the Shenandoah Valley, I returned to General Stuart and the cavalry near Barbee's Crossroads in Fauquier County. General Stuart was not there too long, but moved on and set up his headquarters at Culpepper. While at Culpepper he gave me and two other men the opportunity to stay behind and scout the enemy's lines. During the scouting mission, I learned that General McClellan had been relieved of the command of the Army of the Potomac and that General Ambrose Burnside was now in command. Immediately, General Burnside and the Army of the Potomac moved from Warrenton to Fredericksburg, along the Rappahannock River. I reported these events to General Stuart, who sent my intelligence to General Lee. This caused General Lee to order General Longstreet and his command to Fredericksburg.

Before General Stuart departed from Culpepper, he sent me on another scout with nine men. The scouting mission came about because General Lee was concerned that Yankee Generals Franz Sigel and Henry Slocum's Corps were being pulled closer to Washington and the Potomac River. General Lee believed these Yankee soldiers were going to travel by steamers down the Chesapeake Bay and once more make an attempt to come up the Virginia Peninsula and capture Richmond. But that did not happen. During the scouting mission, we came upon a Yankee cavalry regiment on the old Manassas battlefield. The Yankees had posted a ten-man picket force not far from their main cavalry column near the stone bridge over Bull Run Creek. I ordered my nine men to dismount and charge the Yankees with the Rebel Yell while I shouted to imaginary cavalrymen from General Stuart's cavalry. It was the same ruse I used successfully while scouting for General Stuart on his ride around General McClellan's army earlier in the year. The Yankee pickets fled and this caused great consternation among their comrades, causing them to flee in a panic.

Several days after returning to camp, I read a report in the *Richmond Times Dispatch* that we had killed one and wounded five in the skirmish against the Yankees. General Lee sent me a letter expressing his gratification on the scout and raid.

On December 13, 1862, after crossing the Rappahannock River at Fredericksburg, General Burnside and the Army of the Potomac attacked General Lee's forces. Many of General Lee's men were fighting from behind a stone wall fence at the base of Marye's Heights. General Burnside's force made repeated attacks against the stone wall fence, but our men turned them back, inflicting heavy casualties on the Yankees. General Burnside's men gave up the fight and re-crossed the Rappahannock River. Soon after the fight at Fredericksburg, General Burnside was relieved of his duties and General

Joseph Hooker was given command of the Army of the Potomac.

Shortly after Christmas, General Stuart decided to raid Dumfries, which was located in Fairfax County on General Hooker's lines of communication with Washington. General Stuart took a force of eighteen hundred men from three different brigades for the mission. I was one of them. Our cavalry moved across the Rappahannock River at Kelly's Ford and that evening, we camped at Morrisville. The next morning, some of Fitz Lee's men took the advance, but were soon turned back by Yankee infantry near Dumfires. General Stuart had brought four pieces of artillery along on the raid and began to use it, but the Yankee's long range artillery began to respond against our batteries. As more of our cavalry began to arrive, General Stuart formed the men for an attack against the Yankee position. While this was happening, General Stuart learned from some Yankee prisoners that our force was facing a brigade of infantry, some cavalry and artillery. He decided against the attack because it had taken too long to get the men into position for the fight and the battle would have been too costly in men and blood. He later wrote, "The capture of the place would not have compensated for the loss of life which must have attended the movement, there evidently being no stores in the place." Over the five day raid, we captured two hundred Yankee prisoners, twenty wagons loaded with supplies, and made quite a few sutlers very unhappy. The raid left the Yankees in great confusion and embarrassment.

After the raid, General Stuart asked me to take Fount Beattie and ride ahead of the main cavalry column for fear of an ambush by the Yankees. The forest was very dense and danger was lurking. We came upon a large body of Yankee cavalry. Several officers from the Yankee cavalry regiment made a mad dash at us, firing their weapons, but we did not run from them. General Stuart heard the gunfire and came dashing down the road at the front of the First Virginia

Cavalry. The fight was brief and sharp, but the Yankee cavalry, a Pennsylvania regiment, fled through their camp, leaving their turkey dinners behind.

On December 29, I rode to Frying Pan Church with General Stuart and several other men. One of those men was John Scott, who later served in my Command. We were going to visit with an acquaintance of General Stuart, Miss Laura Radcliff. Miss Radcliff was very loyal to our Cause and had been of great service to us. After some time had passed during our visit, General Stuart rose from his chair and said to Miss Radcliff, "You are such good Southern people through this section, I think you deserve some protection, so I shall leave Captain Mosby, with a few men, to take care of you. I want you to do all you can for him. He is a great favorite of mine and a brave soldier, and, if my judgment does not err, we shall soon hear something surprising from him." I was greatly surprised but happy for the opportunity. It was just what I wanted to do.

After leaving the Radcliff home, I was in high spirits and believed that fortune had finally smiled on me. While we were heading toward Loudoun County on the Little River Turnpike near the Fauquier County border, I rode up to John Scott, who was riding in the advance at the head of the cavalry column. I invited him to join my new Command when it was organized. John agreed to what would soon prove to be an adventurous life.

Later, we arrived at Middleburg, and General Stuart set up his headquarters at Oakham, the home of Hamilton Rogers. At Oakham, General Stuart kept his promise and made it official, leaving me behind to begin my partisan warfare with nine men. My friend Fount Beattie was one of them.

My men and I soon began our career as partisans. During the next week, I took my men back to Fairfax, where we conducted several raids. We chose to attack the Federal outposts because they were the weakest points. Up to that time, the pickets had passed a quiet life in their camps or dozing on the picket posts, but now they were kept under arms and awake all night by a foe who generally assailed them where he was least expected.

During this time, I came across John Underwood from Herndon. John was a short and stocky man, who was alert and intelligent. John's whole appearance was that of a wild man. He was a forester, who knew every rabbit path in the county. I used John as a guide and never in all of the war ever knew one who was any better at his skill.

On January 5, 1863, John guided us on our first raid against a Yankee outpost in the area of Frying Pan Church. We used deep ravines, skirted by massive foliage to conceal our approach. We kept our movements concealed from the unsuspecting foe until we were ready to attack. When ready for the attack, I fired my weapon as a signal to my men. The Yankees gave up without a fight and then we retreated deeper into the pines. We captured seven New Yorkers without the loss of a signal man. On that first raid, we captured some fine horses with their equipment and weapons. Among the weapons were a fine pair of Colts.

The next night was clear, cold and crisp when again I called on John Underwood to guide my men. This time we raided a Yankee outpost along the Little River Turnpike at Cub Run. When we arrived near the outpost, I noticed a campfire and dismounted my horse. I walked up to within a few yards of the outpost. The Yankees were playing a game of euchre and never suspected any danger. I paused, looked on for a minute or two, hating to spoil their game. I fired a shot from my revolver to let them know their relief had come. My men charged and we captured the outpost. I ordered all the New Yorkers to lie on the ground by a fence and had one of my men watch over them. My men captured five of the Yankees.

After raiding the New Yorkers' outpost, I believed that it was too early to call it an evening, so we decided to take our prisoners with us and attack another Yankee outpost several miles down the road. This time there were ten Yankees manning the outpost, who we later learned knew of our presence in the area. As we continued on, we approached a house where the Yankee cavalrymen were sleeping. They had posted a few sentinels near the door. Their horses were tied to the trees around the house. Since we came from the direction of their camps, we were mistaken for one of their patrols until we came close to them. One of the sentinels challenged us. Our response was a charge, surrounding the house and firing our weapons at it. The surprise was great. The Yankees made no resistance and surrendered.

We returned to Middleburg where I had the Yankees sign their paroles. When a soldier was paroled, he removed himself from the war until properly exchanged. In the two nights that my men and I surprised three Yankee outposts, we took twenty prisoners and twenty horses. After the raid, we returned to General Stuart's headquarters near Fredericksburg. On my arrival, I reported what I had done. General Stuart expressed great delight. When I finished my report, General Louis Armistead entered General Stuart's tent. General Stuart requested that I repeat my report to General Armistead and then go and commit it to paper. I complied with his request. When finished with the report, I returned to General Stuart's headquarters. I promised the general that if he gave me some men that in the next two months I would compel the enemy to give up their advance outpost and ten miles of country.

"Very well," General Stuart replied, "Let it be so; we will destroy them in detail."

General Stuart gave me fifteen men to go back and try my luck again. This time, I never returned, but continued my partisan life until the end of the war.

Chapter Ten

My Command

During the war, my men were viewed by the Yankee government and army as no more than a bunch of bushwhackers and ruffians. Nothing could be further from the truth. My Command was formed and operated under the Partisan Ranger Law adopted by the Confederate Congress on April 21, 1862. One day I was on a scout with one of my newest men, John Munson. He said that the men had "an invariable willingness to go where I directed," and "without being in any way informed of the work to be done, or the purpose or reason for it."

"Only three men in the Confederate army knew what I was doing or intended to do; they were Lee and Stuart and myself; so don't feel lonesome about it," said I.

I received all of my orders during the war through both Generals Lee and Stuart. I greatly respected both officers and trusted their confidence.

My warfare was always such as the laws of war allowed. To destroy supply trains, to break up the means of conveying intelligence and thus isolating an army from its base as well as different corps from each other, to confuse plans by capturing dispatches, these are the objects of partisan warfare. The military value of a partisan's work is not measured by the amount of property destroyed, or the number of men killed and captured, but by the number he keeps watching. Every soldier withdrawn from the front to guard the rear of an army is so much taken from its fighting strength. In 1885, General Grant wrote of me in his memoirs, "There were probably but few men in the South who could have commanded successfully a separate detachment in the rear of an opposing army, and so near the borders of hostilities as long as he did without losing his entire Command."

Another interesting incident happened during the war between General Grant and me. After General Grant's memoirs were published, I learned that his train had stopped at Warrenton Junction. The general learned from an agent at the railroad depot that my Command had just passed the depot several minutes before in pursuit of Yankee cavalry. When I look back on that time during the war, I cannot help but to think of how it might have helped our Cause if I would have captured the commanding general of all of the Union armies.

I never was in the habit of doing what the Yankees wanted me to do. While the country afforded an abundance of subsistence, it was open and scant of forest, with no natural defensive advantages for repelling hostile incursions. There were no such shelters there as Marion had in the swamp of the Pedee, to which he retreated during the Revolutionary War. It was always my policy to avoid fighting at home as much as possible, for the reason that it would have encouraged an overwhelming force to come again, and that the services of my own Command would have been neutralized by the force sent against it. Even if I defeated them, they would return with treble numbers. On the contrary, it was safer for me, and greater results could be secured, by being the aggressor, and striking the enemy at unguarded points. I could thus compel him to guard a hundred points, while I could select any one of them for attack. If I could do so, I generally slipped over when my territory was invaded and carried the war into the enemy's camps.

I respected my men. I did not require anything of my men which I was not willing to do. I never took them into a fight and not have a way of getting them out of it. I knew each man personally by name. I rode with them, slept on the ground with them, and fought side-by-side with them.

I never took anyone into my confidence concerning my plans. When I got an idea that was worthwhile, I immediately worked toward its development. All of my men in the Command never asked what I was planning. My silence sufficed. When on a raid, I was usually far in front of my men in thought about some future problem that might materialize during our raid so I did not always speak to the men in a casual way.

My men personally respected me. They respected my rules and authority to maintain organization within the Command. Because of my standards of authority and command, they preferred serving under me as opposed to the Regular army. Every man was treated fairly as long as he took his duty seriously and did his part. I did not permit deserters from the Regular army to join my Command. I understood the claim that the army had on its men. If someone deserted and tried to join my Command, I had him escorted under guard back to the Regular army. I recall that I was highly spoken of by one of my men, John Scott. He wrote that I had "an uncompromising sense of military honor and duty. Instead of allowing his command to become a refuge of deserters, he is, on the contrary, a most efficient ally of the conscript officer. In this way he has obtained the respect and confidence, as well as the admiration of military superiors and officials in Richmond."

In the Confederate army, officers were nominated and voted on by the men who served in the regiment. It was always my practice to nominate my own men, who I believed were best for the position. I presented my Command with a slate of names and would not allow the names of others to be added. The nominations were agreed on and that settled the issue. Not all of my men agreed, but they soon learned the reasoning once they served under the men that I had chosen to command their company.

My men were to be paid the same as Regular troops serving in the Confederate armies. If we captured any military equipment and delivered it to the Quartermaster, we were paid for it, which was an additional benefit to the men. The mules were sent to General Lee's army and were used to furnish a large part of his transportation. The captured sabers and carbines were turned over to his cavalry. We did not have any need for them. But I divided all captured horses by lottery among those who figured in the particular raid in which the animals were secured. Sutler supplies, Yankee greenbacks, and personal property were given to the man who was brave enough to take it.

The men in my Command came mostly from Fairfax, Fauquier, and Loudoun Counties, Virginia, with the exception of a few who came from Maryland. Many lived in the area where we operated. Many of the men in my Command were very flush and in the prime of their youth. They were no more than a bunch of beardless boys, whose looks were far more suggestive of the nursery than of the warpath, and I fear that not all of them were model Sunday School boys. Most of them had run away from their homes to join my Command. I recall that the thing which pleased them most was my commendation of them when asked what in the world I did with such children. I always replied that they are the best soldiers I have. They haven't sense enough to know danger when they see it, and will fight anything I tell them to. They were required to stay awake and fight or be sent to the Regular Confederate army.

Quite a few of my men were veterans before they joined the Command. Reared upon the border, they had passed the most impressionable time of life amid the scenes which attended the flooding and ebbing of the tide of war about their homes. They had become familiar with war in its darkest phase and acquainted with the enemy in his strongest and weakest points. Armies had marched and countermarched about them; battles had been fought around them; their homes had been pillaged and burnt before their eyes; scouts, spies, and deserters were familiar among them. They had become experts in running pickets, and securing and conveying secret information. In short, they had learned a whole lot of things which are not written down in the standard books on the culture of youth, but which admirably fitted them for partisan warfare.

A large number of my Command were veterans from the Regular Confederate army, who had either served out the term of their enlistment or had become disabled for that service. And many of them had already distinguished themselves in that field. Most of my earliest officers were men from the army who, upon some occasion of service with me, had attracted my attention by their bearing, and I had secured their transfer by promoting them to officers.

There were privates, who had been officers in the Regular Confederate army; men of high spirit, who chafed under the monotony of army life. They were attracted to my Command because of the adventure and resigned their officer commissions.

Then, too, we had some grim old sires, which the merciless laws of war relegated to their homes. But the ruthless hands of those who knew no laws had made their homes only dark spots of desolation, or had put upon them some deep outrage that set fire even to the sluggish blood of age. These were men who had some grievous wrongs to avenge, and their implacable and unwavering hate furnished a kind of conservatism to the younger and, perhaps more erratic spirits.

The men in my Command did not have camps, fixed quarters, and never one night did they sleep in a tent. They never boiled coffee, fried bacon, or ate hardtack such as the Regular Confederate soldiers were compelled to do. They had no camp duty to do, which, however, necessary, would have been disgusting to soldiers of high spirit. To put them to such routine work is pretty much like hitching a racehorse to a plow. Not only that, but if I had put my men into camp they would soon have all been captured. We depended on citizens, even the poorest, who were loyal to our Cause to feed and to give us shelter. In return they enjoyed the security of our protection. Their trust in me and my men was unquestionable. They knew the stakes were high if caught by the Yankees, but they were more than willing to take the risk.

In every household, there was a family member who was a spy or a courier in our service. The citizens had their way of warning us of potential danger. At night, they used lights in certain windows, a woman waving some colorful garment, and still the more deceiving, a young lad innocently running and playing across a field carrying the word of Yankee presence to another home. Without their assistance and loyalty, we could not have operated as efficiently as we did. Some of my men stayed with these families in between raids, but for those that did not have family living in the area of operation, those men were treated as a family member by the ones they boarded with. When that man in my Command captured some booty or greenbacks on a raid, he shared his spoils with the family. We paid for everything and worked the property of those who boarded us. Even I paid my own way. There was a deep affection that abounded between the families and my men, who boarded with them. One night on the way to a raid, I overheard one of my men, John Alexander say it best, "A genuine affection inspired the many little offices which softened the roughness of a soldier's life, and it was with actual sense of defending homes and loved ones that more than once a Ranger laid down his life on the threshold of his host. When we started on raids farewells were spoken with moistened eyes and in broken words, and the soldier knew that if he were brought back on a bloody bier there would be gentle hands to lay him to his rest, and some quivering lip to kiss him for a mother."

Quite a few of the local citizens had sons, cousins, sweethearts, and husbands riding with my Command. I felt a personal responsibility to each family and when one of their loved ones was killed in battle against the Yankees, I grieved as much as they grieved. And I took the loss just as personal as they did. Amid fire and sword they remained true to the last, and supported me through all the trials of the war.

The homes where my men stayed were called safe houses. Most of the safe houses were located in and around the villages of Salem, Rectortown, and The Plains. When the Yankees occasionally raided the area and appeared at one of the safe houses, my men would flee off to the mountains or be hidden away somewhere in the house. Some of the families who sheltered my men had huge wardrobes where a man could squeeze into it for shelter behind clothing. There were trap doors in the floor of a certain room, sheltered by rugs and furniture, some leading to a three-foot cellar under that room. And then other residents had garrets where a man could slide down the roof to safety. I had an occasion where I had to flee to safety from capture, using this same way of escape.

I boarded mostly at a place called Heartland, with my servant, Aaron. A very corpulent man by the name of Joseph Blackwell owned the property. I always liked him and will forever remember the friendliness and generosity of his family. On one occasion, Joseph requested something gray, which was required of my Command when in battle, so that he could take part in a raid in Maryland. I granted his request. After his little adventure, Joseph never again took part in another raid. He apparently had his fill of war.

The homes where my men boarded were known to me and everyone else serving in the Command. When a meeting was desired, one which had not already been appointed at the last disbanding, a word of the time and place was sent to one house and the men who were there would bear it to the others, from whom it would pass on with promptness and certainty. In this way, one hundred men could easily be rendezvoused in a few hours. The raid could take place.

    The men in my Command carried two Colt .44 revolver pistols with a third in their boot, or another pair in holsters across their saddles. No sabers were used because they were ineffective at close range fighting, which we engaged in. The men owned more than one horse. The horses were of the best thoroughbreds in the Old Dominion. The men always took the best care of their mounts because their lives depended on the efficiency of the animal. This proved to be a fact because our fights were fast and furious and quickly over, one or the other side withdrawing at a dead run when the pistols were empty. At one time during the war, I owned six horses, giving their care to Aaron.

    Battle was a hard thing. I have known the best of my men to sicken and tremble with nervousness, caused not so much I think by fear for themselves as anxiety about the work that was before them. Killing men is a painful business and to sit quietly in cold blood and contemplate it is a fearsome thing. I never thought less of any man because of this.

    We fought against great odds. Seldom did we wait to receive a charge by the Yankee cavalry, but nearly always sought to make the first attack with a yell. This worked in our favor because the Yankees were either surprised and fled, or quickly became demoralized and surrendered.

    There were times when my men were charged with disguising themselves as Yankee soldiers. They never masqueraded in the uniforms of a Yankee soldier, except through force of circumstances. Then they wore blue overcoats captured from Yankee cavalry. The Confederate government could not always provide proper clothing, so we used them to protect ourselves from the cold. However, Jessie Scouts of the Yankee army will be remembered by the soldiers of both armies because they dressed in Regular

Confederate uniforms with the purpose of deceiving our men.

I was proud to serve beside the men in my Command. I have never witnessed more courage and chivalry among a more organized group of young soldiers.

Chapter Eleven

Partisan Operations

The fifteen men General Stuart gave me were from my old regiment, the First Virginia Cavalry. Out of the lot, I chose twelve Virginians and three Marylanders. From Virginia, my men were Fount Beattie, Jasper and William Jones, John Buchanan, Christian Gall, William Hunter, Ned Hurst, William Keyes, Benjamin Morgan, George Siebert, Charles Wheatley, and John Wild. The men from Maryland were, George Slater, Daniel Thomas, and William Turner. My men were good men. They were twenty to thirty years of age and some of them had already suffered imprisonment or some kind of injustice by the Yankee army during the years of the war.

It was a cold and rainy day on January 18, as my men and I left the camps of the First Virginia Cavalry at King William Courthouse. We crossed the Rappahannock River at Foxe's Mill and rode toward Warrenton. My idea was to make the Piedmont region of the country between the Rappahannock and Potomac Rivers the base of my operations. From that time on until the close of the war the area was the theater on which I conducted partisan operations. It became known as "Mosby's Confederacy."

The area was a rich, pastoral country, which afforded subsistence for my Command, while the Blue Ridge was a safe point to retreat if hard pressed by superior numbers that could be sent against us. The country had been abandoned to the occupation of the Yankees except for a short time when the Confederate army was passing through in General Lee's first campaign into Maryland. Only then did we once more occupy the area. I determined that by incessant attacks, I would compel the enemy either greatly to contract his lines or to reinforce them; either of which would be of great advantage to the Southern Cause. I thought that zeal and swiftness of movement would go far to compensate the deficiency of my numbers. Nearly everyone thought that I was starting on a quixotic enterprise that would result in doing no harm to the enemy, but simply in getting all of my own men killed or captured. My faith was strong, and I never for a moment had a feeling of discouragement or doubted my ability to reap a rich harvest from what I knew was still an un-gleaned field.

When we arrived at Warrenton, we were stopped by the citizens. They expressed surprise when they heard that we had come to make war, for they said we resembled the retinue of an ambassador, or a company of missionaries rather than a band of warriors.

While at Warrenton, we stopped at the Warren Green Hotel to warm ourselves and to enjoy a nice dinner, which I paid a quarter for. After an hour or so, we moved on in a northeast direction from Warrenton where I dispersed my men to find shelter among the citizens of the surrounding area. This would be our habit during our operations in Northern Virginia. Before my men departed for shelter, I ordered them to rendezvous at the Mt. Zion Church along the Little River Turnpike about a mile and one-half from Aldie.

I did not rest or waste my time. Over the next eight days, I collected information about the position of the enemy and gained a more accurate idea of the area in which I would be carrying out operations. Many of the citizens living in the area were faithful to our Cause and were of good use. The population was highly refined and cultivated. They gave me a great amount of information about the Yankees. As the war continued, their stubborn faith in the Southern Cause never wavered.

On January 26, my men gathered at my call like Children of the Mist. We rode down the Little River Turnpike and then turned in the direction of Frying Pan Church where we captured a patrol of two men. Then we headed to Old Chantilly Church where we regained the turnpike. At the church was a picket of nine men from the Eighteenth Pennsylvania Cavalry. I was determined to attack them.

Covering our movements by the pines, I formed the men and moved cautiously forward and planned to attack the Pennsylvania regiment from the front then by the rear. I took one man, dashed forward, and captured two mounted sentinels, who did not offer resistance. The command to charge was given and the Yankees' reserves were attacked. The fight was brief. One Yankee cavalryman failed to halt at my command. As he continued his escape, I fired my revolver, hitting him in the arm and side. The Yankee was taken to a farmhouse where I visited him. I expressed my regret at injuring him. The Yankee cavalryman was paroled and left in civilian care.

The Yankees had been completely surprised by our attack. We captured horses, bridles, and eleven Yankee prisoners on this raid. I sent a citizen with a message of admonishment for Colonel Percy Wyndham that he should arm his pickets with Colt revolvers; their obsolete carbines were not worth capturing. The Yankees' spoils were divided among the men.

After the raid, Fount Beattie and I went to the home of Lorman Chancellor in Middleburg where we enjoyed a hot supper and much needed sleep. Early the next morning, about two hundred Yankee cavalrymen under Colonel Percy Wyndham arrived in the village. Fount and I were awakened by one of the male servants and told what was going on. We easily slipped away from the Chancellor's house without being noticed by the Yankees. At the time, the Yankees believed the village was the headquarters where the men were supplied to attack their outpost. While the Yankees were going from home to home, they complained we did not fight fair. They arrested eight men, who were elderly, crippled, and infirm, and took them as their prisoners. While the Yankees' raid was taking place, I gathered up seven of my men.

My men and I entered Middleburg just as Colonel Wyndham and his cavalry were leaving. I gave the command to charge the rear of the Yankee force. In the short fight, we killed one and captured three of their number and then retreated to the farther end of the village. At the end of the village, I stopped my horse, turned and allowed the Yankees to shoot at me. It was a piece of temerity which greatly astonished the citizens but was not without its good effect upon the men. The enemy gave pursuit. I rode onto a hilltop outside of town, only a few hundred yards in front of the Yankee column. One of Colonel Wyndham's men approached, believing I was one of their command who had gotten too far ahead of them with orders to return. I received the order quietly, but sent the messenger back with the reply that I couldn't come yet. In the fight, I regretted the loss of my good friend, Fount Beattie and several other men of my Command. Fount Beattie was eventually paroled and returned to fight in my Command.

Colonel Percy Wyndham was an English officer, who had fought with Garibaldi in Italy. He commanded a Yankee brigade of cavalry and had charge of the outposts where we had been attacking. He was familiar with the old rules of the schools, but he soon learned that they were out of date, and his experiences had not taught him how to counteract the forays and surprises that kept his men in the saddle all of the time. After the fight at Middleburg, Colonel Wyndham threatened to burn the village to the ground. I was petitioned by some of the citizens to cease my attacks on the Yankees' outpost. I wrote the citizens:

"I am not prepared for any such downgrading compromise with the Yankees, I unhesitatingly refuse to comply. My attacks on scouts, patrols, and outpost, which have provoked this threat, are sanctioned both by custom of war and of the enemy."

On February 8, 1862, I took some of my men dressed in dark blue overcoats, on another raid. We headed in the direction of Frying Pan where I heard that a cavalry picket was stationed and waiting for me to come after them. I did not want them to be disappointed in their desires to visit Richmond. When I got within a mile of it and stopped for a few minutes to make my dispositions for attack, I observed two ladies walking rapidly toward me. One was Miss Laura Radcliff, a young lady to whom General Stuart had introduced me a few weeks before, when returning from his raid on Dumfries. The other lady was Miss Radcliff's sister. Their home was near Frying Pan, and they had information of a plan to capture me, and were just going to the house of a citizen to get him to put me on my guard, when fortune brought them across my path. But for meeting them, my life as a partisan would have closed that day. There was a cavalry post in sight at Frying Pan, but near them, in the pines, a large body of cavalry had been concealed. It was expected that I would attack the picket, but my momentary triumph would be like the fabled Dead Sea's, ashes to the taste, as the party in the pines would pounce from their hiding place upon me. This was not the only time during the war when I owed my escape from danger to the tact of a Southern woman.

We changed our plans and headed in the direction of Herndon Station where we surprised and raided a blockade runner with goods. He was paid for his merchandise in Yankee greenbacks. The trader was surprised.

When we captured prisoners, it was my custom to examine each one of them separately, and in this way, along with the information that I obtained from local citizens, I had a pretty accurate knowledge of conditions in the enemy's camp. On February 11, my Command was moving toward a place called Rector's Cross Roads, which was west of Middleburg. We were heading on a raid to Fairfax County when an unexpected incident took place. A dismounted Yankee sergeant by the name of James Ames, Fifth New York Cavalry, came walking toward us. He was dressed in full uniform. He was large and muscular, with determination stamped in every line of his face. His black eyes were clear, he was intelligent, his bearing was manly, and his manners and conversation pleasing. Sergeant Ames told me that on the previous day, he had deserted from the Union army. He wanted to join my Command. Like many of my men, I believed Sergeant Ames had been sent to entice my men into some kind of a trap. To dispel my suspicions, I required him to pledge his parole of honor not to serve the United States in any capacity during the present war until duly exchanged as a prisoner-of-war. He willingly agreed to the terms and I witnessed his oath. He became known to my men as "Big Yankee" Ames.

I never asked "Big Yankee" Ames what his grievances were against the Union army. I did not find out until a new recruit by the name of Walter Frankland and "Big Yankee" went off to steal some horses from the Yankee cavalry. "Big Yankee" told Frankland that he had deserted because he did not agree with President Abraham Lincoln's Emancipation Proclamation. "Big Yankee" believed the document made it clear that the war was being fought over the issue of slavery and not as he was led to believe, the preservation of the Union. Near Germantown, Ames and Frankland came to the camp of Ames' old regiment. They spoke with some of the Yankee cavalrymen, who Ames had served with. They entered the stable and rode off on two horses and then just as boldly passed the regiment's sentries without incident.

On February 25, twenty-seven of my men met me at Rector's Cross Roads. A heavy snow had fallen the previous night and eventually turned to rain. The roads were all but impassable, but I was determined to ride in the direction of Fairfax County. I met with Miss Radcliff to determine if she possibly had any information for me on a Yankee outpost five miles from Germantown. As always, she was helpful.

The next morning well before sunrise, I stopped at a farmer's house to make an inquiry as to the number of men at the outpost. I recall, he came to the door dressed in his nightdress, and the first thing he asked was, "How many men have you?"

"Seventeen." said I, to deceive him. I asked the farmer, "How many are at the picket post?"

"One hundred. I have been down there this evening. You are certainly not going to attack them with so few men?"

"Yes, it is so dark they can't see us, and will think I have got a hundred too."

I went straight down the road with my Command. We came on a lone sentinel, who challenged us. We did not know the password or counter-sign so he fired on us. The sentinel fled from us, but we were close to his heels. The Yankees were asleep in an old schoolhouse with their horses tied to trees. They should have driven us off with the shelter they were using, but when we charged they ran from the house and tried to gather their horses. At first, my attention was attracted to "Big Yankee" Ames. I don't remember why. Up to this point, I had not allowed "Big Yankee" Ames to have any arms. This was to satisfy my men because of their distrust for him. But, Ames took the carbine of the Yankee soldier that he was fighting and struck him with the weapon. I never again questioned his fidelity after the fight. We killed three and captured five in the raid.

The next morning, Colonel Wyndham and his Yankee cavalry came after us with the hopes of capturing us. But their attempts were futile. After twenty miles they gave up their pursuit and returned to their camps with broken down horses.

Colonel Wyndham became very angry and determined that he was going to stomp out all rebel resistance. On March 1, two hundred men from the Eighteenth Pennsylvania Cavalry and the Fifth New York Cavalry under the command of Major Gilmer were sent to Middleburg to carry out Colonel Wyndham's threat. The weather was cold that morning. It was just before daybreak when Major Gilmer and his men arrived and surrounded Middleburg. It was their intention to arrest all the men, many of them crippled and infirm. News came to me that the enemy was at Middleburg, so, with seventeen men, I started that way, hoping to catch a few stragglers. But when we arrived at the village, we learned they were gone. Women and children came out to greet us. The tears and lamentations of the scene aroused all of our sentiments of chivalry, and we went in pursuit.

I rode in the advance with six of my men and commanded the others to approach at a slower pace. I suspected that Major Gilmer and his cavalry had paused at Aldie, about five miles ahead. But, I was surprised as I later learned from prisoners after the fight, it was the First Vermont Cavalry under Captain Franklin Huntoon, who we would end up fighting. Just as we ascended a hill on the outskirts of the village, we captured two Yankees. I sent orders for the others to hurry along. Just then, I saw two cavalrymen in blue riding along the pike. No others were visible, so with my squad we started at a gallop to capture them. Halfway down the hill we learned that it was a considerable body of cavalry we were confronting. The Yankees had dismounted. Their horses were hitched and they were feeding at a mill. I tried to stop the noble bay I was riding, but he was of high mettle and raced at full speed. I could not control him. The cavalry at the mill were taken absolutely by surprise by the interruption; their sentinels had not fired their weapons. Panic seized the Yankees and they fled without noticing how many of us were there. Without bridling their horses or fighting on foot they scattered in all directions. There was another body of cavalry ahead of us, gazing in bewilderment. To save myself, I jumped from my horse as it reached a narrow bridge over Little River. One of my men, Henry Carter, stopped and gave me his horse. Fortunately the mounted Yankee party in front of me saw those I had left behind coming to my rescue, so they wheeled and started full speed down the pike. The affair was over.

War is not always fighting and killing. There is another side, the humorous side. I recalled one night when I was returning from Fairfax. We were passing a house when I heard a dog bark and someone call, "Come here, Mosby." So I turned, rode up to the house, and asked the man if he had called me.

"No," said he, "I was calling Mosby. I wanted him to stop barking."

So I have had the distinction in this war of having babies and dogs named after me.

Chapter Twelve

Capture of a Yankee General

It was my intention and desire to capture Colonel Wyndham. He had retaliated more than once against the elderly and infirm citizens who lived in Middleburg. Colonel Wyndham believed these good Southern citizens had done everything to support our activities in the area. Colonel Wyndham also took it upon himself to insult me and the men of my Command. He called us a bunch of horse thieves. To this accusation, I replied, "it might be true, but all of the horses had soldiers armed with pistols and carbines mounted on them." Colonel Wyndham had sent me several messages that he proposed to capture me, and I was determined to show him that two could play at that game.

I decided to execute my scheme to capture General Stoughton and Colonel Wyndham at their headquarters at Fairfax Court House. Ames knew the whereabouts of their headquarters and the place was familiar to me as I had previously been in camp there earlier in the war. I also knew from Ames and the prisoners we had taken where the gaps were located in the Yankee lines at night. The safety of the enterprise lay in its novelty because nothing like this had been tried thus far in the war.

In obedience to my orders, twenty-nine of my men assembled at Dover in Loudoun County to carry out my scheme. The men who participated in this raid thought we were simply going down to make an attack on a picket post. While mounting my horse at the home of Hamilton Rogers to begin the raid, I said to him "I shall mount the stars tonight or sink lower than plummet ever sounded." Well that did not happen, but I did not sink. At that time during the war, I had no reputation to lose, but knew I had much to gain if successful.

The weather favored my success. It was dark, there was a mist, and the snow was melting as we began the twenty-five miles we had to cover to get to Fairfax Court House. No one knew my objective point before we started on the raid, but I later told Ames about my plans after leaving the Roger's homestead.

We proceeded down the Little River Turnpike to within three miles of Chantilly. My plan was to reach Fairfax Court House by midnight so that we could be well out of the Yankee lines by daybreak. But we had an unfortunate incident take place that delayed our arrival. So intense was the darkness that, as we passed through a dense body of pines, the Command was separated accidentally into two divisions. I was going forward with some of the men while the rest stopped under the impression that a halt had been ordered. I later learned from one of my men that there were some of the men in the Command who thought of returning to Fauquier while others wanted to press on. They made the right choice. They continued on until they discovered a faint light from a woodman's hut where they located me. We had wasted about an hour riding around in a circle looking for each other. After we united, we started off and struck the pike between Centreville and the Court House. This area was where one of the gaps in the Yankee lines was located that Ames had knowledge of. Ames led us through the gap without a Yankee sentinel seeing us. I do not believe any of the men from my Command knew for certain that we were within the Yankee lines. Before we entered the village, I rode up to Sergeant William Hunter and told him of my intentions. He realized as I did, the difficulties and dangers that surrounded us. I directed my men on until we struck the

Warrenton Pike at a point about four miles from Fairfax Court House. Some of my men cut the telegraph wires. Then we struck the Chain Bridge Road, running north to Fairfax Court House.

Near Fairfax Court House, I noticed the campfires illuminating the sky from Colonel Wyndham's cavalry camps along the road. I knew Colonel Wyndham did not sleep at the cavalry camps but at the village. I led my men off the road into the woods to avoid the Yankees. We entered the village from the direction of the railroad station where only a few sentinels were about the town. As we entered Fairfax Court House, I knew many of my men must have been surprised that they had penetrated the Yankee lines. There was not a question among any of them. There was not a faint heart among them. All seemed to have a blind confidence in my destiny.

It was 2:00 in the morning when we arrived in the village of Fairfax Court House. The streets were deserted, scarcely a light was visible, and everyone seemed buried in sleep, officers, soldiers, and citizens alike. It was so dark that the Yankee sentinels could not distinguish us from their own people. It may have helped because we wore dark raingear, which covered the gray that every man was required to wear on a raid.

On the inside of the village, squads were detailed to go around to the officers' quarters and stables for horses. Men were quickly sent out to capture sentinels. I understood that some of the captured sentinels laughed when informed they had been taken prisoners. They believed that it was a joke, but they soon became believers. One of my men, Joe Nelson, captured a telegraph operator in his tent. The capture took place when Joe noticed a lantern burning in the operator's tent. He approached the tent and apprehended the operator, who mistook him for a comrade who had been playing pranks on him. It was not until Joe grabbed him by the throat with a pistol in his face that the Yankee operator took his capture seriously. Joe captured another prisoner on his way back. The courtyard was where the men were ordered to report once they had finished their duties.

While I was taking six of my men to the residence of Judge William Thomas, where I believed Colonel Wyndham was sleeping, Joe Nelson returned with his prisoners. One of the prisoners informed Joe that Brigadier-General Edwin Stoughton's headquarters was located a block away in a brick two-story house belonging to Doctor William Gunnell. I immediately sent Ames and a few men to capture Colonel Wyndham while I went off with my men to capture the Yankee general.

When we arrived at General Stoughton's headquarters, we dismounted and I knocked loudly on the front door. Soon a window on the second floor opened and someone asked who was there.

"Fifth New York Cavalry with a dispatch for General Stoughton," said I.

The ruse worked. The door was soon opened by a staff officer, Lieutenant Samuel Prentiss. I took him by his night shirt, whispered my name in his ear, and told him to take me to General Stoughton's room. Lieutenant Prentiss obeyed my order because he knew it was useless to resist. I left some of the men to stand guard while I went with the staff officer to the general's room. When we arrived at the general's room, a light was struck and the general was before me, sound asleep. I looked around the room and noticed there were signs in the room of having revelry in the house that night. A half-dozen champagne bottle were lying around, which furnished an explanation for the general's deep sleep. He had been entertaining a number of ladies from Washington City in a style becoming a commanding general. The revelers had retired to rest just before our arrival with no suspicion of the danger hovering over them. I was told the ladies had gone to spend the night at a citizen's house. Loud and long have I been told were lamentations the next morning when they heard of the mishap that had befallen the gallant young general.

There was no time to waste. I drew up his bedclothes, pulled up the general's shirt, and gave him a spank on his bare back, and said, "General, get up."

The general did not realize the situation before him, but thought that somebody was taking a rude familiarity with him. He sat up in bed, rubbed his eyes and asked in an angry tone what all of this meant?

"Did you ever hear of Mosby?" asked I.

General Stoughton answered, that he had heard of Mosby and asked, "have you captured him?"

"I am Mosby, and I have caught you. Stuart's cavalry has possession of the Court House; be quick and dress," said I.

A look of agony and despair was upon General Stoughton's face. He asked if General Fitz Lee was here with the cavalry. In order to deceive him so he would not try to escape, I answered yes to his question.

"Take me to him. We were classmates at West Point?" General Stoughton asked.

I agreed to General Stoughton's request.

General Stoughton took his time and dressed carefully in his best uniform before a mirror. As we departed, he realized that he had forgotten his timepiece, which was retrieved by Frank Williams of my Command. When General Stoughton and his staff walked from the house, his seven couriers and their horses were ready to leave with us. They had been captured by George Whitescarver and Welt Hatcher. General Stoughton wanted to ride his own horse, but I denied his request and gave him a horse of lower mettle. William Hunter was ordered to take the reins of General Stoughton's horse and lead his mount so the general would not have an opportunity to escape.

When we arrived at the courtyard, there were three times as many prisoners as my men and each was mounted and leading a horse. Ames had returned from Colonel

Wyndham's headquarters without the prize possession that we had sought to capture. Earlier in the evening, Colonel Wyndham had departed for Washington City. He had eluded capture, but Ames and the men with him carried off several of the colonel's best horses and all of his finest wardrobe. Ames did not come back empty handed and without prisoners. He returned with Captain Augustus Barker. Captain Barker was Ames' former commanding officer, but now served as an Assistant Adjutant General. Ames treated his former commander with the greatest civility, and seemed to feel great pride in introducing him to me.

It was 3:30 in the morning. I had to get my Command on their way before daylight because I did not desire that the Yankees would discover our small numbers. We were ten miles within their lines. I was in a critical situation, for in addition to several thousand troops in the surrounding camps, a considerable number were quartered in the houses in the village. If there had been the least concern among them, they could easily have driven us out. Although we remained there an hour, not a shot was fired.

To baffle any Yankee cavalry pursuit, my Command departed from Fairfax Court House, using the Ox Road, which was in a different direction. All was quiet and went well for us until we were challenged by a gentleman shouting from a window of a house at the edge of town. He commanded in a loud voice, "Halt! The horses need rest. I will not allow them to be taken out. What the devil is the matter?"

No one in the Command replied. The gentleman again shouted, "I am commander of this post and this must be stopped."

Some of my men laughed at the officer. I ordered several of my men to dismount and capture him. The officer fled and entered the house with both of my men in pursuit. When my men entered the house, the gentleman's wife confronted them and fought like a lioness in order to give her husband time to escape. They next entered his bedchamber, where they found a Yankee uniform on a chair, hat on a table, but as for the officer, he had fled. We were informed by his wife that her husband was Colonel Robert Johnston, Fifth New York Cavalry. He was in command of the cavalry brigade while Colonel Wyndham was in Washington City. My men could not find Colonel Johnston, but I later learned the commanding officer had hidden under an outbuilding and refused to reappear for some time.

When we continued on, General Stoughton did not see General Stuart's cavalry near the village. General Stoughton turned to me and said, "This is a bold thing you have done; but you will certainly be caught; our cavalry will soon be after you."

"Perhaps so," answered I.

Outside of the village of Fairfax Court House, I paused long enough for my cavalry column to close up. Some of the men had been following at a distance and others were on the flanks. This was to prevent any of the Yankee prisoners from escaping. I rode forward to scout the area. There were no Yankees stirring about. I ordered Sergeant Hunter, still holding General Stoughton's horse's reins to move the men forward at a trot. Joe Nelson and I dropped some distance behind the Command and listened for any Yankee pursuit. By now, I thought the alarm had been sounded of our presences at Fairfax Court House and the incident with Colonel Johnston. My heart beat higher with hope every minute; it was the crisis of my fortunes.

There were camp fires burning on the heights around Centreville as we approached the village. I knew it was Yankees. My plan was to go around their flank, and pass between that place and the camps at Chantilly. I soon found Sergeant Hunter had paused with the Command, so I galloped forward. There was a fire burning alongside of the road about one hundred yards in front of us. I slowly rode forward to scout the position, but found no Yankee sentries.

We were about half a mile from Centreville and it was becoming daybreak. I called Sergeant Hunter forward with the rest of the men and we continued on. We turned off that road and went around the forts at Centreville.

I rode in the advance. I noticed the Yankees' camps were quiet; there was no sign of alarm. I saw a cannon bristling through the redoubts and heard the sentinel on the parapet call out to us to halt. We paid no attention to him and he did not fire to give the alarm. No doubt he thought we were a body of their own cavalry going on a scout.

Some time had passed. There was a shot behind me. I turned and noticed one of my men, Jake the Hungarian, chasing Captain Barker toward the redoubt. Jake was about to get off another shot when Captain Barker and his horse tumbled into a ditch. We got Captain Barker and his horse out of the ditch in full view of the sentinel, who just watched and did not sound the alarm. I asked Captain Barker if he were injured. He replied that he was not injured. Some of our prisoners escaped because of the darkness and because there were not enough men to sufficiently guard them. One of the Yankees to escape was Lieutenant Prentiss.

After we passed the forts and reached Cub Run, a new danger arose. The stream had risen because of the melting snow and it appeared to be swift. In full view behind us were the white tents of the enemy and the forts, and we were within their cannon range. We had a choice. Either we could turn back or swim our horses across the stream. Without any hesitation on my part, I rode my horse into the cold water and crossed the stream. General Stoughton followed. As General Stoughton came up the bank, he was shivering from the cold. He said, "Captain, this is the first rough treatment I have to complain of."

No man or horse was lost in crossing Cub Run. I knew we were safe. I left Sergeant Hunter in charge of the Command and rode with one of my men, Private George Slater, ahead of the column to see what was ahead. I did this because I did not want Yankee cavalry to intercept us on the pike we had left that runs through Centreville.

We moved on until we crossed Bull Run Creek at Sudley Ford, at the old battlefield. From the heights overlooking Groveton, the sun had risen. It seemed to me that it never shone with such splendor before because I could see the road was clear to Centreville. There was no Yankee pursuit. Sergeant Hunter and the rest of the Command arrived and were ordered forward. I stayed behind with George Slater as a rear guard.

When my Command and our prisoners arrived at Warrenton, the whole population turned out and gave my men an ovation. General Stoughton and his officers had breakfast with a citizen of the community, John Beckham. General Stoughton had been a classmate with Mr. Beckham's son Robert at West Point. Mr. Beckham's son was a Confederate artillery officer with General Stuart's horse artillery.

We soon remounted and moved south, crossing the Rappahannock River. After crossing the river, I placed all the prisoners to be turned over to the provost marshal into the hands of Dick Moran and some of my men. I took General Stoughton and his other officers with me to General Fitz Lee's headquarters at Culpepper Court House. I recall it was a wet and cold morning when General Stoughton, his officers, and I dismounted at General Fitz Lee's headquarters. We tied our horses and entered the house, only to find the general sitting at a table writing in front of a log fire. I introduced his old classmate, "General, here is your friend General Stoughton, whom I have just captured with his staff at Fairfax Court House."

General Fitz Lee was very polite to General Stoughton and the other officers, but he treated me with indifference. He did not ask me to take a seat by the fire, nor seem impressed by what I had done. I was very angry at the treatment.

I was not a welcome person at those headquarters. So, bidding the prisoners good-by and bowing to General Fitz Lee, Sergeant Hunter and I rode off in the rain to the telegraph office to send a report to General Stuart. The telegraph operator informed me that General Stuart was on his way to Culpepper Court House and would arrive on the train the same evening. I met General Stuart and Major John Pelham at the depot and will never forget the joy his generous heart showed when he met me.

General Stuart handed me a captain's commission from Governor John Letcher. The commission only gave me rank over Virginia troops, which did not exist any longer. All of the Virginia state forces had been mustered into Regular service with the Confederate army. General Stuart thought the Confederate War Department would recognize the commission. I angrily informed General Stuart that I did not want any recognition. Instead, General Stuart published a general order which was sufficient enough gratitude. General Stuart wrote:

"Captain John S. Mosby has for a long time attracted the attention of his generals by his boldness, skill, and success, so signally displayed in his numerous forays upon the invaders of his native soil.

None know his daring enterprise and dashing heroism better than those foul invaders, those strangers themselves to such noble traits.

His last brilliant exploit, the capture of Brigadier-General Stoughton, U. S. A., two captains, and thirty other prisoners, together with their arms, equipments, and fifty-eight horses justifies this recognition in General Orders. The feat, unparalleled in the war, was performed in the midst of the enemy's troops, at Fairfax Court House, without loss or injury.

The gallant band of Captain Mosby shares his glory, as they did the danger of this enterprise, and are worthy of such a leader."

Touching the capture of General Stoughton at Fairfax Court House, I wrote to a friend in Richmond that already you have seen something in the newspapers of my recent raid on the Yankees, though I see they call me Mosely instead of Mosby. The *Richmond Daily Dispatch* wrote:
"*Captain Mosby, of Gen. Fitzhugh Lee's cavalry, has returned from a scout. He captured Brig-Gen Stoughton, a captain and 30 privates, at Fairfax C. H., taking them from their beds. They were greatly astonished at the presence of the Confederate Cavalry and offered but feeble resistance.*"

Great was the surprise at Fairfax Court House the next morning when it was discovered that during the preceding night I had been there and carried off the commanding officer, and a large number of prisoners and horses. Some censured one officer, some another, but it was agreed on all hands that so daring a feat could not have been performed without the aid of accomplices in the town. It was not true; I had no communication with anyone there. But eight citizens of known Southern sympathies were thrown into jail; they were later released.

In a few days, I received a correspondence from General Fitz Lee, informing me that I must return the detail of men I had from his brigade. This attempt to deprive me of a Command met with no favor from General Stuart. I sent him General Fitz Lee's correspondence, and he issued an order for them to stay until he recalled them. When the armies began to move again from winter quarters in April of 1863, the men from General Fitz Lee's brigade went back to him, but a considerable amount of recruits had joined my Command.

After the raid on Fairfax Court House and the capture of General Stoughton, my reputation grew among the Yankee invaders. My reputation even grew with General Lee. He wrote, "Mosby has covered himself with honors."

General Edwin H. Stoughton
Source: *Courtesy Library of Congress*

CHAPTER THIRTEEN

April Fool's Day

A very important aid to me in my successful attacks and surprises was the selection of skillful and intelligent guides and scouts. Men familiar with the section of country in which we operated; knowing all the little roads and cow paths; who could creep through the dense undergrowth or dark ravines like foxes, unobserved, and if discovered easily elude pursuit. John Underwood again proved his worth to me in this vocation.

On March 16, 1863, I met forty of my men at Rector's Cross Roads. John Underwood was one of them. From Rector's Cross Roads, we rode along the Little River Turnpike until we were east of Middleburg. There we turned northeast and rode until sundown, when we came to Ball's Mill along Goose Creek. As we tramped through the mud and snow that day, one man said to another that "I had inspired all hearts that not a man doubted but that ahead somewhere there was a good thing in store for us."

At Ball's Mill, Dick Moran was ordered to take part of the Command to find shelter among the nearby residents. I took the rest of the Command and stayed the night with a friend by the name of Nate Skinner, who lived close to the mill.

The next morning the Command reassembled and we rode toward Dranesville. It was around noon when we crossed the Alexandria, Loudoun, and Hampshire Railroad near Herndon Station. As we rode from a wooded area I noticed about one hundred yards away, fifty cavalrymen from the First

Vermont in a lazy and dull mood. They were not aware of our presence. The order to charge was given and the Yankees were taken by surprise. They did not try to defend themselves, and most of them surrendered. Others tried to escape and took shelter in a home where they were fired upon by my men. They too soon surrendered. One of my men, Sergeant John DeButts, and I entered a nearby mill, and demanded the surrender of the rest of the escaping Yankees or the mill would be burned. They gave up without firing a shot.

After hearing the gunfire from the fight at Herndon Station, another detachment of Yankee cavalry arrived and gave pursuit. I had taken twelve men and formed a rear guard and was able to drive off the Yankee cavalry that was chasing us. In the raid at Herndon Station, we captured twenty-five men, twenty-six horses, and their equipment. I did not lose a man in the fight.

A week later, we got into another little scrap with Ames' old regiment, the Fifth New York Cavalry. We got the better end of the fight and chased some of them down the Little River Turnpike toward their comrades. The tide turned against us when the Yankees ordered a counterattack, driving us for three miles back down the pike. We came to some fallen trees where I had the men dismount. When the Yankees approached the area of the fallen trees, my men fired from the front and flank. The Yankee cavalry quickly wheeled around. My men mounted and we charged and followed the Yankees until we came upon a larger Yankee cavalry force. We gave up the fight, but not before we captured thirty-six Yankees and fifty of their horses.

It was during the time of these raids that I had a recruit join my Command who would always hold my dearest love, affection, unquestionable loyalty and, even after the war continued to be one of my closest friends. He was a preacher by the name of Sam Chapman. Sam previously served as a lieutenant with the Dixie Artillery from Page County,

Virginia. The Dixie Artillery was disbanded by General Lee. Sam was assigned to the conscript business of the war, but soon resigned to join my Command. The first time Sam saw me was in Warrenton. He told me later after joining the Command that the hotel-keeper had said, "If that fellow Mosby attempts that caper again, he will be caught." The hotel-keeper was talking about one of my raids into Fairfax County. Sam and I had a good laugh over the remark. Sam Chapman was one of the best fighters in my Command and I never knew him to ever back down from doing his duty when it came to a fight. After the Chantilly raid, Sam would never serve in any other Command but mine.

Another recruit who I would come to rely on and trust with the most sincerity in a fight, was Sam's younger brother William. Like Sam, William had served in the Dixie Artillery and was enrolling conscripts into the army. William found the service in my Command adventurous. Like his brother, he was a furious fighter and as the war continued, he proved to be a good leader of men. Before the war ended, I promoted him to the rank of lieutenant-colonel.

On March 23, 1863, I was appointed captain of partisan rangers by General Lee. I was ordered to hold elections for officers and to organize the men into a company. Not a single officer, commissioned or non-commissioned, had been appointed yet. I was ordered by General Lee to report from time to time the progress of my Command. The telegram was passed to me from General Lee by General Stuart. General Stuart advised me to call my Command Mosby's Regulars instead of partisan rangers and that I was to be vigilant about my own safety, and not to have an established headquarters anywhere but in the saddle.

Now back to operations. On Monday, March 31, seventy men assembled in the snow at Rector's Cross Roads for another raid into Fairfax County. It was the largest number to serve under me in a raid thus far during the war. It was a Command which was made up of furlough soldiers from different commands, a few convalescences, and new recruits. Patriotism as well as the lore of adventure impelled them. If they got rewards in the shape of horses and arms, these were devoted, like their lives, to the Cause in which they were fighting. They were made no richer by what they got except in the ability to serve their country. My authority over the men had been of such a transitory nature that I disliked ordering them to do anything but fight. And furiously fight they were willing to do.

When ready, we headed east toward Fairfax County, where we passed Mt. Zion Church. Several miles down the road past the church, we turned off the road and headed northeast toward Herndon Station. When we arrived at the depot, we learned the Yankee outpost that I had planned on attacking was now behind Difficult Run. Difficult Run was about five miles from the depot. I knew it would be difficult to attack the Yankee outpost behind the stream because there would be few passable fording areas. Those fording areas would have a heavy picket force to contend with, so I led my men toward the Leesburg Pike.

After reaching the Leesburg Pike, my Command had traveled thirty miles over rough and muddy roads and we were exhausted. We turned west in hopes that I could obtain some forage for the horses from one of the nearby farms. When we arrived at a farm owned by Henry Green, I was informed by him there might be a sufficient supply of forage over at Miskell's farm. Miskell's farm was located where Broad Run enters the Potomac River, about one mile from the Green farm. We continued on toward Miskell's farm while Dick Moran stayed behind to visit with the Green family, whom he was well acquainted with.

It was 10:00 in the evening according to my timepiece when we arrived at the Miskell homestead. I requested of the owner, Tom Miskell, if my Command could bivouac for the night, a request he readily agreed to. I noticed the house Tom lived in was a two-story clapboard dwelling, seated on a ridge, which was located a mile from the Leesburg Pike. I also noticed the property was bordered by a high plank fence with a gate in the corner that opened into an enclosure of cultivated land. Inside of the field was another stone and wooden fence that surrounded a barn and barnyard, which gave shelter to livestock and much needed hay. The only way out of the homestead was the lane we had used from the house to the pike.

That evening, we had corn cakes and some bacon. Many of the men bedded down for the night in the Miskell's barn, sleeping in a blanket on the hay, while some of the others stayed with me and slept on the floor of the kitchen in front of the stone fireside. The horses were unsaddled, unbridled, and tied to the barnyard fence and the other fence surrounding it. I recalled I laid my head on my saddle and used it as a pillow. I was soon in a deep sleep. There was only one sentinel placed around the property. I believed at the time that our position was relatively a safe distance from the Yankees and that no one would be looking for us because of the nasty weather. I did not believe there was a threat. But I would soon be proven wrong.

Bright and early the next morning, I had just risen and put on my boots and buckled on my arms when one of the men came in and said that the enemy on the hill across the river was making signals. It was a Yankee signal station along the Potomac River in Maryland keeping an observation on us. Not only did the Yankee signal station see us, but I learned later from a Yankee prisoner taken that day that a lady, who was loyal to the United States and lived at Herndon Station, had watched us pass by. She sent her brother with the intelligence to inform the Yankees at Union Church about our presence in the area.

While I was looking at the Yankee signal station from the rear door of the Miskell house, Dick Moran came galloping at a fast pace across the field shouting, "Mount! Mount your horses! The Yankees are coming."

No sooner had Dick Moran sounded the alarm, the camp was alive with excitement, and the men hurried to their arms and saddled their horses. I turned and noticed the Yankee cavalry was marching two abreast through a gate into the Miskell's field which separated the barnyard from the woods. More Yankees were moving around the house to gain our flank and rear. The Yankee cavalry had been so sure of their prey that they closed the gate behind them and placed boards over it to prevent our escape. I felt like my final hour had come. Things looked rather blue for us. We were in the angle of two impassable streams and surrounded by at least four times our number, with half of my men unprepared for the fight. But I did not despair.

I ran out to the barnyard, which was no more than one hundred yards away from the house and stood behind the high stake and rider fence. I heard a Yankee officer shout, "Draw sabers! Charge!"

The Yankee cavalry moved at the double-quick gallop across the field toward the barnyard. The officer riding in front of the attacking Yankee column shouted, "Shoot the damned cowards!"

As the Yankee bullets whizzed by, some of my men were looking for a way of escape. The air was soon filled with the sound of snorting horses, the thudding sound of a bullet striking wood, pistols crackling, and the shouting and cursing sworn by men in battle. At first, I ordered my men not to return fire, but to quickly saddle their horses.

To help cover my men, I fired both of my Colt pistols at the charging Yankees. By now, there were about twenty of my men who had mounted. I opened the gate and shouted for the Command to charge them and go through them. I had great faith in the efficiency of the charge; and in the affair at Chantilly, I had learned the superiority of the revolver over the saber. I did not care where the charge was made, only that I wanted my men to get out into the open. I made no reckoning of the numbers of the enemy, I gave it no thought;

I only knew my men were in a trap and did not intend they should be murdered like a lot of sheep in the shambles, if grit and ammunition held out.

As my men charged through the barnyard gate, I was still dismounted. One of my men, Harry Hatcher, from Fauquier County rode up and dismounted and gave me his horse. I was confident that we could at least cut our way through the Yankee cavalry.

When the enemy saw us coming to meet them, they halted, and were lost. My men raced into them and when close enough, they fired their pistols into their adversaries' faces with deadly effect. The Yankees were shocked because they did not expect us to charge and pitch into them. They recoiled under our assault; many of their own had been dropped from the saddle. The Yankees became confused and ran.

An officer tried to rally the fleeing Yankees. He was shot down by one of my men. We always went for the leader of the attacking Yankee cavalry because this had a demoralizing effect on some of the men following him. After the fight, I learned the identity of the officer from a prisoner we captured. He was Captain Henry Flint of Company I, First Vermont Cavalry. He was shot six times by my men. After Captain Flint had been shot down, the combat was short, sharp, and decisive. The Yankees wheeled around and made for the gate which they had closed. The other squadron that had gone around us, when they saw their companions turn and fly, were panic-stricken. They started pell-mell for the gate in order to reach it ahead of us. By this time all of my men had mounted their horses, and like a wild force, were riding and shooting among the Yankees' scattered ranks.

The Yankees broke through the closed gate. They became so packed and jammed in the narrow passage that they could only offer a feeble resistance, and at this point many fell under the deadly fire that was poured in from behind.

Sam Chapman was in front of everyone at the gate emptying his pistols. Even at that supreme moment in my life, when I had just stood on the brink of ruin and had barely escaped, I could not restrain a tendency to laugh at Sam. To give more vigor to his blows, Sam was standing straight up in his stirrups, dealing them right and left, as he came upon the Yankees. Sam was a military Calvinist, singing the Psalms of David as he went into battle. I must confess that his character was more on the model of the Hebrew prophets than the Apostles, or the Baptist in whom he was so devoted a believer.

The disordered and frightened Yankees scattered through the woods, and along the road leading to the turnpike. The dead and wounded were strewn from where the fight began, at Miskell's, for several miles along the road. The Yankees never drew rein or looked back to see how many of us were behind them. I got pretty close to one, who, seeing that he was bound to be shot or caught, jumped off his horse and sat down on the roadside. As I passed him he called out to me "you have played us a nice April fool, boys." This reminded me this was the first day of April.

Among the first fugitives to pass through Dranesville and show the day's disaster in his face, was the citizen who had hurried down the night before to the camp of the Vermont cavalry to tell them where I was. Thinking Captain Flint was going to have an easy thing of it, the citizen had ridden with him as a pilot, to witness my humiliation and surrender. He escape captured, but never returned to his home during the war.

In the fight at Miskell's farm, Sam Chapman was wounded while chasing the Yankees beyond Dranesville. Sam published his account of the fight after the war, which I read. Sam wrote:

"Capturing men in their retreat is by no means a pastime. I remember riding between two men, calling on them to surrender. They fell upon me with their sabers, and one

fellow gave me a blow on the head that seemed to drive it into my shoulder. His blade turned in the stroke and I received a flatwise rather than the edge, or my soldiering would have ended there. As it was, I was considerably stunned, and it might have been worse for me had not a comrade, Sergeant Hunter come up and knock one of the men off his horse, and the other gave up."

Sam's brother, William had been captured by the Yankee cavalry during our pursuit and was with them in a wooded area about four hundred yards off of the Leesburg Pike. After being there for a few minutes, William was rescued by some of my men who had heard about his misfortune. A number of other prisoners from my Command were also rescued from the clutches of the Yankee invaders. After the war William gave his recollections of the fight. He wrote:

"Our men were fresh from having had a night's rest and had warmed themselves at the fire in the house, while Captain Flint's men had been in the saddle most of the night, and had faced a bitter cold. We were armed with Colt's pistols while they were armed with Remington pistols. A great many of their pistols failed to go off, and I never heard of a single instance when a Colt pistol snapped when the trigger was pulled. Some of the prisoners stated that they had been out the day before and had gotten their pistols wet, which they gave for the failure of the Remington pistols to go off."

We left on the field at Miskell's farm nine Yankees killed. Among them a captain and lieutenant and about fifteen too badly wounded for removal; in this lot two lieutenants. We brought off eighty-two prisoners, many of these also wounded. There were certainly not less than two hundred men from the Yankee cavalry. We took all of their arms, equipment, and one hundred horses. I lost one man killed and three wounded in the affair.

The Yankee Lieutenant Josiah Gout, who at the time of the fight at Miskell's farm was believed to be mortally wounded, survived his wounds and became the Republican governor of Vermont. After the war, Sam Chapman and I had the opportunity to visit Governor Gout at the Arlington Hotel. When we sent up our calling cards to his room, Governor Gout and his wife warmly received us. He did not express any animosity toward us. It was a very cordial visit.

On March 26, I was promoted to the rank of Major.

Captain Sam Chapman
Source: *Author's Collection*

Captain Henry Flint
Source: *Courtesy Library of Congress*

Chapter Fourteen

Railroad Raids

General Joseph Hooker, the new commanding officer of the Army of the Potomac was preparing to cross the Rappahannock River. As a preliminary movement, he had sent General Stoneman with the army's cavalry corps up the river to seize the Orange and Alexandria Railroad and hold it as the line of communication with Washington. The line that connects an army with its base of supplies is its most vital and vulnerable point. It is a great achievement to compel an enemy to make a heavy detachment to guard it; it is equally as great a one to destroy the force that threatens it. General Julius Stahal and a division of cavalry was given the responsibility of protecting the railroad while General Stoneman and the rest of his cavalry corps crossed the Rappahannock River to head south and operate on General Lee's lines of communications.

About this time, I received a correspondence from General Stuart. General Stuart believed there was a splendid opportunity to strike the enemy in the rear at Warrenton Junction. The trains were running regularly to that point. He asked that I capture a train and interrupt the operations of the railroad. General Stuart warned me to keep far enough away from the Yankees' camps to give me time to get off with my plunder and prisoners.

Meanwhile, I was willing to let the Yankees down in Fairfax rest while I turned my attention to Joe Hooker and the railroad. The next morning, April 29, I called for a meeting of my Command at Upperville. Eighty men assembled for the raid. The first thing I did was send out Tom Richards and several other men to scout in the area of Middleburg, about eight miles away, to watch some Yankee cavalry. If possible, I wanted to slip away from them undiscovered.

In order to execute my plan of capturing a train on the Orange and Alexandria Railroad, I made a detour by Salem, going on toward Thoroughfare Gap in the Bull Run Mountain. We were marching very leisurely because I did not want to get to the railroad until after dark.

Just as I reached Thoroughfare Gap, two of my scouts, Alfred Glasscock and Norman Smith, returned with the news that the enemy was pursuing us. The scouts had stayed behind at Salem and watched the Yankee cavalry march through the village, using the same road we were on. The Yankees were only about one hour behind us. I knew the roads forked at a village called The Plains, where one road led to Thoroughfare Gap and the other to Hopewell Gap in the Bull Run Mountain. The idea of attacking the railroad was abandoned and it was determined to harass the Yankees.

After receiving the news I said to my men, "the Yankees are the same men whom we whipped at Chantilly and at Miskell's and we could do it again." I wheeled my horse around and with the rest of my Command headed back to The Plains on the Hopewell Road. I knew the Yankees outnumbered us. My intentions were to cut off the Yankee rear guard before it passed the fork in the gap. When I got on a high hill which overlooked The Plains, I noticed that instead of meeting the Yankee cavalry's rear guard, it was his advance that had just arrived at the fork of the road. We drove back their advance until we came upon their main body. The whole Yankee column rapidly deployed in line of battle, and their artillery guns were placed in battery. From a hill near Kinlock I could observe the Yankee general on a milk-white steed, surrounded by a brilliant staff sending off and receiving couriers. We stayed facing each other for about an hour until it grew dark. Nothing came of the affair, so I disbanded the men for the night with orders to reassemble in the morning.

It had never entered my head that the Yankees, so great in numbers, were going to run from me. So Fount Beattie, who had returned to my Command, and I stopped for the night at the home of George McArty. About daybreak, George came running to where we were sleeping and called out to us, "Boys! Get up quick. The Yankees are all around you."

Fount and I jumped up. We noticed about two to three hundred yards away, the field was blue with Yankees. We quickly bridled and saddled our horses and rode off without incident.

* * * *

A partisan commander who acts in cooperation with an army should always, if possible, operate against troops in offensive movements. My plan now was to strike General Hooker. The moral effect of a blow from behind might have an important influence on the results since the two armies were again campaigning against each other. I would try my hand with a raid on the Orange and Alexandria Railroad. On May 2, I gathered about one hundred men for the raid at Upperville. Forty of those men came from Colonel Butler's Second South Carolina Cavalry. They were in the area gathering horses when they heard of my intentions. They had heard that I was going to lead a raid and they wanted to ride along. I led my Command toward Warrenton, where the residents turned out in the street, cheering and giving us something to eat. We had not been in Warrenton for several months. That night, we camped several miles on the outskirts of Warrenton, where our horses were plentifully fed on the grain which had been left behind by the Yankees.

The next morning, May 3, at daybreak, it appeared that it was going to be a bright, sunny morning. We started on the road to Fredericksburg I was sure General Hooker would not repeat the blunder of General Burnside, but would cross at some of the upper fords of the Rappahannock. It was toward one of these fording areas that my course was directed. Off in the far distance, the roar of the guns at Chancellorsville could be distinctly heard, and we all knew that the two armies were once more in the deadly embrace of battle. It was not more than fifteen or twenty miles off; and we could easily reach there early in the day. I wanted to contribute my mite of support to the Southern Cause by striking one of General Hooker's wagon trains.

All was going well until we came within a couple of miles of Warrenton Junction. A bugle was heard. I turned the Command aside and marched toward the sound, believing I could do some damage to any Yankees that we found. Before we had gone much further, we captured a Yankee infantryman, who warned me that I was marching right into an infantry brigade. I learned from him that there were some cavalry along the railroad at another point, so I turned in that direction.

When we approached the railroad station from the direction of Warrenton, we entered a nearby wooded area. From there, I noticed the Yankee cavalrymen were lounging on the grass while their horses, with nothing but halters, had been turned loose to graze on the young clover. They were lazily listening to the sounds of battle at Chancellorsville, and had no idea that danger was near. The Yankees had not a single picket or patrol placed anywhere in sight. I said to some of my men that you can have a fight now in short order.

When we rode out of the woods, the Yankees mistook us for some of their own men, and had no suspicion who we were until I ordered a charge. The sounds of pistols crackling and the yells of my men caused the Yankees' horses to scatter and stampede over several hundred acres while their riders took shelter in some nearby homes. Those Yankees in the homes quickly surrendered, but the largest body of men were hiding in the large framed depot near the railroad. I immediately ordered a charge on them because I did not want to give the panic-stricken Yankees time to recover. Our charge was momentarily checked by a miry branch over which we had to pass. This gave the Yankees a little time to recover.

I had about thirty men with me when I attacked the railroad depot. I came up in front of two windows by a chimney where the Yankees had been firing from. They had brought down two of my men with their gunfire. The building was densely packed with them. It was almost impossible to fire into it without hitting somebody. I took my two revolvers and emptied their chambers into the windows at the Yankees. Sam Chapman with three men charged into the building. The Yankee soldiers in the lower rooms quickly surrendered, but those above held out. I was concerned with the amount of gunfire, because the noise would alert any Yankees nearby and they would come to their comrades' assistance. Already, the fight had continued for thirty minutes. There was a haystack nearby so I ordered some of the hay to be brought into the dwelling and fire set to it. The Yankees were not willing to be burned alive, so the ones on the floor above held a white flag out the window and surrendered. Twenty Yankees surrendered to us. The Yankee commanding officer, Major Steele, was mortally wounded, and there were many others in the same condition. The Yankees were men from the First West Virginia Cavalry. The fight also came at a cost to us. One of General Jackson's scouts, a soldier by the name of Templeton, was found dead near a house. The raid had been his first and last with my Command.

After a severe fight at the depot, I had taken three times my own number in prisoners, together with all their horses.

After the fight, most of my men had dispersed over the field in pursuit of the frightened horses. I was sitting on my horse giving directions to leave with the prisoners and spoils when one of my men, John Wild, who had been chasing a horse some distance down the railroad came galloping at full speed. He told me that a large body of Yankee cavalry was quickly approaching from the direction of Cedar Run Bridge.

I tried to rally my men, but we were so scattered gathering horses and equipment that we were unable to offer any kind of resistance against the approaching Yankee force. When the Yankees came closer to us, they split their force in two trying to gain our rear while the rest of their force charged from the front. At the time this fight took place, I was with a small party of my men in a body of pines. I stayed on this ground until the Yankee cavalry was fifty yards from me and I was nearly captured. So there was nothing to do but for every man to take care of himself. We broke and ran from the field in small groups of four and five, leaving behind prisoners, booty, and other plunder. This was called the "skedaddle."

After leaving the depot, many of my men managed to escape capture from the Yankee cavalry by riding off on forks in the road, by-lanes, and different roads. The men were so familiar with the surrounding area that it was easy to escape the pursuing Yankees.

It was the first time I had to order a retreat in the four months we had been operating together against the Yankees. Some of my best men had been captured. Dick Moran, Tom Richards, Sam Underwood, and David Jones, General William Jones' cousin, were all captured.

The Yankees claimed to have captured thirty prisoners, some who were badly wounded, and a large number of horses. It was the First Vermont and Ames' old regiment, the Fifth New York, who attacked us.

The loss at Warrenton Junction was like a wet blanket on the men's morale, but it did not hinder my operations against the Orange and Alexandria Railroad. On May 9, I gathered forty men for another raid on the railroad. We removed some train rails between the Catlett and Bristoe stations, causing a train to run off the track. My Command had little effect against the Yankees and we could not do much to hinder them. Yankee pickets were stationed at all the principal bridges and exposed places. Patrols were sent from post to post and each train had its own infantry guard.

Shortly after May 10, my men and I learned of General Stonewall Jackson's death. General Jackson had been wounded during our victory at Chancellorsville. He had an arm amputated, but what the physicians called pneumonia set in and he died not too far from the battlefield. There was not a man in my Command that did not grieve over his loss.

* * * *

I felt that in order to retain my men, it was necessary for me to stimulate their enthusiasm with something more tangible. War to them was not an abstraction; it meant prisoners, arms, horses, and sutler stores; remote consequences were not much considered. So, I sent Fount Beattie with a letter to explain the situation to General Stuart. I wrote:

"If you would let me have a mountain howitzer, I think I could use it with great effect, especially on the railroad trains. I have several experienced artillerist with me. The effect of such annoyance is to force the enemy to make heavy details to guard their communications. I have not attacked the railroad trains, because I have no ammunition for my carbines, and they are pretty strongly guarded with infantry."

I strongly believed that this action would not only draw Yankee troops from the front, but prevent those doing duty in Washington from being sent to General Hooker to make up for his losses from the fighting at Chancellorsville.

May 29, 1863 was a beautiful day, with every tree full of bloom and flower. Forty men answered the call to meet me at Patterson's. It was my intention to cause some harm to the Orange and Alexandria Railroad. As my men arrived, I showed them the new twelve-pound mountain howitzer that General Stuart had sent me. Many of the men were amazed because they did not know the difference between a howitzer and a saw log. I had fifteen rounds of ammunition for the gun stored in a limber-chest. Since Sam Chapman had been an artillery officer, I had him choose enough men to man the gun and instruct them in its use. Sam spent a little bit of time instructing them in artillery tactics, showing them the difference between the muzzle of the gun and the touch-hole.

I knew a brigade of cavalry and one of infantry were lying between Manassas and Catlett's Station. The two places were about twelve mile apart. Between these two places was the only possible chance of reaching the railroad without being discovered by the Yankees. So we decided to attack a train in that area, camping in some pines near Greenwich that night.

The next morning, we were awakened by the reveille in the Yankees' camps, which were a mile or so distance on either side of us. There was a narrow pathway through the pines, along which we marched until we came within one hundred yards of the railroad. The first thing we did was cut the telegraph wires and conceal them in the pines from a passing Yankee cavalry patrol. We then unfastened a rail to allow the train to run off the track.

We were all under cover. I was in fear every moment of a patrol coming on the road that might give the alarm and stop the train. That did not happen.

We did not have long to wait for a train. When the train approached from the direction of Washington City, one of my men concealed in the pines, gave the signal. He pulled the rope attached to the loosened rail, causing a gap in the train track. The gap threw the train from the track and the locomotive tumbled to one side. Our men rushed the train and were fired into by the infantry guards. Sam Chapman and his men fired the howitzer. The ball from the howitzer slammed into one of the train cars. The Yankee infantry guards protecting the train fired one ragged volley at my men before fleeing into the nearby woods.

All soldiers, you know, acquire an investigating turn; in fact, they acquire it more readily than they do the drill. The men carried off such luxuries as genuine coffee, sugar, fresh shad, oranges, lemons, and pineapples. There was hay and corn for the horses, and hardtack, salt pork, and flour for the men. The train cars were carrying leather for boots, the U. S. Mail, and Northern newspapers. When finished with plundering, my men set fire to the train cars.

Now we wished to disable the engine. Sam Chapman moved the gun up to within seventy-five yards of the locomotive and fired another shot. After the war I later read one of Sam's articles about this fight. Sam wrote, "the round went 'through the dome,' and such a noise and spray of steam never enveloped us before."

The sound of the cannon had given the alarm. The long roll was beaten and the bugles sounded throughout the Yankee camps. The howitzer was limbered and we mounted our horses and began to move out. When we got about one mile from the railroad, we met a New York regiment coming from the direction of Kettle Run. I believed they were going to try and cut us off. We halted and the howitzer was unlimbered. A shell was sent at them, which burst at the head of the cavalry column, killing the commanding officer's horse. This created a stampede among the Yankee cavalry, and they scattered before another shell could get to them. The way of escape was now open. I was expecting the enemy every moment at my rear. We were now girt with foes on every side. It would have been easy to save ourselves by scattering through the woods, but I was fighting on a point of honor. I wanted to save the howitzer, or if I had to lose it, I was determined to exact all that it was worth in blood.

After we got about one mile further on, the New York regiment of cavalry we had broken rallied with reinforcements and came on again in pursuit. At the edge of a wooded area, we sent another shell at the Yankees. I ordered Sam Chapman to take the howitzer and to go ahead while I stayed behind with six men as a rear guard.

The Yankee cavalry which had been attracted by the firing were now seen in different directions moving toward us. As they approached, I slowly withdrew my Command to a nearby wooded area. The Yankee cavalry's advance guard, twelve to fifteen men, suddenly dashed towards us. We wheeled our horses around and engaged them in a hand-to-hand fight where we finally drove them off. They left behind several of their dead and wounded.

Seeing that no hope was left to us but to save our honor and stand by the gun, I sent an order by Willie Foster to Sam Chapman to halt and unlimber the gun in a narrow lane on a hill. There was a high fence bordering the lane, property owned by Warren Fitzhugh. The narrow lane and fence offered some protection against a flank attack from the Yankee cavalry. I knew we could only hold the position as long as the ammunition for the gun lasted. What was disappointing to me was that many of my men had gone their own way with their booty and now I needed every man that I could get to help beat off the Yankees.

When the Yankee cavalry came into sight, they were several hundred yards away from us. Sam Chapman and his gun crew sent them a shell that exploded in their ranks. The Yankees fell back into the woods in confusion. They made several more attempts at the gun, but we drove them off. The Yankee cavalry again charged, this time up the lane in columns of four. Our little howitzer, which was about eighty yards away, raked them with grape and canister. The Yankee cavalry made several successive onsets like this, but Sam

Chapman and his gun crew drove them off. By now, the ground over which the Yankee cavalry had crossed was strewn with their dead and wounded men and horses.

I was sitting just behind the howitzer when Sam Chapman rammed home the last charge. As the Yankees charged up the lane one more time, the gun fired, belching forth flame and smoke. A number of the Yankee horsemen and their mounts tumbled to the ground.

After the howitzer fired its last round, we charged. That day I was riding a spirited sorrel horse. When we charged, my sorrel carried me with so much force that I could not hold him up until I had gone some distance through the Yankee cavalry. As I passed by, one Yankee struck me on the shoulder with his saber, nearly knocking me off my horse. At the same instant, my pistol flashed and he reeled from his saddle. Charlie McDonough had followed me through the Yankees. Both Charlie and I found ourselves hemmed in by a high fence. Seeing that my men had abandoned our gun, the Yankees dashed for it, leaving us alone.

I dashed by the Yankees and their captured howitzer, receiving no injury from them. In the fight at the Fitzhugh farm, I left behind some of my best men. Among them, Fount Beattie and Sam Chapman, who were both captured.

The saber thrust from the Yankee cavalryman caused me little harm. This fight did not discourage my morale. I began to look for my next opportunity against the Yankees.

Chapter Fifteen

The Gettysburg Campaign

In early June 1863, I narrowly escaped capture by the Yankee cavalry. My wife Pauline, and the children, May and Beverly, were boarding with James and Elizabeth Hathaway. The Hathaway's lived on a large plantation in a three-story brick home not far from Salem. It was one of the few times the Yankees had an opportunity to capture me. I will now tell you about my near capture.

The Yankees knew very well that they couldn't capture any of us during the daylight, so they made up their minds to try their luck by night. They had left Berryville, and crossed the Shenandoah River earlier in the evening and commenced their search for game, as the Rebels were known to them. They had raided some homes and were in possession of a number of my men and their horses. Some of them made good their escape.

Earlier that same evening, Fount Beattie had warned me the First New York Cavalry had passed through Salem. While at Salem, they learned from an informant that I was staying at the Hathaway homestead and decided to come down and pay me a little visit.

Around midnight the Yankees arrived at the Hathaway homestead. They quickly surrounded the house. I heard the noise and looked out the window. Someone began to noisily beat against the front door. I heard a lady's voice ask, "What's the matter?"

"Open the door quickly or we'll burst it open," replied a Yankee cavalryman.

"Who are you?"

"Never mind who we are, but come down and let us in."

While the lady and the Yankee officer continued their fiery exchange, Mr. Hathaway came down the stairway and opened the door. An officer entered the house and wanted to know where I was.

Mr. Hathaway did not answer. The Yankee officer took the light from Mr. Hathaway and came looking for me, but I was gone. Outside the second story bedroom window where I had been resting was a large walnut tree. I had dressed and gotten out the window onto the tree branch. I quietly watched the Yankees as they entered the bedroom and spoke with Pauline. There were even a few of the rascals who were walking below me looking for my whereabouts. Little did they know I was watching them from above.

The Yankees arrested Mr. Hathaway, taking him away. They also took some fine horses, one of them being my sorrel mare.

On June 10, the Forty-Third Battalion Virginia Cavalry was organized. I had stopped at Caleb Rector's home. In his parlor, I prepared the order for the formation of Company A. In compliance with the Partisan Ranger Act, I had to go through the formality of an election. I really appointed the officers, and told the men to vote for them. This was my rule as long as I had a Command, but with two or three exceptions, their conduct vindicated my judgment. James Foster, formerly with the Seventh Virginia Cavalry was elected captain. Thomas Turner from Maryland was elected first lieutenant. William Hunter was elected second lieutenant. Thomas Turner and William Hunter were from the First Virginia Cavalry. They were from the original fifteen men, who had begun partisan operations with me six months ago. George Whitescarver was elected as third lieutenant. I chose these men because they had proven their courage and bravery in battle. Unfortunately, Lieutenant Whitescarver was killed the next day.

The previous day, June 9, General Stuart fought a bloody battle against General Alfred Pleasanton's Yankee cavalry at Brandy Station, south of the Rappahannock River. On the very day I formed Company A, General Lee's infantry began to move north toward the Shenandoah Valley. His invasion would begin one of the greatest and most bloodiest campaigns during the war. The two armies would meet at a little town in Pennsylvania, called Gettysburg.

* * * *

Early on the morning of June 17, I visited with General Stuart at "Yew Hill," the home of Miss Kitty Shacklett, just south of Piedmont Station. General Stuart's headquarters' tent was located in Miss Shackett's front yard along the roadside. General Stuart cordially greeted me. It had been three months since I last saw him. He was in his usual gay humor. Always in buoyant spirits, he inspired with his own high hopes all who came in contact with him. I felt the deepest affection for him. My chief ambition was to serve him. We spoke and I told General Stuart what I knew about the position of the enemy. I assured him that I was ready to perform any service he wanted. We agreed to meet again later in the afternoon.

General Stuart's cavalry moved on to Middleburg, where I met with him again that same afternoon. I recall, General Stuart had never seen my Command before and made humorous remarks about them as they passed by. I told General Stuart that he would hear from us. General Stuart and I had a short conference about the situation. He approved of the expedition that I wanted to undertake across the Potomac River. My idea was to create a diversion for General Lee, who was marching his army through the Shenandoah Valley. I also wanted to keep General Lee informed of the enemy's movements. I had already been to Seneca along the Potomac River, and I did not think they would expect me to come back that way.

On our way to Seneca, the weather was very hot, so we stopped at the Gulick homestead, north of Aldie, to rest and drink buttermilk. Off in the distance we heard artillery fire in the direction of Aldie. This indicated to me there had been a collision between General Pleasanton's Yankee cavalry and ours.

We mounted our horses and in a few minutes we were on a hill where I could see clouds of dust rising on every road. This showed me that General Hooker's army was heading in the direction of the Potomac River. After going a little farther, two to three miles, we captured some prisoners. From the prisoners, we learned General Hooker's army was all around us. The information I got from them, I sent to General Stuart. With the turn of events, I could not get to Seneca without passing through General Hooker's infantry. I decided to go down the Little River Turnpike and operate on his line of communications between General Pleasanton's cavalry and the general headquarters. I knew I could gather some prizes there, so I did not move across the Potomac River as planned.

We kept ourselves concealed from the Yankees in the woods until night and then sallied out in quest for game. Well after dark, we moved to a point about four miles below Aldie and on the pike leading to Fairfax Court House, where General Hooker's headquarters was established that evening. My Command was now well inside of General Hooker's lines and surrounded on all sides by the camps of the different corps.

I noticed along the pike there was a continuous stream of Yankees pouring along. I took three men with me, Joe Nelson, Charlie Hall, and Norman Smith, and rode out of the woods and fell in with the column of Yankee troops as they passed along the road. Since it was still dark, they had no suspicion who we were, even though we were dressed in Confederate uniforms. We came to a house alongside of the road. There were three horses standing by the front gate with a soldier holding them by the bridles. I was sure they were officers' horses. We rode up and asked him to whom the horses belonged. The soldier replied they were Major William Stirling and Captain Benjamin Fisher's horses and they were just from General Hooker's headquarters.

I called the soldier closer to me. I took him by the collar, and leaning from my horse, whispered in his ear: "You are my prisoner. My name is Mosby."

The soldier, an Irishman angrily replied, "You are a damn liar. I am as good a Union man as you are."

The Yankee Irishman saw my pistol and was quiet.

In a few minutes, the officers came out of the house. I saluted them and asked where they were from and where they were going. They never suspected our hostile character. They said they were from General Hooker's headquarters and were carrying dispatches to General Pleasanton.

While I was politely talking to Major Sterling, my men dismounted. Joe Nelson walked up and politely extended his hand, asking for the major's pistol. Charlie Hall demanded Captain Fisher's weapon. Resistance was useless and they surrendered.

All of us mounted and both Yankee officers burst out laughing. I asked them what they were laughing about. They said they had laughed so much about their people being gobbled up by me that they enjoyed the joke being turned on them.

I knew the Yankee officers had dispatches for General Pleasanton. I ordered the dispatches turned over to me. Major Stirling promptly complied. I then went to a farmer's house and read them. The dispatches were just the information General Lee wanted. The dispatches disclosed the fact that General Hooker was looking to Aldie with concern, and that General Pleasanton, with infantry and cavalry, occupied the place, and that a reconnaissance in force of cavalry was meditated toward Warrenton and Culpepper. The dispatches also gave the entire number of divisions, from which we could estimate the approximate strength of the enemy. I wrote a note to General Stuart to go with the dispatches, and sent it under the charge of Norman Smith. Charlie Hall and Joe Nelson took charge of the prisoners and also departed leaving me for the night to sleep not too far from the Yankees at Gum Springs.

Several days later, On June 23, General Stuart told me General Lee was anxious to know if General Hooker's army was moving to cross the Potomac River. He did not ask me to go. I had constantly been in the saddle for three days, but I volunteered to return and find out for him the needed information. On the scout, I took two men with me. We used a bridle path across Bull Run Mountain and rode down into Fairfax, even among the Yankee camps. As I gathered information, I would send a man back to General Stuart with the intelligence until finally I was alone. During this time, I went on near Dranesville, along the Potomac River, to learn more information. Since General Hooker's army corps were scattered over the country, it was not difficult to pass between them.

All was quiet; there was no sign of any movement by General Hooker's army. After learning this information, I started on my return trip. I did, however, make one stop at Miss Radcliff's home. Miss Radcliff had previously given me information about the Yankees, so I wanted to speak with her and learn what she might know of their movements, and if she had any Northern newspapers that I could read. When I arrived, I was invited into her home, leaving my horse at the front gate. Miss Radcliff's sister took my horse from the gate and led him behind the barn, staying out of sight with the horse until I was ready to leave. I was not uneasy or concerned about the Yankees. I was in no hurry.

Once I departed from the Radcliff home, I knew I could not travel the main roads, so I used fields to avoid being caught. While traveling across the fields, I got lost. After riding a little further, I came to a house to ask the nearest way to the Little River Turnpike. The house belonged to John Coleman. Just as Coleman was walking toward the front gate, I noticed two cavalrymen approaching. I knew the best way to handle the situation was the safest way, and that was to meet them and inquire where they were from. When asked, the Yankees said they belonged to the Fifth New York Cavalry, with General Reynolds's corps. They were camped about a mile away and had stopped along the road to pick some cherries. They did not have the slightest suspicion who they were speaking to because I was wearing a waterproof cape. It was drizzling rain. The whole time we spoke, I had my pistol drawn under my waterproof cape, pointed at them. They were unarmed and could do nothing but surrender.

Coleman was standing about fifty yards away and witnessed my capture of the two Yankee cavalrymen. I turned with my two prisoners and asked Coleman where the road to the pike was. He did not answer. He thought it was some kind of trick. It wasn't until I showed him my star on my gray jacket, and told him my name that he cooperated with me.

The two prisoners' horses were tied together by a halter strap so they could not escape. I took my prisoners and headed west. It was near sundown and I wanted to get over the mountains because it would be difficult to find the path through the mountain in the darkness. I had important information for General Lee and I wanted to get to General Stuart's headquarters with that information as soon as possible.

My prisoners and I had been riding for about an hour when we reached the Little River Turnpike. There was a long wagon train using the turnpike, escorted by a heavy Yankee cavalry guard. It would take an hour for the train to pass and clear the way so I concluded to take the risk of crossing it in the midst of the cavalry escort. The rubber cape partially concealed my gray coat; but I did not have much reliance in the cape. It would be presumed by the Yankees that no Confederate soldier would dare to be there in uniform riding among them.

The two Yankee prisoners knew who I was because they had heard me when I told John Coleman. I made my prisoners ride close to me, still with my pistol drawn under my cape. I told my prisoners if they opened their mouths or did not stay close to me they would be dead men.

We rode slowly alongside of the wagon train as it passed the Birch house, where I had captured Major Stirling and Captain Fisher several days ago. There was a high fence on each side of the road, but there was no gap in it anywhere. I was afraid to dismount and open one because I did not want to raise any suspicion. I knew that a hundred yards further down the road was a crossroads leading toward the mountain, so I decided to ride on with the Yankee cavalry until we reached that point where I could turn away from them. When we reached the crossroads the wagons slowed to a point to allow me and my prisoners to get through a gap created by them. A company of cavalry had dismounted and were resting under the trees, but they took no notice of us. They must have thought that I was some kind of a general with my orderlies.

We turned from the pike and took off at a brisk pace. By now it was dark and I knew I could not get back to General Stuart. I paroled my prisoners, took their horses, turned them loose on foot, and slept that night in a fence corner during a drenching rain. The two Yankee prisoners had actually deceived their own friends, who never dreamed they were anything other than my escort or companions.

Early the next morning, I reported to General Stuart and informed him that General Hooker's army was still in camp where it had been for a week. We discussed the best route for him to go into Maryland. I knew all the roads, as well as the location of each of the seven corps of the enemy. I thought General Stuart ought to go through an unguarded gap of the Bull Run Mountain, cutting his way right through the middle of the enemy's army, and cross the Potomac River at Seneca. It was the shortest route. General Stuart could go into Maryland, and there have the opportunity to destroy General Hooker's transportation as he went along, and to cut off communications between Washington City and the north. Two of General Stuart's brigades would be left behind to observe the enemy while the other three passed through General Hooker's army into Maryland. I would be the one to lead General Stuart's cavalry to Rowser's Ford along the Potomac River. I believed the plan was practicable.

* * * *

General Stuart received his final instructions from General Lee, authorizing him to move into Maryland, doing as much damage as possible to General Hooker's transportation and communications.

I started across the route I had been traveling for the past week to connect with General Stuart. We stopped at a mountain side spring to have breakfast on some sutler stores. Two men had been sent forward on picket, when suddenly bullets were whistling around us. We sprang to our horses; the two men did not return. I believed the Yankees had set an ambush for us, but I escaped harm and capture.

We made a detour around the Yankees and hurried to join General Stuart, as we heard his cannons booming around the Haymarket area. We got to the Little River Turnpike, below Aldie, which was our point of junction with General Stuart. Instead of meeting him, we struck the head of General Hancock's Yankee columns moving in the direction of the Potomac River. Things had suddenly changed.

I spent that day and night riding about among the Yankees, and with great difficulty trying to extricate myself from the dilemma in which I was placed. I could not locate General Stuart or any of his men because General Hancock's divisions were between us. So, I retraced my steps through the Shenandoah Valley, passing General Robertson, who commanded the two brigades General Stuart had left behind to observe the Yankee army. General Robertson's command was resting in Ashby and Snicker's Gaps in the Blue Ridge Mountains.

My Command crossed the Potomac River at Hancock, Maryland. It was my intention to join General Lee in Pennsylvania and scout for him. When we crossed the Pennsylvania border with Maryland "Big Yankee" Ames said, "Well, I am going with you, but I will not fire a shot. When the Emancipation Proclamation was issued and I saw the war was for the Negro and not for the Union, I joined the South, and am willing to fight to repel the invasion of her soil, and am willing to give my life in her defense, but I will not fight on Northern soil."

We reached Mercersburg, Pennsylvania where we expected to find a portion of General Lee's army, but it had moved on. Our numbers being so small, and we were unfamiliar with the Pennsylvania country, we determined to return to Virginia. We had gathered up two hundred and eighteen head of cattle, fifteen horses, and twelve Negroes.

As we were driving our cattle along toward the Maryland line, an old lady said to Ames in a bitter voice, "Well, now, you've got them, but my earnest prayer is that you may not get across the river with them."

"Old lady, did you ever hear of Mosby?" said Ames.

"Yes."

"Well these are Mosby's men."

The old lady seemed somewhat shaken by the news. She abruptly turned away, saying, "Oh, then, you'll get off safe enough, I'll be bound."

We returned to Washington County, Maryland and re-crossed the Potomac River without any interruptions. Our fate was much better off than many of those that had entered Pennsylvania.

CHAPTER SIXTEEN

After Gettysburg

I was in Winchester, Virginia, turning over the beef cattle that we had captured in Pennsylvania to the commissary, when I heard the news of General Lee's defeat at Gettysburg. I understood we suffered severe losses in the fight, men we could not afford to lose. On July 14, General Lee and the army re-crossed the Potomac River at Williamsport.

General Meade, who now commanded the Army of the Potomac, was not too quick to follow General Lee. Even though General Lee's army was crippled after its defeat at Gettysburg, it still had a lot of fight left in it. They re-crossed the Potomac River on July 16.

By the middle of July, 1863, General Meade and his army had crossed the Potomac River and were now again in Virginia. Now that the Yankee army was again on Virginia soil, my Command was involved in incessant activity against them. Scout, raids, and pitched battle followed each other in rapid succession. We destroyed supply trains, broke up the means of conveying intelligence, thus isolating troops from their base, confusing plans by capturing dispatches, while at the same time compelling the use of large forces to protect Washington City and the Potomac River.

After returning to Virginia, I went to Richmond on official business. When I returned, I called for my men to meet me at Rector's Cross Roads, but the advance of General Meade's army occupied the place. Instead, I changed the place to rendezvous to Rectortown. Thirty men answered my call. In order for us to reach the rear of the invading army, we had to take a roundabout way to The Plains, where we camped in sight of the Army of the Potomac's Eleventh Corps. On the way we met up with Bush Underwood and several men, who had captured several officers and an orderly. This was at Mountsville in Loudoun County.

Early the next morning, we captured three sutler wagons and forty-five prisoners. While engaged we fell in with General Carl Schurz, who was riding out from his camp. We chased him back toward the camp. The horses were divided among the men who participated in the raid and the prisoners sent off to Culpepper Court House.

Several days later, we came in sight of some Yankees with nine wagons, on a foraging expedition. They had no guards with them. The nine wagons were captured and fire set to them. We took off fifty-six horses in the raid.

I began next to operate farther to the front of General Meade's army, between Salem and The Plains. As we were marching from the latter place, we captured two cavalrymen with spoils. They told me that a large number of mules had been turned out to pasture near The Plains, guarded by forty artillerists. We quickly swooped down on the mules and the artillerists in full view of the enemy's camp. We carried off all of the mules and their guards. Yankee infantry gave pursuit, trying to catch us, but we laughed at them as we headed back into the mountains with our spoils.

During this time, I did have one adventure, which was quite striking to me, and that was that I again escaped capture. It happened near the Hathaway house. Fount Beattie, who had been released from prison, and I were sleeping in the nearby woods when a Yankee cavalry patrol came to the Hathaway house looking for me. While the Yankees were at the house, one of their comrades rode into the woods where Fount and I were sleeping, to look for some horses that might had been concealed from them. As the Yankee cavalryman was about to capture me, I awoke, sprang to my feet and fired my pistol, wounding the Yankee soldier's horse in the head. The surprised Yankee turned to run, and I fired again, striking the horse's saddle. Before his comrades could come to help him, Fount and I made good our escape.

General Meade's army had taken a position in the vicinity of Warrenton. While the movement was being made, we hung upon their rear looking for any opportunity to strike them. After the last corps had passed, a major and thirty of his men chased several of my men back into the mountain. When I rode up to a nearby house, a woman by the name of Mrs. Lewis implored me to save myself and flee. The Yankee major, who had breakfast at her house earlier that same morning, had declared that if he captured me, he would hang me from the first tree. I laughed. At this moment, the Yankee cavalry were seen coming from the mountain toward me. At the same moment, eighteen of my men arrived and the order was given to charge them. Up across the mountain the Yankees fled, leaping over two stone wall fences, which lay across their path. The Yankees fled around and around the mountain, followed by us.

The boastful Yankee major was caught while squatting under a bush. Thirteen of his men were captured, but one lieutenant would be the last to surrender. The Yankee lieutenant struck out in the direction of a pine forest with me fast upon his heels. I chased him for a bit, but my horse was entirely spent and did not want to continue on. The Yankee lieutenant was still a good fifty yards in front of me on a hill when I fired my pistol and ordered him to halt. The officer turned and rode back toward me with his pistol drawn and at his side. I thought he wanted to fight, but instead it was to surrender. The Yankee officer had been riding a splendid horse.

"You won't take my horse, will you?" The lieutenant asked in a piteous voice.

"The devil I won't, what do you suppose I was chasing you for." said I.

The Yankee lieutenant was from the Seventeenth Pennsylvania Cavalry.

During the month of July after General Lee's defeat at Gettysburg, we harassed the Yankee army, capturing one hundred and eighty six prisoners, one hundred and twenty three horses, twelve wagons, and fifty fine harness and arms.

On August 24, thirty-five men assembled to go with me down to Fairfax County to look for some game. Near Annandale, I left Lieutenant Tom Turner with all but several men sheltered in a wooded area. Norman Smith and Jack Barnes were the ones who accompanied me on a scout along the Orange and Alexandria Railroad. Our scout had taken some time. It was late in the evening when the three of us stopped at Ravenwood, which was a private residence, and slept in the barn on some hay. The next morning, we awakened in full view and in close proximity to an encampment of Yankees. We saddled our horses and quickly departed. On the way back to Lieutenant Turner and the rest of the Command, we found three unguarded railroad bridges, which I wanted to burn.

While in the wooded area near Annandale, we came across forty Yankee cavalrymen, who were herding some horses in the direction of General Meade's army. They were men from the Second Massachusetts Cavalry. The horses and chance for booty changed events. I decided instead to postpone the railroad bridge burning until later that night and follow the Yankee cavalrymen for a while, looking for an opportunity to strike them. The Yankee cavalry was soon joined by a second group of thirty men. I did not expect them. At that point, I decided to attack and capture as many horses as possible, and stampede the horses that I could not carry off. I divided my Command, sending Lieutenant Turner with fifteen men to attack the Yankees in the front. I took the rest of the Command and would attack the Yankees from the rear. The Yankees soon halted their herd at Billy Gooding's Tavern along the Little River Turnpike to water and rest their horses.

When everyone was ready, the men with me charged the Yankees. When my men let out with a terrific yell, many of the Yankees, who were dismounted, were completely taken by surprise. The charge routed their guards, and they surrendered. Because of the firing of weapons, a number of the horses stampeded in the direction of the tavern building, giving the Yankees an opportunity to scatter into some of the houses and resist our assault. At the very moment of victory, I was shot in the side and right thigh by a Yankee. Upon seeing that I was wounded and in trouble, Doctor William Dunn, who was more fond of fighting rather than curing, and who had just recently joined my Command, came to my assistance and led me off to a pine forest area. My men did not know I was injured and took this as an indication that we were giving up the fight. Their following me gave the Massachusetts boys time to make good their escape, or we would have captured the whole party.

As soon as I was aware that my men had given up the fight, I ordered them back in. About this time, Lieutenant Turner came charging up with the men that had been assigned to him. They had also routed the enemy they had been ordered to attack.

During the fight with the Massachusetts cavalry, I lost one of my best men, Norman Smith. Norman Smith left the memory of a name which will not be forgotten. He was virtuous and courageous.

Lieutenant Turner, with the greater portion of the Command, pushed on with the prisoners and horses, leaving a few men behind with Doctor Dunn and me. My injury was very painful. I could only move slowly because of the nature of my wounds.

I was taken south to my father's home, Idyle Wilde, near Lynchburg, to recuperate from my wounds. I was away from my Command for the next month. While I was gone, my Command continued to look for any opportunities to attack the Yankees.

While at my father's home, I read in a Northern newspaper, the account of an eyewitness in the *Washington Star*. The eyewitness, a woman, said she saw me two days after the fighting at Billy Gooding's Tavern being transported in a wagon near Uppersville. In her account, she said she had seen my face and it had "the ghastly hue of death upon it." I know that many in the north surely thought that I was dead, but they would soon learn differently.

* * * *

On September 27, I decided to undertake another daring raid. I struck out with ten men down some infrequently used roads, which followed in the same direction as the Little River Turnpike toward Alexandria. When we came to Fairfax Court House, I decided we would go around the village. We slept in some pines that night.

The next morning we spent some time collecting information and picking up stragglers. Six of the stragglers we captured were sent off under guard. This reduced my party to five men.

Soon after sunset, we started again toward Alexandria and in a short time, arrived at the City Hotel in Alexandria. It was my intention to capture the bogus governor, Francis Pierpont, who was considered the provisional governor of Virginia for the Union. I learned from the hotel keeper that Pierpont had gone off to Washington City. It was a missed opportunity, but after the war, I understood he was quite angry when he received my message, "you did not see the farmer who rode by your hotel on a hay wagon yesterday, did you Governor? My driver pointed out your window, and I marked it plain. It's just over the bay, and I'll get you some night, mightily easy." Of course, as fate would have it, I was never able to capture him.

I soon rode south with my men on the Telegraph Road from Alexandria. I stopped at a house, two miles from Alexandria to inquire where Colonel Dulaney was residing. Colonel Dulaney was Francis Pierpont's aide. I was informed that Colonel Dulaney had passed but a few hours before on his way to his residence, Rose Hill. He had been to Fairfax Court House earlier in the day. We soon located Rose Hill.

I approached the main door at Rose Hill and knocked for admittance. An upper window was opened and I asked if Colonel Dulaney was in, that I had some dispatches for him from Governor Pierpont. Instead of a staff officer giving me admittance to the house, Colonel Dulaney soon appeared at the door.

"Is this Colonel Dulaney?" I asked.

"Yes sir. Walk in gentleman and be seated."

"My name is Mosby," I said, approaching the Colonel.

The startling announcement confused Colonel Dulaney's staff officer, who was by his side. It was soon understood that Colonel Dulaney was my prisoner. Serving in my Command was Colonel Dulaney's son, Daniel. When Daniel walked through the door, he said, "How do Pa? I am very glad to see you."

"Well, Sir, I am dammed sorry to see you."

Just as we were leaving Rose Hill, Colonel Dulaney said to his son that "he had an old pair of shoes he had better take as he reckoned they were darn scarce in the Confederacy."

Daniel laughed, held up his leg and showed his father a new pair of cavalry boots that he had taken from a sutler in a previous raid.

On the raid, we destroyed a railroad bridge at Cameron's Run. Combustible material was collected by the men and the bridge was burned in sight of two Yankee forts and their batteries. They did not challenge us.

On October 1, 1863, the Command was assembled at Scuffleburg, a tiny hamlet in a small valley on the eastern side of the Blue Ridge Mountain between Markham and Paris. I called for sixty men to be mustered into Company B. I handled the election of officers in the same fashion as I did with Company A. I proposed the slate of officers I wanted and did not give the men the opportunity to cast their vote for another. I did this because I always believed the law of Congress, which ordained the election instead of the appointment of officers, would, if executed, prove even more destructive in my Command than it had done in regular service. I chose William Billy Smith as Company B's new captain. Captain Smith had served as a lieutenant with the Black Horse Company, the Fourth Virginia Cavalry before joining my Command. As one of my men John Scott said of Captain Smith: "He was a man in the prime of life, remarkable for his personal strength, is cool, bold, and possesses in a remarkable degree the qualities necessary to command."

The rest of the slate of officers for Company B were Frank Williams who was promoted to first lieutenant; Albert Wrenn was promoted to second lieutenant; and Robert Gray, third lieutenant. All of these men had served gallantly in the Command. Since George Whitescarver had been killed back in June, Joe Nelson was elected third lieutenant to take his place in Company A.

The next day, Captain Smith set out with forty-five men from the Warrenton area. On Lee's Ridge near Warrenton, Captain Smith came across a Yankee cavalry encampment. About 4:00 in the morning, Captain Smith and his company attacked the encampment, completely catching the Yankees by surprise. The Yankee officers were able to rally their men, and drive off Captain Smith's Company, but not before the Command captured six prisoners and twenty-seven horses. The men in Company B always recalled and spoke of the "Billy Smith Raid."

On October 10, my younger brother came from home to Fauquier County. He enlisted with Company A, and eventually became my adjutant. Willie was twelve years younger than me.

At 6:00 in the evening, on Monday, October 26, I left Salem with seventy-five men. It was my intention to raid the stream of abundant supplies that were being transported by the Yankee army between Gainesville and Warrenton. All of us had knowledge of the surrounding area of operation, but as was our habit, we always scout before a raid. Under the cover of darkness, we were able to penetrate ten miles inside of General Meade's army's cavalry screen of pickets and find a wooded area along the Warrenton and Gainesville Turnpike. A wagon train appeared along the road, guarded by cavalry and infantry in the front of the wagon train and cavalry and infantry marching in the rear of the wagon train They were supported by artillery. But, the middle of the wagon train was pretty much unprotected.

To attack the wagon train would bring the cavalry and infantry escort and they would drive us off since there were so many of them. So instead, I came up with a plan to stop the middle of the wagon train. This would raise less suspicion. To pull off the ruse, I sent William Chapman with ten men to stop the middle of the wagon train. William, posing as a captain with the Eighteenth Pennsylvania Cavalry on provost marshal detail, asked one of the wagon teamsters who was in charge of this section of the wagon train. After learning the name of the officer, William rode forward, identified himself and had the officer placed under arrest. He ordered about fifty of the wagons to be parked along the side of the road, and the mules unhitched. My men and I rode from the woods and were going to fire the wagons, but a cavalry detachment appeared and there was no time to destroy the wagons. We were able to escape and get off with one hundred and three mules, forty-two horses, and thirty prisoners without the single loss of a man from the

Command. I divided the horses among the men and sent the mules off to General Stuart.

* * * *

On Monday, November 2, 1863, there was a meeting at Rectortown. The Command was drawn up in line and letters from Generals Lee and Stuart were read by William Chapman, complimentary of my Command. The men were furnished with printed certificates of membership, signed by me. This was a necessity because men wearing Confederate uniforms, many of them deserters or absent from their commands without leave, were roaming about the country representing themselves as Mosby's Rangers. I ordered my men to arrest all horse thieves and deserters and bring them in to me.

The region in which we operated was without any kind of civil authority. Only my men and I could protect the defenseless people from the roving band of deserters from both armies. The mountains were infested with horse thieves and desperadoes, who were ready to prey on the inhabitants, regardless of their loyalties to the North and South. We performed duties of police as well as soldier. Sometimes I had to be military ruler and judge, settling not only military issues, but differences among the people.

Not everyone remained loyal to my authority and continued to serve in my Command. Such as it was with Charles Binns. Binns had been a resident of Falls Church, serving in my Command since General Lee's retreat from Gettysburg. He got himself into some trouble. While on a drunken frolic, he committed an act of rascality. Binns had abducted two Negro women and was preparing to sell them as slaves. For his crime, I ordered his arrest. In order to escape the punishment he deserved, he fled to the Yankee camps at Fairfax, where he betrayed us. Since he knew the locations of some of the houses where my men were boarding, Binns agreed to lead the Second Massachusetts Cavalry in a search for my men. Under the cover of darkness, twelve to fifteen of my men were taken from their beds and arrested by the Yankee cavalry. The Yankees also took their horses and equipment. Binns led several other raids for the Yankees. One of the raids was on Christmas Day, when they captured eight more of my men.

Long after the war, Charles Binns was still regarded in Virginia as a traitor for his deeds, so much so that he wrote in a newspaper he wanted to put aside the war and hear of it no more. I replied to his article that he would never find rest but would forever hear, ringing in his ears, the raven calling, "Nevermore," and would still be wandering the hills crying "respite, respite, Nepenthe."

The Command was assembled at Rectortown on December 7. I read the order forming Company C. The officers chosen were William Chapman as Captain. Captain Chapman had served with the Dixie Artillery from Luray in the Shenandoah Valley before joining my Command. First lieutenant was given to Adolphus Richards, or as we called him, "Dolly." Lieutenant Richards came from Loudoun County and had served on General Jones' staff before joining my Command. He had distinguished and covered himself in glory with a number of raids, where he served gallantly. Promoted to second lieutenant was Frank Fox, who had served as an officer with the Seventeenth Virginia Infantry, and promoted to third lieutenant was Frank Yager.

In July, Sam Chapman was released from prison and returned to General Lee and the Army of Northern Virginia. For a short period of time he served in the Thirty-Eighth Artillery Battalion. I had Sam transferred to my Command in January of 1864. After his return, Sam told me that being an artilleryman was "a pleasant life, but a very inactive one." He was glad to return to an adventurous life with my Command.

Chapter Seventeen

A Battle in the Snow

On January 1, 1864, it was anything but a pleasant day. The snow had been on the ground for two weeks, thawing in the daytime and freezing at night, until it was absolutely dangerous, because of the mud, to travel on horseback. The sun had risen briefly with all of the grandeur of imagination one could conceive. But clouds began to cover the sky, and by noon, snow was falling. I ordered the Command to assemble at Rectortown for a raid into Fairfax County. Sam Chapman informed me Maryland cavalry under Major Henry Cole had been seen at Upperville. I had not as yet arrived at Rectortown, but sent word for Captain Smith to take charge of the Command, who would assemble there. I went on to Upperville with a few men to scout the Yankee position. By the time my men began arriving in the area, they noticed the Yankee cavalry had occupied Rectortown. My men began to ride from hill to hill, observing the Yankee cavalry in the railroad town, but did not approach them. My Command was outnumbered three to one, but fortunately, the Yankees did not stay long.

As soon as Cole's Yankees departed from Rectortown, Captain Smith and about twenty-five men followed them on the Salem Road for five miles. The Yankees turned off the Salem Road and crossed a field in the direction of Middleburg. Since Captain Smith was familiar with the area, he cut across the country in order to come upon their flank and rear near Five Points, a place where five roads meet.

Three of the men under Captain Smith, who were riding in advance of the main column, Richard Montjoy, John Edmonds, and Henry Ashby, attacked the rear of the Yankee column. When gunfire was heard, Captain Smith quickly brought up his men. The enemy had taken a position in the road. On one side of them was a high stone wall, while on the other was an open, clear country, extending almost as far as the eye could see. The Yankees had formed and were awaiting Captain Smith's attack. With a yell and pistols in hand, Captain Smith and the Command charged the Yankees and went right through them. Their leader's horse was hit during this part of the fight and fell on him. He was trapped beneath the dead horse and quickly captured by my men.

After Captain Albert Hunter, the commanding officer of the Yankee cavalry had been captured by my men, many of Hunter's men fled. An effort was made to rally them in an open field, on the right of the road, but it failed. My men chased them. Some three hundred yards away was a body of heavy-timbered land, in which a large number of Yankees took shelter, hoping my men would not pursue them. Generally woods do afford great protection from the attacking party; but, in this instance, they sought their own captivity. Back of these woods was a little stream called Carter's Run, which was very shallow and narrow, while the banks were high. As we began to push the Yankees from the woods, their horses were so frightened that they refused to jump the stream and instead, tossed their riders into the water. They were captured.

The field showed how complete the fight had been. I noticed the Yankees had thrown bags of corn, sabers, carbines, pistols, and everything they could rid themselves of. Some, as though thinking their horses not fleet enough, jumped off and, leaving them in the road, ran on foot. We captured thirty-five men and fifty horses. The Yankee commanding officer, Captain Hunter, managed to escape.

This would not be the last time we would battle these Marylanders.

* * * *

On January 7, I received a message from Captain Frank Stringfellow, one of General Stuart's most reliable scouts, who was very knowledgeable of the Northern Virginia area. He was an officer I considered trustworthy. Captain Stringfellow had been scouting with some men around the Harpers Ferry area and believed it was possible to conduct a raid on Major Cole's Yankee cavalry, which was camped along the eastern base of Loudoun Heights. Major Cole and his command were picketing the Harpers Ferry and Hillsborough Road. Major Cole's only support was infantry, which were located about a mile away at Harpers Ferry. Captain Stringfellow believed that if properly executed, we could capture all of Cole's command without firing a shot. The attack would take place once Cole's men were asleep. I was eager to capture Major Cole because of his rough treatment of the people living along the border of Virginia and Maryland. I believed our chances were good and it was agreed upon that the raid would be conducted.

On the afternoon of Saturday, January 9, one hundred and six men assembled at Upperville. We rode until it was well after dark when I halted the Command at Woodgrove, the home of James Heaton. When we arrived, Mr. Heaton had fires blazing in every room for our warmth and a plentiful supper had been prepared for both officers and men. Mr. Heaton's son, Henry served in my Command. It was around 10:00 o'clock in the evening when I received a message from Captain Stringfellow. He reassured me in his message that everything was in order for an attack on Cole's men. We resumed the march.

Once we were two miles from Major Cole's camp, we were joined by Captain Stringfellow and ten men near Saint

Paul's Church. They reported favorably. Major Cole was reported to have between one hundred and seventy five to two hundred men. It was made known to me that his headquarters was in a two-story, white weather-board house on the crest of a ridge, which overlooked a stream and was near the Yankee cavalry's camp.

We rode across a narrow skirt of country toward the base of Short Hill Mountain. The night was clear, the stars shone brightly. The cold was sharp and very bitter, so much so, that many of the men would dismount at times and run or walk beside their horses to keep their feet from freezing. Others kept their hands under their blankets as they held the horse's reins between their teeth. There was no talk of the prospective fight, and indeed there was little conversation among the men. No sound broke the stillness of the night except the dull, heavy trump of horses as they walked along the snowy path. Fields, roads, trees, and shrubs were alike clothed in the white robes of winter, and it seemed almost a sacrilege against the beauty, and holy stillness of the scene to stain those pure garments with the life blood of man, be he friend or foe.

Near Piney Run, along Short Hill Mountain, Captain Stringfellow and I rode on to scout the position while the men fed their horses. What I learned was, Major Cole had a picket force along Piney Run, on the Harpers Ferry and Hillsborough Road, not too far from his camp. I knew if we could pass by the picket post and gain Major Cole's cavalry's rear, we would be successful. After about two hours, we returned to the Command. Things were going as planned and I was confident of success. The Command moved slowly onward, using paths and ravines.

Once we reached the Potomac River, we turned west toward Harpers Ferry. There were no Yankee pickets. I noticed the yellowish glow of the Yankee campfires burning on the Maryland side of the Potomac River. The whistle of an engine fell on the ears of some of my men. I believed they were under the impression that we were going to attack a train. They would soon know differently.

We arrived at a steep wooded cliff, which overlooked the river. On reaching this point, without creating any alarm, I deemed the crisis had passed, and the capture of the enemy a certainty. My men dismounted and begin to lead their horses by single file up a very dark and steep, narrow path. At times we had to grab onto the bushes to keep from falling because the ice-covered slope was so slippery. About one hundred yards away from the Yankees' camp, I halted the Command to allow them to close up. There was not a sentinel to be found. The camp was sleeping.

The plan called for Richard Montjoy and six men to capture the Yankee picket post, one-half mile south along the Harpers Ferry and Hillsborough Road at Piney Run. I ordered him to hold this area of the road because it would be used as an escape route. Captain Stringfellow and his ten men were to capture Major Cole at his headquarters about one hundred yards away from the Yankees' camp. Captain Smith was ordered to take some men and capture the Yankees' horses at another building. I took the rest of the Command with me, with intentions of dismounting some them to capture the first tent rows.

It was 3 a. m. according to my timepiece. All my plans were on the eve of consummation, when suddenly, there was the report of yelling and the crackle of pistols blazing. I was not ready for an attack because my men were still strung out on the narrow path leading up from the river. Contrary to orders, Captain Stringfellow and his men attacked the Yankees, but at the time of the first report of their gunfire, we thought that it was Major Cole's men. Great confusion resulted because of this misjudgment.

In response to Captain Stringfellow's attack, I ordered a charge. Captain Smith and Lieutenant Turner with what men were available to them shouted, "charge them, boys." Without any knowledge of who they were charging, they pitched into Captain Stringfellow's men, killing and wounding several in the attack.

While Captain Smith and Lieutenant Turner's men were charging, my dismounted men quickly approached and captured the first row of tents with their sleeping Yankees. They were captured without a fight.

Taking advantage of the confusion, Major Cole's men began to pour a withering fire into my men. But we soon pitched into them. A severe fight ensued, in which the Yankees were driven from their tents. Some of them took shelter in an old log house, firing on us from the door, windows, and through the chinks. Men cursed and yelled as their horses fell and shrieked in pain or kicked wildly. Some combatants stood almost in reach of one another, firing into each other's face. Still, others cried out, "Surrender!"

"No, I won't! You surrender!"

Many of the Yankees, driven from their tents, sought refuge among the thick bushes higher up the mountain side and from this advantage poured a galling fire into our ranks. The balls striking the ground threw up the frozen earth in our face. Lieutenant Turner was shot down by the Yankees while courageously leading his men. He was seriously wounded and removed from the field by several men from his Company.

Captain Smith was soon reinforced by Captain Chapman and Company C. Captain Smith ordered the tents to be set on fire so they would have some light and could see the Yankees. Captain Smith shouted, "fire the tents and shoot 'em by the light." While he was giving this command, Captain Smith was shot by a Yankee. After the fight at Loudoun Heights, Captain Chapman told me the Yankees fired a volley and he noticed Captain Smith leap into the air and fall from his horse. Captain Smith's head was in the snow and his feet were still dangling in the horse's stirrups when Captain Chapman tried to help his comrade back into his saddle. As he did so, he realized that he was dead. He placed Captain Smith's body on the ground. He made every effort to try and recover Captain Smith's timepiece to give to his wife and children, but his hands were so numb from the cold that he could not unbutton his comrade's overcoat. He could still see the Yankees in the same position as when they fired at them, but they made no further demonstration by trying to fire on, or capture him. He could not understand why. But he had no other choice than to leave Captain Smith's body behind. This was something that always troubled him.

During this time, I heard an artillery gun sound from the direction of Harpers Ferry. I knew it was some sort of a signal to General Sullivan and the Yankees garrisoned at that town. The Yankees were only about a mile away and I realized that it was hazardous to continue in my position, so I shouted for the men to retreat because there were too many of them for us. The Yankees did not attempt to follow, but kept up a steady fire while we were leaving the field. We retired in good order, carrying off seven prisoners and fifty to sixty horses.

Lieutenant Turner was taken by his men to the home of Levi Waters. Mr. Waters was a Unionist, who lived about a mile south on the Harpers Ferry and Hillsborough Road. I took the opportunity to visit with Lieutenant Turner before moving on with the Command. I was greatly affected when I saw some of the men from Lieutenant Turner's Company standing around his bed. They had followed him in so many fights; but hope still kept her vigil by his bed, and in cheerful accents, he assured his sorrowing comrades that in another week he would be with them again. That would not be so and I knew it. When I looked upon his face and saw his piteous condition, I wept as I had never done so before. He died the next day. My loss was severe; more so in the worth than the number of the slain. Lieutenant Turner was one of the men, who came with me from the First Virginia Cavalry when I began partisan operations.

I also grieved greatly over the loss of Captain Smith. He left behind a wife and four children. He died two days short of his twenty-eighth birthday. Captain Smith and Lieutenant Turner were two of the noblest and bravest officers of this army, who thus sealed a life of devotion and of sacrifice to the Cause they loved.

The march homeward was indeed a gloomy one. A sad and sullen silence pervaded our ranks and found expression in every countenance. All that we could have gained would not compensate for the loss we sustained. I could not conceal my disappointment and keen regret of the enterprise. I knew and felt that I had suffered a loss which could not well be repaired. I was sorry I had made the attack on Major Cole's camp. If my plans had been carried out, the expedition would have been a success. Captain Stringfellow failed to carry out his part in the attack. I would never enter into another enterprise with him during the war. This affair would be known in the Northern newspapers as "A Battle in the Snow."

Chapter Eighteen

Anker's Shop

At the end of January, 1864, I went to Charlottesville to see Pauline and the children. She had moved there for the children's and her own safety to avoid capture by the Yankees. After visiting her, I went to Richmond. While in Richmond, I procured the transfer of Sam Chapman to my Command with the rank of first lieutenant. I was also informed that I had been recommended by General Lee and promoted to the rank of lieutenant-colonel. General Lee wrote Secretary of War James Seddon:

"During the past year Major Mosby, of the partisan rangers has been very active in harassing the rear of the Federal army operating in northern Virginia. He is zealous, bold, and skillful, and with very small resources has accomplished a great deal. I beg leave therefore to recommend his promotion to be lieutenant colonel. I do this in order to show him that his services have been appreciated, and to encourage him to still greater activity and zeal."

My promotion took effect on January 21, 1864. After leaving Richmond, I returned to my Command.

I had often been in the habit, before the Harpers Ferry disaster, of attacking the enemy's camps in the nighttime; but even after this, I could not be induced to entertain such a proposition, except under peculiar circumstances. This resolution was not arrived at so much from fear of the enemy's inflicting injury on us, as from danger of my own men firing into one another. In this case it was conceded, by all the men, that three out of five killed at the Loudoun Mountain were killed by our own men. So great was the despondency of the men, at the result of this affair, that nothing was done for some time. But even though my men's spirits were dampened their ardor was so great that soon we were engaged in new enterprises as though we had sustained no reverse.

On February 21, 1864, the men were gathering at Piedmont for the funeral of James McCobb. Private McCobb was from Baltimore. He had been killed the previous day when Yankee cavalry under Major Cole surprised him and several others from my Command at their boarding house near Upperville. McCobb tried to escape by mounting his horse, and, in attempting to leap a fence was thrown, and there killed.

As the men began to assemble for Private McCobb's funeral, I was at the Jeffries' house writing a report to General Stuart of the proceedings of the last few days. I had not finished my report when one of my scouts arrived and informed me that Yankee cavalry, the Second Massachusetts and Sixteenth New York, were in Fauquier on a raid. I was sure they were looking for me. It was reported by the scout that they were near Middleburg. Without waiting to pay the last sad tribute of respect to our comrade, the Command, numbering one hundred and fifty marched under Captain William Chapman in the direction of the enemy. I moved on ahead of them with a small party to reconnoiter the Yankee position.

When we arrived at Rector's Cross Roads, the Yankee cavalry had already departed, heading toward Mountsville. I sent Sam Underwood and another man to follow their trail and report to me. I took the Command and headed toward Dranesville with the intentions of intercepting the Yankees on their way to their camp at Vienna. Underwood reported that the Yankee cavalry had proceeded in the direction of Leesburg. With the object still in view of keeping between the Yankee cavalry, I marched the Command to Carter's Mill along Goose Creek. I left instructions with Captain Chapman to feed the horses from the corn-crib of a Union man in the neighborhood. Captain Chapman was then to take his men to Harrison's farm, lower down on Goose Creek, which was in the direction of the Leesburg and Dranesville Pike and await my orders. I took several men with me to use as couriers and proceeded toward Leesburg, for the purpose of watching the movements of the enemy and directing the Command. I now felt sure of success; for, while my men were moving on the shorter interior route, the Yankee cavalry were marching on a longer circular route. I sent a courier to Captain Chapman to move the Command closer to the pike.

That night, the Yankee cavalry camped at Mr. Kephart's farm along the Leesburg and Dranesville Pike. They were joined by the Thirteenth New York Cavalry. My Command camped near Dranesville in some thick pines where we built fires. Most of the men retired to their saddle blankets and slept on the frozen ground later than usual as the imminence of a splendid fight made sleep impossible to many. The hot-headed youngsters wanted to begin the attack at once. I disagreed and said to my men that I had been running the Yankees parallels all day, but had headed them; that they would come down the Leesburg Pike and we would attack them in the morning.

Early the next morning, I reassured my men that it was all right, and they would certainly catch the Yankees before they got to their camp. I then marched the Command farther down the pike in the direction of Vienna. The Command was posted in a body of pines on the right of the road, a little beyond Anker's Shop, a few miles west of Dranesville. I left Walter Whaley on the pike where a road branches to the right. The Yankees, I thought, might use this road, instead. If they used this other road, it was still possible to strike across country and get in front of them.

Walter Whaley soon came in with intelligence that the Second Massachusetts was coming along the pike in our direction and that the other Yankee cavalry, who had camped with them the previous evening was using the other road. I began to position my men. Company A and part of Company B, under Lieutenant Frank Williams, were placed along the edge of the pine woods in columns of fours, to charge the front of the advancing Yankee cavalry. Company C with the balance of Company B, under Captain Chapman, was to charge the Yankee cavalry's rear. Fifteen men with carbines were posted in the pines under Richard Montjoy. They would strike the center of the Yankee cavalry. After I had made these arrangements, I said to my Command, "Men, the Yankees are coming and it is likely we will have a hard fight. When you are ordered to charge, I want you to go through them. Reserve your fire until you get close enough to see clearly what you are shooting at, and then let every shot tell."

I wanted to use a diversion, so I sent Frank Rahm and two other men down the road to attract the attention of the approaching Yankee cavalry. As for the rest of the Command, I gave them strict orders not to fire on the Yankees until they heard the blast of my whistle. All were near the road, but hidden in the woods from the sight of the Yankee cavalry. The men sat motionless in their saddles, every ear was strained and eyes watching and waiting in anxious expectation. There was an unnatural, an unearthly stillness around us at that moment. I knew my men were eager to begin firing, but they knew that my commands were not to be disobeyed.

Very soon, the Yankee cavalry was seen moving slowly down the pike, two videttes riding about two hundred yards ahead of all, then the advance of about twenty, and lastly the main body. The videttes had passed without noticing us. When they came upon Rahm and the other two men, who had been on a hill in full view of the road, they turned around and seeing my men formed along the edge of the pine forest, a vidette waved his hand to his men, calling to them to charge. At that moment, I blew my whistle.

Company A and part of Company B charged down the pike. My men were yelling and were like wolves on the fold as they scattered the Yankee advance. When my men came to the main body, the Yankees stood firm until we were upon them. At first they made a hot fight. Captain Chapman's men were among the Yankees and it was a hand-to-hand fight. I later learned from Captain Chapman during that part of the fight about some of the Yankee trickery. He told me the commanding officer of the Yankee cavalry, a Captain Reed had made some motion of surrender by throwing up his hand to Barron Von Massow, a Prussian officer in my Command. As Von Massow charged at Captain Reed, he believed the Yankee officer had surrendered. As Von Massow rode by Captain Reed, the officer shot him in his back. Captain Chapman saw Captain Reed's trickery and made his shot tell, dropping the Yankee officer from his saddle. Von Massow looked up at Captain Chapman and said, "I am much obliged to you." Von Massow recovered from his wound.

Another incident of this same kind of deceit took place involving John Munson. I heard Munson later telling some of my men that "he got the drop on a Yankee cavalryman, who threw up his hand and exclaimed, 'I surrender.' I took it for granted he meant what he said, and rode past him, firing at a man beyond who was trying to work his way through a wedge of his men, on the roadside. Then the man who so readily surrendered turned and shot me in the back as I passed him. Lud Lake, who was an eyewitness to his attempt on my life, shot and killed him."

The Yankees were unable to withstand the intensity of our charge. They broke and fled in every direction. Some fled down the pike toward Leesburg, closely pursued by my men. Along the Leesburg and Dranesville Pike, they attempted to crowd through a gate on the roadside, which opened into a barnyard where some of my men were waiting. Many of the Yankees were shot down. A number of Yankees jumped over the fences and across the fields. Their officers tried to rally them, but to no avail. The pike and fields around us were strewn with the Yankee dead and wounded. Their arms and clothing were scattered all around. The raiding party was led by Charles Binns. Great exertions were made to capture him in the pursuit, but, mounted on a swift horse, he made good his escape in the direction of the Potomac River.

In the fight at Anker's Shop, my Command killed ten and wounded seven of the enemy. We captured fifty-five and one hundred of their horses with their equipment.

Mosby and his Command
Source: *Courtesy of Forrest R. Martin*

Private Samuel Underwood
Source: *Carol Underwood Sharpe*

Private Bushrod Underwood
Source: *Carol Underwood Sharpe*

CHAPTER NINETEEN

Stuart's Death and the Calico Raid

On March 8, 1864, I assembled the Command near Paris, Virginia with the intention of forming Company D. I presented to the Command my slate of men, who I believed should be chosen as officers of the new company. Richard Montjoy, a Mississippian, who had served in the Seventh Louisiana Infantry before joining my Command was chosen as the new captain for Company D. Alfred Glascock was chosen as first lieutenant. He had served under Colonel Turner Ashby. Charles Grogen was chosen as second lieutenant. Before joining my Command, Lieutenant Grogen served on General Trimble's staff. He was captured at Gettysburg and was successful at escape from Johnson's Island. All of these men had proven themselves in a fight.

During the months of March and April, there were but few opportunities offered for making any successful attacks on the enemy. We continued our annoyances to which they had been subjected during the winter, causing them to exert great vigilance in guarding against our surprises and interruptions of their communications. I myself was engaged in scouting the enemy's rear for General Stuart and collecting information, which was transmitted to his headquarters, concerning movements, and distribution on the enemy's forces both east and west of the Blue Ridge.

In May, General Grant crossed the Rapidan River with the Army of the Potomac to begin his campaign against General Lee and the Army of Northern Virginia. While this was taking place, I took forty men and moved down the north bank of the Rappahannock River to assault General Grant's communications wherever there was an opportunity. Captains Richards and Chapman were to operate against General Sigel's army in the Shenandoah Valley. They attacked one of his wagon trains near Strasburg, bringing off thirty prisoners and horses. During the same time, I captured an ambulance train near Belle Plain, and brought off seventy-five horses and mules and forty prisoners. A few days later, I wanted to make another attempt near the same place, but such a heavy force was used to guard their trains and line of communication that it made an attack impracticable. My raids incessantly continued on the Yankees. After General Sigel's defeat at New Market, he was stripped of his command by General Grant and replaced with General David Hunter.

* * * *

It was about this time I learned the grievous news of General Stuart's death after suffering a wound while fighting General Sheridan's cavalry at Yellow Tavern, north of Richmond. I recalled the first time I met General Stuart at Bunker Hill when my company joined his regiment, his generosity during a cold snowy evening when he invited me to spend the night at his headquarters near Frying Pan Church, his confidence in my scouting abilities during the Richmond and Gettysburg campaigns. General Stuart was a distinguished officer, who had a great injustice done to him. There were those officers in the Army of Northern Virginia, who accused him of our failure at Gettysburg because he did not interpret his orders correctly from General Lee. That is not so. I have, even until this day, spent my life defending what I consider the greatest injustice done to any army officer. It is an argument that I will not write of at this time in my narrative. It was my fortune to serve under the direct orders of Generals Lee and Stuart, and for both I have always felt a deep affection. An article appeared some time ago in the *Rockbridge County News* that I have held onto because it best describes General Stuart's service:

"*We have said that James E. B. Stuart was a warrior by instinct, and his whole life showed it. He was a born soldier. From his youth he was noted for a daring enthusiasm which gave promise of what the man would be; and his genius soon showed it.*"

Since the article in the *Rockbridge County News* came into my possession, another article has since been written:

"*On a summer morning a solitary man was seen beside the grave of Stuart, in Hollywood Cemetery, near Richmond. The dew was on the grass, the birds sang overhead, the green hillock at the man's feet were all that remained of the daring leader of the Southern cavalry, who, after all his toils, his battles, and the shock of desperate encounters, had come here to rest in peace. Beside this unmarked grave the solitary mourner remained long, pondering and remembering. Finally, he plucked a wild flower, dropped it upon the grave and with tears in his eyes, left the place. This lonely mourner at the grave of Stuart was Mosby.*"

* * * *

On May 20, I had one hundred and fifty men with me near Strasburg, with the intention of inflicting damage and capturing General Hunter's wagon train as it moved up the Shenandoah Valley. General Hunter's trains had about six hundred infantrymen and one hundred cavalrymen guarding his wagons. We got into a little fight with their cavalry, routing them, but when they fell back on their infantry, we gave up the fight. We did not capture any of General Hunter's wagons, but we did accomplish one major objective, and that was, we forced the Yankees to detach heavy forces to guard their lines of communications, which would take them out of a fight.

On June 8, I chose thirty-five men to meet me at Rectortown, for the purpose of accompanying me to Alexandria, with the hope of capturing Governor Pierpont. The next day, we set out. We moved slowly until near sundown when we halted in a body of pines. During the interval, I made my dispositions for the raid. Two men had already been sent off to procure a covered wagon, and have it in readiness at a designated point on the Telegraph Road, near Alexandria. The first part of my plan called for me to take some men to the picket post in the covered wagon, claiming admittance that it was a supply wagon. While I was speaking to the pickets, thus throwing them off their guard, the men concealed inside of the wagon would capture the Yankee pickets. With the way to the town open, my Command would divide into three detachments and march in. The rest of the plan called for me and the men in my detachment to capture Governor Pierpont while Captain Richards and his men captured General Slough, who was the Yankee military governor in this area. Sam Chapman was to capture the government stable, and gather horses to be used by the prisoners.

But the best of plans sometimes miscarry, as would be the fate of this one. The guide who we were going to use got lost on his way to the rendezvous, and in consequence, it was too late to attempt the capture of Governor Pierpont and General Slough that night. If I would have been successful, I would still have needed several hours of daylight to elude pursuit, which would have certainly been made. I postponed the raid until the following night. During the next day, we stayed concealed with some friendly citizens, who fed us.

While waiting, the passing hours were tedious, but as I would soon learn, my plan would come to naught. A Unionist citizen informed the Yankees of the plot to capture

Governor Pierpont and General Slough. There was no other alternative, but to give up the effort, which I did.

* * * *

In June, I took two hundred and fifty men and crossed the Shenandoah River at Shepherd's Mill. It was my intention to raid Duffield's Depot, along the Baltimore and Ohio Railroad, which travels through Jefferson County to Martinsburg. When we arrived at Charlestown, we camped for the night. The ladies of the town brought us bread, meat, pies, and an abundance of milk. For a time we had quite a picnic.

The next morning, I left Lieutenant Nelson and twenty-five men from Company A at Charlestown. They were ordered to move a few miles north of Charlestown with the purpose of intercepting and notifying me of any approach in my rear from the Yankees at Harpers Ferry. I moved on with three companies and a howitzer toward Duffield Depot with a guide from the area. Near Duffield Depot, we captured a Yankee cavalry officer from the Twelfth Pennsylvania Cavalry, and were informed by him that sixty-five men were fortified in a stockade. He also informed us that we had just missed a westbound train, but there would soon be an eastbound train coming. I wanted to capture the depot without alerting the Yankees and wreck the eastbound train.

After we cut the telegraph wires, I sent Captain Richards and Walter Whaley under a flag of truce to demand the unconditional surrender of the post. I told Captain Richards to inform the officer in command by whom and with what force he would be attacked. While Richards and Whaley were carrying out my orders, I moved my Command to within a quarter of a mile of the Yankee stockade. I placed my Command on a ridge with the howitzer trained on the stockade.

When Captain Richards and Walter Whaley arrived at the picket post, they delivered my demands for surrender. The commanding officer of the stockade appeared at the picket post where he inquired as to the terms of surrender of his force. He was informed that there were none offered, but that he was at liberty to see the attacking force. He mounted Whaley's horse, and came out to see me. I demanded his surrender and at the same time pointing at my howitzer and the Command stationed near it. The Yankee officer knew he had no alternative because he was greatly outnumbered. He used prudence and surrendered his force without any bloodshed. The Yankee command was the First Maryland Potomac Home Brigade Infantry.

My men rode into the Yankee camp and set fire to it. All of the government goods in the depot were confiscated. Union men's shoes, and ladies' and gentlemen's dress and fancy goods were also confiscated. Groceries were found in great quantities with which each man filled his sack. There was a sutler among the Yankees. My men helped themselves to his stores. They carried off all of his calicoes and other types of cloth. They even filled our limber with bags of coffee.

I ordered the howitzer to be advanced so as to command the expected train from the west. We waited for an hour for the eastbound train, but it did not arrive. I gave up the effort and ordered Captain Montjoy, with his company to take the howitzer and the prisoners and head directly toward Charlestown. Captains Richards and Chapman with their companies were to follow at intervals of a quarter of a mile, so as to deceive the enemy by the cloud of dust raised. This would help to disguise the strength of my Command. While riding back to Charlestown, I looked around at my men. They had the appearance of a group of men so laden with merchandise that it reminded me more of a caravan than a column of soldiers.

As I anticipated, a large body of Yankee cavalry, superior in number to ours, moved against Lieutenant Nelson's men. I was riding in the advance of my Command, approaching Charlestown when I received the news by a courier sent from Lieutenant Nelson. Lieutenant Nelson informed me that he had been attacked. When we arrived, Company A was already drawn up in line of battle and giving us enthusiastic cheers. The howitzer was placed in the center of the line with Companies A and D on the left and right of the howitzer. Captains Richards and Chapman, with their companies, were concealed in a wooded area half a mile back on the road to Duffield Depot. They had orders to simultaneously attack the enemy's flank as soon as the firing on the road was heard. I made these dispositions because I believed that the enemy would charge down the road at Companies A and D when they saw them. But the Yankees declined another engagement.

After the raid, I had the chance to speak with Private James Williamson about the fight at Charlestown. Private Williamson was on picket duty along the Charlestown Pike when he and another one of my men reported to Lieutenant Nelson that a Yankee cavalry force was approaching the village. Williamson said, Lieutenant Nelson "ordered the men to ride through a narrow strip of woods in a parallel line with the Charlestown Road towards the advancing enemy. They rode in two's instead of four's, giving the Yankee cavalry the idea they were a larger force. As we moved on, the Federal column appeared, rushing over the hill, and seeing Lieutenant Nelson and his men for the first time, they halted and gazed at us in amazement. Some of our men had been scattered into the houses in the neighborhood to fire from them. The Yankees fired a volley, doing no damage other than to shower a few leaves on our heads from the trees beside of us. 'Now, boys, charge them,' Lieutenant Nelson ordered. The men yelled and charged in among them, firing in their faces. They turned their horses, and as those in front pressed on the ones behind them, the whole body became panic stricken and retreated in the utmost disorder. Those behind the hill seeing the head of our column driving back their comrades, did not wait to ascertain our force, but joined the flight."

Lieutenant Nelson and his men chased the Yankee cavalry to Halltown, which is four miles east of Charlestown. Lieutenant Nelson and his men killed and wounded several Yankees. My men took nineteen prisoners and twenty-seven horses. We sustained no loss. James Williamson captured a Yankee prisoner who said to him "Why, we had enough to have whipped you fellows!"

After my Command had united, quite a large body of Yankee cavalry was sent out from Harpers Ferry. They followed us for some distance, and twice we formed a line of battle, but each time they declined an engagement. I sent the prisoners and horses forward with the other companies, leaving Company A as a rear guard. As was my custom, I lingered in the rear of the column and again was almost shot by a Yankee cavalryman when my horse became unmanageable. Private David Carlisle shot my antagonist. We re-crossed the Shenandoah River at Shepherd's Mill and camped for the night without food for man or beast. Many of the men made beds with their captured merchandise.

After returning from the raid at Duffield Depot, I had a lady approach me and compliment our success. And then she said, "I hear you have a large supply of calico, an article which I greatly need, and I suppose you will sell it very cheap?"

"Madam, you have mistaken my profession: I am a soldier," said I.

Many of my men would remember this expedition with fondness as the "First Calico Raid."

CHAPTER TWENTY

Point of Rocks and Mt. Zion Church

On the afternoon of July 2, 1864, I was at Rectortown with Fount Beattie. While there, I met Captain Hugh Swartz from General Jubal Early's quartermaster's department. From him, I learned of General Early's march down the Shenandoah Valley with the Second Corps of the Army of Northern Virginia. Captain Swartz informed me General Early and the Corps intended on marching north through the Shenandoah Valley, cross the Potomac River and raid into Maryland. They were going to camp for the night at Winchester.

I knew I could best support General Early by operating on the Yankees' line of communication, the Baltimore and Ohio Railroad at Point of Rocks. I immediately dispatched runners to collect my men. Two hundred men of my Command assembled at Upperville the next day. We started at noon with one twelve pound cannon. Our march was very leisurely because the day was very warm. Quite a few of the men brought cloth sacks along to gather up booty. I led my men along by-roads and narrow paths to avoid villages where Unionists were living; neither did I allow them to straggle. Any citizen that my men encountered, they were told to inform them that General Longstreet's Corps was following. We camped for the night at Wheatland.

The next morning, the Command marched until we came to the Potomac River, where Berlin, Maryland rested on the northern shore. We continued to march east along the

Virginia shore until we came to a farm where the Command rested while I took a few men with me in the direction of Point of Rocks. Point of Rocks is an important station on the Baltimore and Ohio Railroad, just across the river from Loudoun County, Virginia, and about twelve miles east of Harpers Ferry. The area is a high outcrop of solid rock in which a range of mountains terminate close to the river's bank that the Chesapeake and Ohio Canal barely squeezes past it. West of the railroad tunnel for miles up the river, steep and rocky bluffs bind the railroad track on the north. East of the tunnel lies the village. On the mountain slope back of the town was the Yankees' camp. The only way from the west was along the narrow towpath between the canal and river, and from a wooden-framed bridge over the canal into the middle of the town. In this area, the Potomac River is about a quarter mile wide, but is split by a narrow island. At the head of the island is a ford passable for horses. In this area of the Potomac, the water is very low.

On the scout, I determined the Yankees were about the size of several companies of infantry and a company of cavalry. They were behind an earthen fort near the depot, not too far from the village.

When I returned to the rest of my Command, I began to cross the Potomac River with some of my men. Yankee pickets began firing on us from the island. My men and I returned without a fight to the Waterford road where the rest of the Command was well out of sight of the Yankees on the island. I called for sharpshooters. At least two dozen men dismounted with carbines and responded to my call. Some of the sharpshooters rushed across the river bottom and got behind some trees and fallen logs, while I moved others into the water as a long range advance guard. The higher the water came around them, the more exasperated they became, as the Yankee sharpshooters on the other side continued to fire on them. I noticed there was one Yankee sharpshooter firing from the canal bridge and greatly annoying my men. I paused long enough while crossing the river to ask Emory Pitts, "can you stop that Yankee over there from sucking eggs?"

"I'll try." Pitts replied.

While standing in waist high water, Pitts aimed his carbine and fired; the sharpshooter fell. Meanwhile, I had earlier ordered the cannon placed on a small rise to support our effort. The gun was in position and had begun to fire.

My sharpshooters floundered through the water, shooting, yelling, stumbling over round river stones getting ducked overhead, rising and firing. The cannon fired another round and the Yankees became demoralized and fled down the river toward Point of Rocks. A number of Yankees sought safety in the bushes on the river bluff beyond the railroad. While still other Yankee soldiers were joined by some excursionist from Washington City, who had come up the canal in a boat on a Fourth of July outing. They got mixed up with the Yankee soldiers and scrambled up the steep hillside.

The mounted men of my Command had followed closely and got across the river before the sharpshooters. The mounted men dashed off down the towpath, leaving the sharpshooters behind. Since the sharpshooters had to wait for their horses to be brought across the river, they began to go through the boat which lay in the canal lock. My men were out for a good time. They took the choicest brands of liquors, cigars, and all kinds of dainty foods. While my men were plundering, a train came into sight from Harpers Ferry. The men prepared to seize the eastbound train. Just then, the cannon fired, sending a shot toward the train. The train slowed down and then stopped on a curve. Some of the passengers piled out of the train. As my men rushed toward the train with the intentions of capturing it, the passengers took refuge among the bushes. A shot or two fired after them, purely in sport, seemed to paralyze some of them and they lost their footing and rolled back down a hill they had been climbing. We did not disturb them any further. The engineer was able to move his train back toward Harpers Ferry. We did not follow.

Meanwhile, my men, who were mounted, rushed on until they came to the bridge across the canal. The canal bridge flooring had been torn up by the Yankees. My men tore down a building near the bridge and used the planking to reconstruct the bridge flooring while the Yankees from their earthen fort kept up a brisk fire. Once the work was competed, my men hurried across the bridge to dislodge the Yankees. They scattered into the forest in their rear, not wanting their defenses stormed by my men. The retreat of the Yankee, Loudoun Ranger Cavalry, was so precipitated that they neglected to carry off their flag. Captain Richards with a small party started in pursuit of them, but they might as well have undertaken to follow a crow. Captain Richards and the men under his command did manage, however, to capture one lieutenant and three privates who belonged to the infantry. We sustained no injury.

Once the Command entered the village, the plundering began, first the Yankee camp and then the storehouses. Most of the men went into the dry-good business, and soon four shops and one sutler establishment were emptied of their contents. Some of the men appropriated calico, some one article, and some another; while another element in the Command, represented by our surgeon, supplied themselves abundantly with confectionaries of various kinds to carry to their favorites whom they had left behind.

We re-crossed the Potomac River at the fording area and proceeded to a wooded area where we came to a halt. While there, a humorous incident took place that I witnessed. A mountain woman approached, after hearing the sound of fighting at Point of Rocks. She came first to Sergeant Charlie Hall. I heard her ask for a pair of shoes that Charlie had in his possession. Charlie replied, "Certainly, but you must give me a kiss in return."

On these terms, the bargain was concluded. The shoes were handed over to the mountain woman. She smiled and blushed, turned her cheek to Charlie, who kissed her. They both parted and went their own way.

I sent some men, mostly Marylanders from my Command back across the Potomac River at Noland's Ferry to cut down telegraph poles and wires, breaking communications between Harpers Ferry and Washington. Walter Bowie told me after the foray, they raided a Yankee cavalry camp, carried off some prisoners, horses, and stores. When they were returning along the towpath, they had Yankee cavalry approaching on the towpath from the direction of Harpers Ferry and coming up behind them from the direction of Washington City. Among the prisoners he had taken was an elderly black man who knew the area. The elderly man was promised his freedom if he helped Bowie and the men under his command to escape across the river. He showed them a sandbar just below the water where they could cross. Bowie and his men escaped capture.

Late in the evening, the Command resumed the march toward Leesburg, but after hearing from a local citizen that Yankee cavalry had possession of the town, I sent several men to scout in that direction. I was having my supper at Temple Hall, the Ball homestead, when the scouts returned and reported the presences of the Second Massachusetts and Thirteenth New York Cavalries under Major Forbes. I moved the Command to an area about one mile north of Waterford, where we camped for the night, using our saddle blankets to cover the ground and saddles as pillows.

* * * *

The fight at Mount Zion attracted great attention at the time, especially in the North and made my name redoubtable. My name became an awe-inspiring one. The fight that I am about to tell you about will explain why.

Early the next morning, July 6, three of my scouts, Lieutenant Hatcher, John Thomas, and Albert Fox, brought news from Leesburg that Major Forbes and his Second Massachusetts Cavalry, were looking for us. I thought our presence in the neighborhood must have been known by the many Unionist sympathizers living in the area and he had been informed by them. After receiving the report, I ordered my Command toward Leesburg to give Major Forbes an opportunity to fight us.

When we arrived near Fort Johnson, about a mile from Leesburg, we noticed the Yankees were moving in the direction of Aldie. There were about two hundred and fifty of them. They had the reputation of being well mounted, well equipped, disciplined, and good fighters. I had less than two hundred men and I knew we were not going on some picnic.

When we reached Leesburg, we heard from the citizens how Major Forbes and his men were anxious to meet us in battle. It was no light circumstance that these taunts were communicated to my men by the pretty ladies of Leesburg, who had lined the streets of the town as we passed by. The ladies gave us trays laden with a most acceptable breakfast. I heard one of my men, John Alexander say that he believed the taunts and breakfast gave the men a "greater determination to wipe Major Forbes and his men from the face of the earth." When it came to my men, I never let valor get the better of my discretion. I always tried to secure for them every advantage for a fight. The loss of one of my men was a much more serious matter to me than the loss of many Yankees.

I determined not to follow Major Forbes and his men, but instead to take a road leading to Ball's Mills, along Goose Creek, where I hoped to get in front of them on their way back to Fairfax. My plan called for placing men with carbines among the bushes at the top of the bluff overlooking the stream, while men who were still mounted would attack the Yankees while they were crossing the water. I left Captain William Chapman in charge of the Command while I took my brother, Willie, and Walter Bowie, Bush Underwood and a few others on to ascertain the whereabouts of Major Forbes and his men. We soon encountered a detachment of the enemy at Aldie. We returned to Ball's Mills, hoping the Yankee cavalry would follow. I believed we would soon be attacked by Major Forbes and his entire force. We waited for some time, but much to my disappointment, they did not come at us. Therefore, I went in search of him, leading the Command toward Gum Springs and then south on a farm road that cut into the Little River Turnpike.

We located the Yankee cavalry in a field where they had halted to feed their horses. I noticed to the west of their location was a large brick dwelling and grounds. To the east, leaving the field and crossing the turnpike, was a body of woods about one hundred yards wide. This wooded area gave shelter to the Yankees from our view when we came out on the pike on top of a hill nearly a mile below them. I believed that their pickets in the wooded area had discovered us; that there would be no surprise, but we would just pitch into them over an open road. They would be prepared to receive our charge. Our only advantage was the position we held. It was between them and their home. It would make them fight more desperately.

Lieutenant Hatcher led twelve men with carbines toward the Yankees in a sweeping gallop, while our twelve pound cannon was being placed on the hill, in the road. Lieutenant Glasscock and Company D were given the task of supporting Sam Chapman's men and the cannon. The Yankee pickets fired some shots with little effect at my men with carbines. Lieutenant Hatcher and the men with the carbines did not get within a hundred yards before the Yankee pickets ran back upon their main body of men.

We occupied the woods where the Yankee pickets had fired on us. I looked from the wooded area and saw a grand sight. Several hundred yards in front of us, the Yankees were drawn up on the slope of the hill in the old field in two lines, one behind the other, facing us. Their alignment was just as perfect as if on dress parade. They were ready for us.

I watched as our cannon fired a shot. The cannon shot was ineffectual with the exception that it did cause some consternation along their battle line. In order to get to them, we had to ride along the pike and endure their fire. I left the wooded area and led my men at a leisurely pace, not giving the horses full rein. There was a gap in the fence that I was going to use. I ordered the men not to fire their weapons until we got into the field. They obeyed.

Once through the gap in the fence, my men yelled and pitched into the Yankees like a hurricane. The men fired with fearful rapidity, threatening to completely envelop them. At first the Yankees stood their ground and made a good fight, but they could not stand the rain of our pistol balls. We managed to split their front ranks asunder and thus broke their spirit. Half of the Yankees retreated into the next field where Major Forbes tried to rally them. Major Forbes was a gallant officer. They began to fight as gallantly as any command could fight. My men pitched into them and the battle became a hand-to-hand fight. Our revolvers were crackling into the very faces of the Yankee cavalrymen. It was a mass of struggling, cursing frenzies, each striving to slay his enemy.

About six hundred yards in their rear, the Yankees were checked by a high fence. A party of twenty-five Yankees turned upon us and fought with great determination, but it was useless valor. Half of this gallant band were either killed, wounded, or dragged by their wounded horses. The fence gave way because of the horses' weight against it. The retreat became a rout. The pursuit was continued for ten miles, to Sudley Church, where the fleeing Yankees put up another little fight, but they soon continued their retreat.

We captured Major Forbes in the fight when his horse was killed and fell on his leg. When I saw Major Forbes, I recalled that during the fight he tried to thrust me with his saber and instead, it went through my coat doing me no harm. When I spoke with him, he told me that he was in the center of his men, Company A, trying to rally them when one of my men, who I later learned was Tom Richards, came to do combat with him. At the time, Major Forbes said he was standing in his stirrups with saber drawn fighting as desperately as he could. In the one-on-one fight with Tom Richards, he thrust his saber through Richards' shoulder. Richards tried to discharge his revolver at Major Forbes, but it misfired. The capture of Major Forbes was an important incident in my life because after the war, Sam Chapman and I dined one evening with him at The Arlington. At that dinner, Sam returned a watch to Major Forbes that had been taken from him by one of my men after the fight at Mount Zion Church. I recall with many fond memories that our families were very close after-the war.

After the fight at Mount Zion Church, John Munson, Johnny Edmonds, and I found the dead, wounded and wounded horses all along the road and in the fields. We found a man kneeling near a fence by the roadside with his head bent forward touching the ground in front of him and his left hand clutching a gaping wound in his side. I ordered John Munson to dismount and go to his assistance. When Munson tried to raise him, he was already a corpse.

The fighting and the rout had lasted until late in the afternoon. There were so many wounded men to help and so many prisoners to care for that we did not leave the field of battle until long after dark.

My loss from the fight at Mount Zion Church was one killed. He was eighteen year old Henry Smallwood, who died the next day. Seven of my men suffered wounds.

Major Forbes' command loss fourteen men killed in the fight, thirty-seven men wounded, and fifty-five men captured. We also captured one hundred Yankee horses and equipment.

After the fight at Mount Zion Church, when there was opportunity, our raids against the Yankees continued from the Potomac River to the Shenandoah Valley. A large number of men continued to take part in these raids and desired the opportunity to be a part of my Command. On July 28, I formed Company E. I handled the elections as I previously did by giving the men a slate of names, who I believed should be elected as officers. I chose Sam Chapman as captain. On more than one occasion since joining my Command, he had served gallantly and for this reason, I promoted him. Fount Beattie, my good friend since the very beginning of the war, I made first lieutenant. Another man of my Command, who had fought in a number of fights and honorably displayed his gallantry was William Martin. I made him second lieutenant, but he did not serve for too long. About a month after his promotion, he was accidentally shot and killed by a comrade. William Martin was replaced by Channing Smith. Channing Smith had served in the Fourth Virginia Cavalry before joining my Command. He had earned praises for his scouting abilities and gallant conduct from both Generals Lee and Stuart. Ben Palmer was promoted to third lieutenant. He had attended the Virginia Military Institute in Lexington and would have graduated in 1866, if it had not been for the war. He was known for his gallantry in battle.

Since Lieutenant Sam Chapman had been promoted to command of Company E, it became necessary to organize an artillery company. On July 28, 1864, Peter Frankland was promoted to captain of the new artillery company. John Fray was promoted to first lieutenant, John Page, second lieutenant, and Frank Rahm, junior second lieutenant.

Chapter Twenty-One

The 1864 Shenandoah Valley Campaign

After General Jubal Early's raid into Maryland and his fight along the suburbs of Washington City, he retreated back across the Potomac River into Virginia. General Early's force remained along the Potomac River as a distraction and threat to Washington City and the Baltimore and Ohio Railroad. General Early and his men caused much damage to bridges, destroyed tracks and harassed the railroad without any Yankee opposition. He sent a cavalry force up to Chambersburg, Pennsylvania to seize a ransom of five hundred thousand dollars because of the destruction of civilian property in the Jefferson and Berkeley County areas by General David Hunter's Yankee army. When the citizens of Chambersburg failed to meet General John McCausland's demand, his four hundred cavalrymen torched the city, burning it to the ground. One newspaper reported that "Two hundred and sixty-five of the most valuable and elegant public and private buildings were destroyed." The shifting of the scene and invasion of the north by a portion of an army whose surrender had been daily expected, created not only astonishment, but severe criticism of the military policy of the Administration at Washington City.

In order to stop General Early, General Grant sent Major-General Phil Sheridan to Harpers Ferry to command the Middle Military Division, which at the time took in the Middle, Washington, West Virginia, and Susquehanna Departments. It was General Grant's desire that General

Sheridan and his force would wipe out General Early's army and make war on the civilian population by destroying all of the crops in the Shenandoah Valley. General Grant hoped through his strategy that he would destroy the Confederate army under General Early and break the will of the people in the Valley. General Grant also knew this would break General Lee's line of communication with the southwest, and the inevitable results would be the fall of Richmond and the end of the war. General Grant gave General Sheridan fifty-six thousand men to destroy General Early's army of seventeen thousand men.

During the campaign against General Sheridan in the Shenandoah Valley, which took place in early August of 1864, my battalion of six companies was the only force operating in the rear of his army. The main object of my campaign was to vex and embarrass General Sheridan and, if possible to prevent his advance into the interior of the state. But my exclusive attention was not only given to General Sheridan, for alarm was kept up continuously by threating Washington City and occasionally crossing the Potomac River.

As for General Sheridan's army, he had already moved up the Shenandoah Valley and he now kept his headquarters near Winchester. This meant that he had to haul his supplies for his army from Harpers Ferry. This would give me the opportunity I was looking for to embarrass, and cause him to pull more men away from his force to guard his trains.

On Friday, August 12, I assembled my Command at Rectortown. Around noon, we moved toward the Blue Ridge Mountain. We passed through Snicker's Gap, crossing the Shenandoah River at Castleman's Ferry after sundown. That night, a few miles from the river, we rested at Josiah Ware's homestead, where some of the men unsaddled their horses and slept on the landscape. I sent John Russell, who was from the Berryville area, and a few men to scout west in that direction.

Before dawn the next morning, the 13th, I was resting on my saddle when John Russell brought in the intelligence that a large wagon train with supplies and with a heavy guard of cavalry and infantry was on its way from Harpers Ferry. I trusted Russell. He had a thorough knowledge of this section of the Shenandoah Valley. He was bold and shrewd in the performance of his duties. I immediately went with Russell and two other men to scout and see what was going on. Captain William Chapman was ordered forward with the rest of the Command. They took up a position concealed in some woods, four miles from Berryville, and one mile from the turnpike leading to Charlestown.

In a few moments we came across an ambulance drawn by four mules, with a Yankee guard of two men. They approached us. I concluded that possibly I could learn something from them regarding the wagon train, so I rode up to them, and before letting them know who I was, I began to inquire from one of them how long it had been since the Yankee wagon train had passed. One Yankee replied that it had just passed. At once, I demanded his surrender and sent him and his comrade back to the Command. John Russell and I pushed on to ascertain the whereabouts of the wagon train. The other two men followed.

Near daybreak, we came near Berryville. I knew we were near because we could distinctly hear the rumbling of the Yankee wagon train on the hard surface pike from the direction of Charlestown. They were marching at night on account of the intense heat in the daytime.

When we arrived on the crest of a ridge, about one mile north of Berryville, overlooking the turnpike to Charlestown, we found a long line of wagons winding along the road and stretching away into the darkness as far as the eye could see. We rode among the drivers and the guards, looking the stock over and chatting with the men in a friendly way. John Munson, one of the men with us asked one of the Yankee cavalrymen for a match to light his pipe, which the Yankee quickly complied. It was still too dark for the Yankees to distinguish us from their own men and we mingled with them so freely that our presence created no suspicion. I asked them whatever questions I chose to, and learned that there were five hundred and twenty-five wagons in the train, with more than one thousand head of horses, mules, and cattle guarded by about two thousand men, consisting of two ninety-day Ohio regiments, one Maryland regiment, besides cavalry distributed along the line; all under the orders of Brigadier-General John Kenly.

Many of the wagons pulled into a large grassy meadow near Buck Marsh Creek, others kept moving. John Munson was sent back full speed to tell Captain William Chapman to hurry forward with the whole Command. We were within two or three hundred yards of our prey, but they were unconscious of danger. We waited for Chapman with breathless expectation. While waiting on Captain Chapman and the Command, I looked at the wagon train. I knew it was heavily supported, as John Russell had informed me, with cavalry and infantry. I felt some of the oppression and awful forebodings, which it is said that even the great soul of Caesar felt when he halted on the banks of the Rubicon. I was about to do what all men would say, if I failed, was an act of desperation. A successful blow struck then at General Sheridan's communication would, I knew, make a deep impression on him and have much influence on the result of the campaign. Failure meant, in all probability, the loss of my Command. I decided to play for a great stake.

The sun began rising in the east as Captain William Chapman and the Command came up at a trot. The men were eager for the fray; silence was golden. All spoke in whispers. We would attack in an open pastoral country with stone fences. A small clump of trees concealed us from the unsuspecting enemy. My plan of attack called for Captains William Chapman and Alfred Glascock's companies to charge from the ridge down into the meadows where the

Yankees had their wagons parked and their horses and mules grazing. Captain Dolly Richards was to take his squadron and attack the wagons rolling toward Berryville. Captain Sam Chapman's company was placed directly behind the ridge to support the artillery, and to be ready to be used if needed to support either Captains Chapman's or Richards' men. In a few words the order for the attack was given by me.

As I had written before, I had two howitzers for the fight. But unfortunately, one of the guns suffered some damage to its carriage and would be of little use to me. The one remaining howitzer came up at a gallop and was unlimbered on the crest of the ridge that commanded the pike. Lieutenant Frank Rahm commanded the gun crew.

Just as my men began to ram down a charge, a new enemy, on whose presence we had not counted, made his appearance on the field, drove the men from the gun before they could fully load it. It came near upsetting all my plans. It was a swarm of yellow jackets. They were home-rulers, like the Boers, and instantly flew out to repel the invasion of their territory. They came flying out of the ground where the howitzer had been placed. They appeared to have no fear of cavalry or the artillery, and evidently regarded our presence as an invasion of their right to local self-government. As they were under ground and we on top, I thought they ought to have stayed where they were. All we asked of the yellow jackets was, in the language of Mr. Jefferson Davis, "to be let alone." But this was the thing that they were not willing to do. They flew at the gunners and settled down on the battery horses; the drivers could not hold their horses and fight yellow jackets at the same time. They could stand bullets, but the sting of insects was too much for them. Gunners, drivers, and horses all ran off, taking the limber and caisson with them.

That day I was riding a fine sorrel mare. A swarm settled down on her; the stinging made her perfectly frantic, and she began rearing and plunging. I could with difficulty keep my seat in the saddle, and almost forgot that there was anything in the world but yellow jackets. During this scene, we were in plain view and within one hundred yards of the enemy. But fortunately, through the mist the Yankees could not distinguish gray from blue. We were soon relieved from our predicament by one of the men running up, seizing and dragging off the howitzer. The yellow jackets held the field, but seeing us retreat, they did not pursue us. The men soon got the howitzer back into action. The lone howitzer fired its first shot at the wagon train, knocking the head off of a mule. Another shell was fired and exploded like a clap of thunder out of a clear sky and was followed by yet another which burst in the midst of the enemy. The whole train stopped and writhed in its center as if a wound had been opened in its vitals. The rapidity with which Frank Rahm moved the howitzer from point to point created the impression among the Yankees that several batteries were firing upon them.

At this time, Captain Dolly Richards and his men charged the Yankee infantrymen while Captain's William Chapman and Glascock went at their rear. The companies charged from the slope, each man doing his best to out yell his comrades and emptying his revolver. The whole wagon train was thrown into a panic. Teamsters wheeled their horses and mules from the meadow into the road, plying the black-snake whips, sent the animals galloping madly down the pike, crashing into other teams, which in turn, ran away. Infantry stampeded in every direction. Cavalry, uncertain from which point the attack came, bolted backward and forward without any definite plan. Wounded animals all along the train were neighing and braying, adding to confusion. Pistols and rifles were cracking singly and in volleys.

After my men charged down the slope at the Yankee wagon train, I recall that I was dashing up and down the line of battle, urging the men by voice and gesture. I was never so interested in the total demolition of things. My men were creating pandemonium among the Yankees everywhere.

Captain Dolly Richards' men chased the wagons into the town of Berryville, causing great consternation among the Yankee infantry guards. Mules were taken from the wagons and the wagons then set on fire. The braying of the mules and the lowing of cattle were heard together with cries and groaning of the wounded. Some of my men, who were riding alongside of the wagons, would set fire to them, and as the smoke curled up, the frightened mules rushed frantically along until they fell exhausted or were released by dashing the wagon against a tree or some obstacle in the road.

A body of Yankee infantrymen rallied in a brick church in the suburbs of Berryville, from which they kept up an incessant fire. A few shots from our howitzer soon demoralized them. Captain Richards and his men charged the church and took most of the Yankee infantrymen prisoner.

Across from the slope and along the pike to Charlestown where we had commenced the attack, a strong body of Yankee infantrymen formed behind a stone wall fence, in an orchard near the road, from which for some time they kept up a murderous fire. They seemed determined to hold their ground, but they did not stop Captain's William Chapman and Glascock's men for a moment. They rode over the stone wall fence and killed or captured many of its defenders. I recall at that time, I was directing the fire of the howitzer when one of my men, Guy Broadwater galloped up to me and said, "Colonel, Lewis Adie is killed."

"I can't help it," I replied. He was a fine boy.

It was in the crisis of the fight, and no time to indulge in tender emotions. Private Aldie of Company D was a noble boy, and Sergeant Broadwater knew my attachment for him. I was told that he followed Captain Chapman and was killed while leaping the stone wall fence.

By eight o'clock in the morning, the fight was over, the enemy was ours. I ordered all of the teams unhitched and fire set to the wagons. It made for a grand picture. I later learned in a newspaper that a wagon burned, containing a safe with Yankee greenbacks, said to be over one hundred thousand dollars. We overlooked it unfortunately, and it was recovered the next day by the enemy.

We did face one serious problem. How were we going to get two hundred prisoners, nearly eight hundred head of captured stock, and the other spoils of war out of General Sheridan's country and into our own. News of the raid, I thought, had gone in every direction and we were, I was sure, going to be threatened with an overwhelming assault. Not only that, but my Command had been in the saddle for the last twenty-four hours and was pretty well broken down. I decided that we would go directly to Rectortown and take all the prisoners, animals, and booty with us. My decision was the only thing we could do.

Another problem came about. What were we going to do with the howitzer that had a disabled carriage? I asked Frank Rahm. He said, "I'm going to take it back home on the other gun, if I have to hold it there." He did exactly what he had promised.

At a trot, we herded the animals in one drove down the pike to the Shenandoah River. The organization of my Command was entirely broken up returning with our booty and prisoners. The cavalcade of horses, mules, cattle, and prisoners was stretched out several miles along the road. It was a most extraordinary procession. Our captives were on foot while we were mounted. My men chatted freely with them even though the prisoners exceeded the number of my men.

The Command was in a spirit of gayety. They had decked themselves out in fine uniforms, which had been appropriated from the Yankee officers' baggage wagon. The Yankee officers enjoyed seeing my men swelling in their new uniforms, which had been provided for them with so much expense in New York. I noticed that some of the men had taken the coats and turned them inside out so as to display the fine lining.

Another humorous incident took place while we were marching to the Shenandoah River. I wished that I could have had a sketch of it. From one of the captured wagons, the men had resurrected a lot of musical instruments and the leaders of our mounted vanguard made the morning hideous with attempts to play plantation melodies on tuneless fiddles. Bob Ridley was playing the tune "Dixie," and at the same time swearing all kinds of oaths at a mule. There was a song on every man's lips and those who had yelled or sung themselves hoarse waved captured flags. My men always knew how to amuse themselves. No more motley throng ever came back from a successful raid.

It was strange to say, but not a man or an animal was lost crossing the Shenandoah River. We crossed the mountain at a breakneck pace, made a rapid decent through Snicker's Gap and into the Piedmont Valley. When the people of the eastern side of the Blue Ridge Mountain saw the long column coming through the gap, they thought it was General Sheridan's army. The men were whooping and yelling with joy, and the mules were braying. A more grotesque sight, I never witnessed. By now, my vexations about the episode of the yellow jackets had vanished. How narrowly we escaped disaster on account of that unexpected attempt of those bees was never officially known. At 4:00 o'clock that same afternoon, we arrived at Rectortown and divided the captured property.

My loss during the wagon train raid at Berryville, was two men killed and two men wounded. I could not ascertain the number of the enemy's casualties in killed and wounded. We did, however, capture one hundred of the enemy's wagons. After dividing the horses and plunder among the men, I sent the mules and a large number of the cattle to General Lee for the use of the army.

By August 16, the *Richmond Daily Dispatch* had written about out raid in the Shenandoah Valley. The newspaper wrote:

"A few days ago Mosby attacked one of the enemy's wagon trains at Berryville, in Clarke County, destroyed it, and captured a quartermaster's wagon, with a large amount in greenbacks. He also took some two hundred or three hundred prisoners. Good for Mosby."

The raid at Berryville would teach General Sheridan the danger that was in his rear. He never forgot the lesson. As long as he was in the Shenandoah Valley he seemed always uneasy about his supply trains.

General Philip Sheridan
Source: *Library of Congress*

CHAPTER TWENTY-TWO

Retaliation

On Tuesday, August 16, after the wagon train raid at Berryville, General Sheridan began to move his army down the Shenandoah Valley from the area of Cedar Creek, where General Early had his lines established. Our raid against General Sheridan's wagon train on the 13th, had greatly annoyed General Grant. General Grant sent a telegram to General Sheridan, "If you can possibly spare a division of cavalry, send them through Loudoun County, to destroy and carry off crops, animals, Negroes, and all men under fifty years of age capable of bearing arms. In this manner you will get many of Mosby's men." To carry out General Grant's orders against my Command and to prevent our raids, General Sheridan requested the Eighth Illinois Cavalry, the largest and regarded as the finest in the Army of the Potomac, be given the task of dealing with us. They set out on August 20, after my Command with the intentions of carrying out General Grant's orders "to break up and exterminate any bands or parties of Mosby's, White's or other guerrillas which may be met."

The Eighth Illinois Cavalry marched from their camp at Muddy Branch to Aldie, Middleburg, and Upperville to Snicker's Gap and then back to their camp on the Potomac River. On their way, they picked up and carried off a number of citizens, among others, two preachers. General Sheridan had hoped this would clean out the Loudoun Valley. Yet this fond hope was not realized, and another and more formidable expedition was planned. The next expedition included the Sixteenth New York Cavalry. This time, the Yankee cavalry were commanded to bring in all males between the ages of eighteen and fifty; impress all wagons and bring them in loaded with forage; destroy all hay, oats, corn, and wheat they could not bring in and seize all horses. Their raid was not successful as they had hoped. They brought in only thirty men and thirty horses. No wagons could be found to bring off the supplies in any quantity. But no manner of threat from Generals Grant or Sheridan brought fear upon my men. We continued our raids.

On Thursday, August 18, Jim Wiltshire and several other scouts having been sent in the advance, crossed the Shenandoah River at Castleman's Ferry. While on their scout in the Valley, they came across four Yankee pickets from the Fifth Michigan Cavalry of Brigadier-General George Custer's cavalry brigade. Near the Ferry, Wiltshire and his men got into a fight with the Yankee picket post. They killed one Yankee cavalryman, wounded another and brought off two captured. The two Yankees captured escaped.

On Friday, August 19, I moved my men across the Shenandoah River, where I divided my Command of two hundred and fifty men. Company B, under Captain Dolly Richards moved toward the direction of Rippon, where he was allotted that portion of road between that village and Charlestown. Companies C, D, and E, under Captain William Chapman, were ordered to operate on the section of the turnpike between Rippon and Berryville, while I proceeded with Company A to the road between Harpers Ferry and Charlestown. This partition of the Command was resorted to because it was too large to be kept together safely in the midst of the hostile army, and particular sections were assigned to particular officers for the twofold purpose of prolonging the line of attack and of preventing collisions during the night.

General Custer became angry over the attack on his picket outpost along the Shenandoah River. General Custer believed some of the local citizens in the area had given my men information that led to the attack on his picket outpost. He decided to make them pay. In retaliation for our attacks, the Yankees, acting under General Custer's orders, proceeded to wreak their vengeance on the defenseless citizens, and the burning and destruction commenced by General Hunter, was resumed. General Custer soon learned this was a great mistake.

After leaving three companies in a wooded area near the Shenandoah River, Captain Chapman took John Hefflebower and another man and proceeded to the house of Hefflebower's father. They wanted to obtain additional information on the Yankees' camp around Berryville. Near the Yankees' camp, Captain Chapman fell in with three Yankees cavalrymen upon whom he imposed himself for a provost guard. He captured them without resistance. On his way back to his men with his prisoners, Captain Chapman passed near the Josiah Ware homestead, where he noticed that farm animals and sheep had been slaughtered. The animals were lying dead everywhere. The outbuildings had been torched with fire. The Yankee cavalrymen of the Fifth Michigan saw Captain Chapman and immediately started in pursuit. The Yankee cavalrymen gave up the chase and Captain Chapman rejoined his Command.

Not long after this took place, Captain Chapman noticed smoke and flames bursting from the homestead of Province McCormick. Captain Chapman hastened to the spot, which was about two miles. When Captain Chapman arrived at the McCormick homestead, he found the family standing outside of their burning stone house. Captain Chapman was told that their house had been fired by a detachment of Yankee soldiers. That the Yankees had threatened to leave their grandson inside of the house when they fired it because he would grow up some day to be a rebel. The Yankee raiders took the family's meat from their smokehouse; officers rode off loaded with the richest part of the plunder. The entreaties of the women and children had been of no avail. The order had been given and the order had been obeyed. After learning this news, Captain Chapman ordered up the rest of his men. When they arrived, they immediately started on the tracks of the burners.

When Captain Chapman and his men reached the homestead of William Sowers, they likewise had been embraced by the cruel order. The house was wrapped in flames from the basement to the garret, as was also the barn, stable, corncrib, hay, and wheat stacks. The roof of the house had already fallen in, and the ladies and children of the family were gathered in a corner of the yard near the roadside without a shawl or cloak, exposed to the rain that was falling in torrents. As soon as they saw Captain Chapman, they pledged their loyalties to our Cause. Though weeping bitterly when Captain Chapman and his men passed by, the ladies sudden cries of vengeance, "smite and spare not, for, though we have lost our home, we are still for the South, yes, as true as ever." At this proclamation, the men raised a shout, "No quarters, no quarters!" On they went, like bloodhounds on the trail. Captain Chapman and his men quickened the pace after the inhuman Yankees who had just destroyed the Sowers family's house and barn.

About one-half mile from the Sowers' homestead, Captain Chapman and his men came to the elegant residence of Colonel Morgan. Colonel Morgan's house, hay, wheat, and barn had already been torched with fire. The men were worked up to madness by this scene, as well as what they had just witnessed. After noticing Colonel Morgan's homestead ablaze, Captain Chapman gave the order, "Wipe them from the face of the earth! No quarters! No quarters! Take no prisoners!"

The Yankee cavalry, numbering about ninety, were still on Colonel Morgan's ground when they saw the hand of vengeance lifted to strike them. After the Yankees fired an ineffective volley, they tried to hastily form their ranks to receive Captain Chapman's attack. Captain Chapman and his men charged with fierce impetuosity, and immediately broke, every Yankee seeking safety in flight. The only way out for the Yankee cavalry was a narrow lane that they themselves had earlier barricaded. As the Yankee cavalrymen fled for their life, they tried to get through a narrow passage in the fence, which many of them could not do. Captain Chapman's men cornered a number of Yankee cavalrymen crouched along the corner of the fence. The Yankees turned and surrendered to Captain Chapman's men, but were killed as they surrendered. Captain Chapman's men pursued the Yankees for a mile and then returned to put to death all the prisoners who had been taken, and all the wounded who had fallen by the way. Some of the dead and wounded Yankees had carried off all kinds of jewelry, blankets, and wine.

When I learned of the villainy, I wrote General Lee that such was the indignation of our men at witnessing some of the finest residences in that portion of the state enveloped in flames that no quarters was shown the Yankees. The anger of the burnings in Clarke County was still evident among my men when James Williamson of Company A wrote many years later, "The man who could stand within the glare of burning dwellings, and witness unmoved the pitiful spectacle of pleading mothers with their frightened little ones clinging around them, and see the merciless savages who wrought this ruin gloating over the wreck they had made, and proceeding to a repetition of their cruel deeds of incendiarism, and not feel an impulse which would drive him to avenge such savagery, would not deserve the name of man."

Twenty-nine Yankee soldiers thus perished, victims of the bloody code of retaliation. This is what "No quarters" is all about.

* * * *

On September 13, 1864, the Command was assembled at Piedmont where Company F was organized. Walter Frankland was elected as captain. He had been with the Command and serving as its quartermaster since the winter of 1863. "Big Yankee" Ames was elected first lieutenant. Ames had more than once in battle proven his daring gallantry, and his loyalty to my Command. Walter Bowie was elected as second lieutenant. Walt had quickly caught my attention because of his gallantry and his natural ability as a scout. Frank Turner was elected as third lieutenant. Frank had served with great honor and had also shown his loyalty and gallantry in more than one battle. Frank Fox of Company C had been wounded near Berryville, therefore, Frank Yager took his place and John Russell, my most trusted scout, was promoted to third lieutenant of Company C. For the Company's first scout, I sent a detachment under John Russell into the Shenandoah Valley, while I took some men down into Fairfax.

The next day the Command was returning from a raid at Falls Church. I sent the Command back to Fauquier County, but two of my men, Tom Love and Guy Broadwater, lingered behind with me. After leaving the home of a local resident at Fairfax, we met an advance guard of five men of the Thirteenth New York Cavalry on the turnpike to Centreville. I believed that they had been on a scout to Aldie in search of my Command. I was dressed in full uniform, and made for an easy target. It was by a feigned retreat that we induced the Yankees to follow us for the distance of a quarter of a mile, and then we turned suddenly upon them and charged. Being only a few yards from each other, all fired at the same time. Two of the enemy's horses fell dead and I was seriously wounded. One ball shattered the handle of my pistol while another ball entered into my groin. Two Yankee cavalrymen were trapped under their horses. The other three fled full speed with Love and Broadwater after them until I called them back to my assistance. I was able to keep my saddle and ride with great difficulty, until my men procured a wagon and carried me off.

I was taken to the home of Major Foster, in The Plains, where I was kindly cared for by the family. As soon as it was raised through the neighborhood that I lay wounded, the ladies and gentlemen of the country around flocked to see me, and vied with each other in expressions of admiration and sympathy for me. In a few days, I was removed to my father's home in Lynchburg to recover from the injury. Captain William Chapman was given command over the battalion in my absence.

* * * *

Late September 1864, revives the memory of a painful episode of the war. But it does more; it proves that heroic sentiment still survives and that those who died for their country's cause did not die in vain. "Their country conquers with their martyrdom."

At the time, I was still away from my Command wounded; General Sheridan with an overwhelming force was pushing General Early up the Shenandoah Valley; he had sent General Torbert with two divisions of cavalry to cut off his retreat at New Market. General Wickham in command of General Fitz Lee's cavalry division had repulsed them at Milford, between Front Royal and Luray. General Torbert retreated down the Valley.

Captain Sam Chapman had been wanting to strike a blow to impede General Sheridan's march by breaking his lines of communications. Therefore, on September 22, Sam gathered one hundred and twenty men and headed into the Shenandoah Valley with the intention of capturing the picket outpost of the Sixth New York Cavalry. He had been informed that the outpost was stationed in Chester Gap, one of the breaks in the Blue Ridge Mountain, not far from Front

Royal. He marched his men to a point midway between Front Royal and Chester Gap, where they camped for the night. That evening, Sam was informed that no such picket had been posted at that place, but a large body of Yankee cavalry had the day before marched from Front Royal toward Luray. It was General Torbert's cavalry. General Torbert's cavalry had been repulsed by General Wickham's cavalry at Milford.

About daybreak, the next morning, Sam called for John Gray, my brother Willie, and several other men, and rode to Mr. King's, on the Gooney Manor Grade. From this point, Sam could see the Yankees' camp, a mile or two below Milford.

In a short time, it was reported to Sam that an ambulance train, escorted by about one hundred and seventy-five men had started from the Yankees' camp, and was moving down the turnpike toward Front Royal. Acting upon this information, Sam and his scouts returned in the direction of Front Royal. When near Front Royal, he halted his party midway between the road leading from Chester Gap and the turnpike leading from Milford. The area was bordered by the Shenandoah River on the west and steep cliffs on the east. This was where he would attack the Yankee wagon train and its escort. Sam sent for the rest of the Command to join him.

When the Command arrived, he divided it into two parts; one he placed fifty men under the command of Captain Walter Frankland to make a circuit over Graveyard Hill, and assail the front of the Yankee escort, as it was about to enter Front Royal. This would put him about two hundred yards closer to the village on the Luray Pike. The other men, Sam would attack it in the rear at the tollhouse, at the angle of the Luray Pike, one-half mile out of Front Royal, as the pike turns toward the river. Sam's position placed him nearer the advancing escort. Sam and his men were sheltered by the woods. Sam watched them as they turned the angel of the road. Later after I returned to the Command, Sam told me about this fight. That, "down towards the river, a quarter of a mile off, I could see distinctly what was coming. Further back, up the river, my view was concealed by a field of tall corn, on the rise to the left." Sam noticed that cavalry followed without intermission. Sam counted three stands of colors and knew he was greatly outnumbered. Sam became concerned about Captain Frankland and his men. He called out to Fount Beattie to "take the men and get back to Chester Gap. I'll go after Frankland!" He also sent Lieutenant Harry Hatcher and Company A back to Chester Gap, while he dashed off to Captain Frankland and his men to call off the attack. Sam raced his horse along the Yankee cavalry's flank, hidden by the woods, not more than fifty feet from them.

Before Sam could get to Captain Frankland and his men to call off the attack, they had already pitched into the front of the Yankee cavalry escort, driving them back among the ambulances.

When Sam met Captain Frankland, he ordered him to call off his men. Sam informed Captain Frankland that he was attacking a brigade of Yankee cavalry. Captain Frankland asked Sam why; that they had already whipped them. Sam repeated the order, but it was slowly obeyed because the men had tasted blood.

In the meantime, the Yankee cavalry enveloped Captain Frankland's men like a cloud. Captain Frankland's men charged them in front, beating them off from the flanks and rear. But still the Yankees continued to crowd around them. They would beat off an attack and continued the retreat.

Sam and his men continued to retreat until they reached the Criser homestead, which stands near Chester Gap Road. There, one of Sam's men came to him yelling, "Captain, the Yankees have blocked the road in our front!" The Yankee cavalry was posted to cut off retreat in that direction. It did not look good for Sam and the men. Sam told the soldier to go back and inform the men "to charge them, as that was our way of escape, and that the whole Federal column was pressing our rear." The men rallied and made a desperate charge.

A Yankee lieutenant, by the name of Charles McMaster had led the small party of Yankee cavalry up the Chester Gap Road to intercept some of Sam's men, while attempting to make their escape by crossing Hominy Hollow. Lieutenant McMaster thought he had Sam's men in a pen. But Lieutenant McMaster found that he and his men were cut off by the interposition of Captain Sam Chapman. The lieutenant himself was dismounted from his horse, it is supposed, intending to surrender. But he imprudently retained his arms, and was riddled with bullets by Sam's men as they passed him. Lieutenant McMaster was killed in the excitement of a fight, by men who were seeking to escape from a superior force, and who were fighting for their lives. Sam recalled this incident, and wrote about it some time later:

"As I rode up I beheld a young officer wounded, and dismounted, standing by a large rock with his hands up. Some men new to the business, and in their panic, fired at him, which I promptly stopped. The truth is, McMaster was never a prisoner. He attempted to cut off the retreat of my men when attacked. He cut himself off and got killed. My men shot him and rode over him; they had no time to rob him if they had wished to do so; General Merritt's whole division was behind us and McMaster was in front of them. He may have intended to surrender, but it does not necessarily follow that my men knew it. They had no time to take prisoners or parley. They were surrounded by thousands and their only way of escape was to break through the ranks that enclosed them. McMaster got in the way; they shot him and rode on. It was not their business to ask him what he wanted to do."

Sam lost no men in the fight, but the blood among the Yankees flowed freely enough. A vindictive and sanguinary spirit prevailed among the Yankees. The Yankees accused my men of killing Lieutenant McMaster after he surrendered.

They claimed that my men fired into the wagons of wounded and defenseless soldiers. They captured six men from my Command who either had their horses shot out from under them or they had been cut off from the rest of the Command. The Yankees wanted to exact revenge on them. The captured men from my Command were Thomas Anderson, David Jones, Lucian Love, Thomas Overby, and a man by the name of Carter, whose first name I do not recall. The Yankees captured a seventeen year old boy, by the name of Henry Rhodes, who did not belong to my Command. His widowed mother entreated the Yankees to spare the life of her son and treat him as a prisoner of war, but the demons answered by whetting their sabers on some stones and declaring they would cut his head off and hers too, if she came near. They ended by shooting him in her presence. It is said that Generals Torbert and Merritt turned the prisoners over to General Custer for the purpose of their execution.

These acts of vengeance at Front Royal against my men even dispirited some of General Custer's men. Many years after the war, Henry Avery who served in the Fifth Michigan Cavalry, published a journal. Avery was a witness to the brutality, and wrote:

"We made a move up above Front Royal, capturing a few of Mosby's men at Front Royal. They were recognized as a part of the band that had recently captured a lieutenant and some men of our advance guard and murdered them. Being caught and recognized by the lieutenant before he died, they were sentenced without court or jury, and two of them were given over to our regiment. Being brought in front of us, the colonel said, 'If any of the Fifth had a spite against Mosby's men to ride out.' We all had a spite against them, but did not feel like murdering them in cold blood. The only proper way would have been to detail a firing party, under orders. Only two men rode out.

The boys, one about sixteen, the other eighteen years old, were to be shot. They begged of the chaplain a chance to run for their lives, but no such boon was allowed them. They were placed a short distance away, and the two men began firing at them. The first shot killed the younger, but the other received two or three balls before he fell. I pronounced this barbarous, and some of the boys muttered to me, but I did not care, why should we be obligated to see those boys shot down like dogs, right at their doors in this savage style? Two others were led along to a piece of wood and hung to a tree. This was a terrible warning to bushwhackers, and this kind of work was carried on until Mosby was glad to quit."

As to Henry Avery's term of "bushwhacker," I will say this in defense of my men. By this time in the war, I believed my Command had reached the highest point of efficiency as cavalry because they were well armed with two six-shooters and their charge combined the effect of fire and shock. Yes, we were called "bushwhackers," as a term of reproach, simply because our attacks were generally surprise, and we had to make up by celerity for lack of numbers. I never resented the epithet of "bushwhackers" because bushwhacking is a legal form of war, and is just as fair and equally heroic to fire at an enemy from behind a bush as it is breastworks or from the casemate of a fort. The Yankee cavalry, who met us in combat knew that we always fought on the offensive and at close range.

Now I will return to the atrocities by General Custer and his men against my Command. Another article appeared in the *Richmond Dispatch* about the Yankees' retaliation against my men at Front Royal, Virginia. It was written by information supplied by a citizen of the village, who witnessed the uncivil atrocities. The newspaper published:

"Custer determined to wreak summary vengeance upon these men. Rhodes was lashed with rope between two horses, dragged in plain sight of his agonized relatives to the open field of our town, where one man volunteered to do the killing, and ordered the helpless, dazed prisoner to stand up in front of him, while he emptied his pistol upon him.

Anderson and Love were shot in a lot behind the court house. Overby and Carter were carried to a large walnut tree upon the hill between Front Royal and Riverton, and were hanged. The writer saw the latter under a guard in a wagon lot. They bored themselves like hero's, and endured mien. One of them was a splendid specimen of manhood, tall, well knit frame, with a head of black, wavy hair, floating in the wind, he looked like a knight of old. While I was looking at them, General Custer, at the head of his division, rode by. He was dressed in a splendid suit of silk velvet, his saddle bow bound in silver or gold. In his hand he had a large branch of damsons, which he picked and ate as he rode along. He was a distinguished looking man, with his yellow locks resting upon his shoulders. Rhodes was my friend and playmate, and I saw him shot from a distance, but did not at the time know who it was."

Two of the prisoners had placards around their neck with the inscription: "Hung in retaliation for the Union officer after he had surrendered, the fate of Mosby's men."

After I received the news of the brutality served on my men at Front Royal, I was greatly dismayed. Retaliation would come in my time.

Chapter Twenty-Three

Railroads Raids II

The Orange and Alexandria Railroad runs south by Gordonsville and Charlottesville to Lynchburg. From Manassas Junction, twenty-five miles from Washington City, a branch road runs west through the Blue Ridge Mountain to Front Royal and Strasburg. It was assumed that if the Northern army held the Manassas Gap line, my Command would retire south of the Rappahannock River. In this way a double purpose would be effected; a more convenient line of supplies would be secured, as well as the annexation of more territory to the United States. This line would be used to supply General Sheridan's army as it moved further up through the Shenandoah Valley. The valuable service which my men and I could render in conjuncture was to retard, and, if possible, to defeat this enterprise. The undertaking was great, and my means small. Yet by activity, and courage, and skill, I hoped to accomplish that result.

As we operated in General Sheridan's rear, the Manassas Gap Railroad that brought his supplies was his weak point and consequently our favorite object of attack. For security it had to be closely guarded by detachments of troops, which materially reduced his offensive strength. We kept watch for unguarded points, and the opportunity they offered was never lost. General Sheridan and General Halleck did not lose sight of the dangers we posed. General Halleck sent General Grant a telegram about his concern:

"In order to keep up communications on this line to Manassas Gap and the Shenandoah Valley, it will be necessary to send south all rebel inhabitants between the railroad and the Potomac, and also completely clean out Mosby's gang of robbers who have so long infested that district of the country, and I respectfully suggest that Sheridan's cavalry should be required to accomplish this object before it is sent elsewhere."

* * * *

On September 29, I returned to my Command. I was still on crutches recovering from my wound but I was ready to carry out my scheme against General Sheridan and his army.

On October 4 my scouts reported a body of Yankee infantry, with a construction force, coming up the Manassas Gap road; they could not have anticipated any resistance, as they had only a single company of cavalry for couriers. I decided to attack them. The next day, I assembled about two hundred men and rode toward Salem, which was along the Manassas Gap Railroad. By 3:00 o'clock in the afternoon, I had my men and my howitzers well placed on Stevenson's Hill, a little south of Salem, and half a mile from the Yankees' camp. The Yankees did not expect the attack. When the howitzers fired, the Yankees formed a skirmish line, but soon believed that my force outnumbered them. The Yankees offered little resistance and gave up the fight, fleeing toward Rectortown. When my men raced into the Yankees' camp, I told them to help themselves to the plunder. They took tents, rubber cloths, blankets, and well-filled knapsacks, all new. What they could not carry off, they torched with fire.

I followed the retreating enemy with about eighty men while Captain William Chapman and his men were left behind to do all the damage that they could to the railroad by tearing up the track. The Yankees' trail was easy to follow, for as they fled, they threw away everything likely to impede their flight, such as clothing, arms, ammunition, and equipment. In our pursuit of the Yankee infantry, we came to a turn in the road at Rectortown, where we found them drawn up in line of battle in a strong position. They opened a brisk fire as we dashed forward. I ordered the men to withdraw. In the fight near Salem, we killed and wounded a number of Yankees. We captured fifty of them. My loss was two wounded.

I will, however, conclude this part of the narrative of this fight with an anecdote, which strikingly illustrates the courageous spirit which animates the maidens of "Mosby's Confederacy." While the fight near Salem was progressing, Miss Anna Morgan of Clover Hill, was standing in front of her father's residence, watching the smoke as it rose from the guns on Stevenson's Hill. While thus absorbed, three Confederates soldiers approached, coming from the direction of Salem. As they rode up and saluted Miss Morgan, she said, "You are going in the wrong direction, gentleman. Every Southern soldier ought to be there," pointing to the scene of combat. Southern women are the fiends that drive men into battle. That evening after the fight, we bivouac between Rectortown and Salem.

On Thursday, October 6, we moved on to Salem to continue our attacks on the railroad. I had a howitzer. Near the village, I had the howitzer placed on a hill with a commanding position overlooking the railroad while the men set about destroying the track. A train came up from the direction of The Plains, but was driven back. A second attempt was made. As the train drew near, it stopped. Yankee infantry guarding the train jumped from the cars and formed along a body of woods. Our howitzer fired a shot, but the shell fell short. While the men of my Command formed near the edge of the village, the howitzer was moved closer to the Yankee infantry. The Yankees decided to give up the fight. They boarded the train and hurried off.

On Friday, October 7, the Command was assembled at Joe Blackwell's near Piedmont to continue another day's attacks on the railroad. We kept up the work of shelling and driving back trains with four cannons. As the Yankees replaced the track, we would once more tear up and demolish it. It was my intention to annoy the enemy with everything at my disposal.

The locomotive and train cars on the Manassas Gap Railroad were compelled to run at a low rate of speed. They were concerned that we would by some means throw them off the track. The trains were sometimes escorted by infantry guards, who walked by the side of the cars. With all of these precautions, mishaps would still occur.

For instance, on Monday morning, October 10, Lieutenant Glascock, with a few men, displaced a few rails and lay in wait for a train. The train came slowly along and was allowed to pass. Lieutenant Glascock and his men fired a volley into the rear of the train. The engineer immediately put on steam, running the train ahead to escape, when a general smash up was the consequence. As a result, four Yankee officers were killed, four Confederate prisoners on the train escaped in the confusion.

On the following day, I had a narrow escape. I was scouting the Manassas Gap Railroad with Captain Montjoy and Company D. While in the woods near The Plains with Company D, I took thirteen men in sight of a Yankee camp. About fifty Yankee cavalrymen of the Eighth Illinois Cavalry started in pursuit, but instead of charging, they stopped, dismounted, and took up a position behind a stone wall fence to fight at long range. I then sent my brother, Willie, for Captain Montjoy and the rest of Company D. While falling back to the woods to draw the enemy out, the Yankees followed, thinking we were retreating. I then turned and charged them, when they, no doubt fearing an ambush, wheeled and fled. A Yankee cavalryman whom I passed in the chase, shot my horse. My horse immediately fell, pinning me to the ground in the midst of the enemy. After seeing my situation, my men hastened to release me. Captain Montjoy charged and drove off the Yankees. I suffered a sprained ankle.

The men of my Command were so vigilant in their efforts against the Yankees and the Manassas Gap Railroad that their commanders wanted vengeance, even to the determination of taking their anger out on civilians. I came across a message in the *Official Records of the Union and Confederate Armies* that was written on October 12, 1864, by General Halleck. The message was sent on behalf of Secretary of War Stanton to General McCallum, General Manager of the U. S. Railroads. General Halleck wrote:

"The Secretary of War directs that, in retaliation for the murderous acts of guerilla bands, composed of and assisted by the inhabitants along the Manassas Gap Railroad, and as a measure necessary to keep that road in running order, you proceed to destroy every house within five miles of the road which is not required for our own purpose, or which is not occupied by persons known to be friendly. All males suspected of belonging to, or assisting, the robber bands of Mosby, will be sent, under guard, to the provost marshal at Washington, to be confined in Old Capitol Prison. The women and children will be assisted in going north or south, as they may select. The inhabitants of the country will be notified that for any further hostilities committed on this road or its employees an additional strip of ten miles on each side will be laid waste, and that section of country entirely depopulated."

If destroying civilians' homes and depopulating the area was not enough punishment, the Yankees in retaliation resorted to the inhuman expedient of arresting prominent citizens of the Southern type residing in Fauquier and Alexandria, and making them ride on every train which ran on the Manassas Gap Railroad. In addition some of my captured men were sent along. That did not stop my attacks ad. I was so determined to fight that even if my ... ie, and children were on board I would still throw ... n cars.

... attacks and raids continued on the Manassas Gap ..., all work stopped, and both the soldiers and workmen went to building stockades for their own safety. A courier was sent immediately to Gordonsville with a telegram to General Lee informing him of the movement on the railroad. General Lee sent a reply to me, "Your success at Salem gives great satisfaction. Do all in your power to prevent reconstruction of the road."

* * * *

During our raids on the Manassas Gap Railroad, my Command suffered the loss of James "Big Yankee" Ames. It all happened on Sunday, October, 9. I was not present when the mishap took place. I was told about "Big Yankee's" death by one of my men, Lemuel Corbin. He said that a Yankee cavalry patrol had arrived near Piedmont depot. He was with several other men from the Command, eating their breakfast at the Shacklett homestead. Corbin and his comrades hastily departed the Shacklett house to sound the alarm. Corbin rode off to inform the Chapman brothers, Ludwell Lake, and Ames near Piedmont. After learning of the Yankee patrol at the depot, "Big Yankee" wanted to ride over to the Chappalear homestead to gather some of the men. Captain William Chapman agreed. After "Big Yankee" departed, the Chapman's and Ludwell Lake heard the sound of approaching Yankees, so they headed off in the direction of the Shacklett homestead.

When the Chapman brothers and Ludwell Lake came near the Shacklett homestead, they heard the sound of a rifle, coming from the direction of the Shacklett's orchard. After the gunshot sound, they noticed a horse running down the lane. The two Chapman's took off to capture the horse while

Corbin and Lake continued toward the Shacklett's house. As Corbin and Lake rode closer to the house, they noticed a Yankee soldier robbing the body of a dead Confederate. Corbin and Lake approached the Yankee. When the Yankee stood and turned toward Corbin and Lake, Lake asked, "Are you a Yankee?"

"No" was the answer. The Yankee soldier turned and began running down the lane away from Corbin and Lake. Lake fired once at the Yankee, but missed. Corbin lifted his pistol and took aim, but it misfired. Corbin shouted at the two Chapman's that a Yankee was running down the road. They easily captured him.

Ludwell Lake dismounted and noticed the Confederate soldier was "Big Yankee." He ran down to the captured Yankee, leveled his pistol and fired, killing him. When the dead Yankee was searched, some of "Big Yankee's" personal things were found. "Big Yankee" had long been a brave and faithful follower. His death was regretted by all. He was a universal favorite with the Command.

* * * *

I kept up an incessant warfare on General Sheridan and his communications. For some time I had been contemplating an attack on the Baltimore and Ohio Railroad in the Shenandoah Valley. One of my men, Jim Wiltshire from Jefferson County, knew the area where the Baltimore and Ohio Railroad crossed. I sent him off into the Shenandoah Valley to get information on the railroad. His scout proved to be very successful. And now I shall tell you of the famous "Greenback Raid."

On October 13, I assembled eighty-four men and moved off to the Shenandoah Valley with the intention of disrupting the railroad. The greater part of the day had been spent along the turnpike between Winchester and Martinsburg, hiding in a section of woods. From an elevation, my scouts watched

ankees moving along the pike in squads of
...es and on various missions. I decided to have
... with them. When one such squad came in sight a
... our camp would slip off around the hills to appear
...ront; and when they ran back from them they would
meet another of our parties which had been sent out in
another direction to intercept them. With variations, this
thing was kept up pretty much all day, most of the
experience being confined to the realm of comedy.

Around dusk, we marched away. I recall the march was
brisk. It was a lovely night, bright and clear, with a big Jack
Frost on the ground.

While on his scout, Jim Wiltshire had discovered a gap
through which we might penetrate between the guards and
reach the Baltimore and Ohio Railroad near Duffield Depot
without exciting an alarm. It was a hazardous enterprise
because there were Yankee camps along the line and
frequent communications between them. I knew it would
injure General Sheridan to destroy a train and compel him to
place stronger guards on the railroad. There was great danger
of our being discovered by the Yankee patrols on the road
and our presence reported to the camps that were near. The
situation was critical, but we were so buoyant with hope that
we did not realize it. I resolved to take the risk.

Jim Wiltshire had acquired a train time-table. In this way,
we knew the minute when the trains were due and so timed
our arrival that we would not have to wait long. The western-
bound passenger train was selected from the time-table
schedule because I knew it would create a greater sensation
to burn it than any other. It was due about 2:00 o'clock in the
morning.

It was around midnight when Jim Wiltshire led us to a
body of woods where we dismounted and left our horses
with a detail of men. We marched a few hundred yards
across a field, where we reached the railroad. At our
position, the railroad was at a long, deep cut about two miles

east of Kearneysville. No Yankee patrol or picket was in sight. I preferred to derail the train in the cut to running it off an embankment. There would be less danger of the passengers being hurt. Lieutenant Harry Hatcher and fifteen men raised the rail with fence posts from the cross-ties, causing a slight elevation.

While the track was being readied for the derailment of a train, pickets were sent out. The rest of the men were ordered to lie down on the bank, out of sight of the railroad, and keep quiet. Many of the men quickly fell asleep because they were exhausted from riding all day. I wrapped myself in a blanket and also slept soundly. We slept so soundly that none of us heard the approaching passenger train until it got up into the cut and exploded and crashed. The displaced rail caused the engine to run off of the track. The boiler exploded, and the air was filled with red-hot cinders and escaping steam. The derailment came so suddenly, that it stunned and bewildered my men. I knew the Yankee guards would soon hear of it and that no time was to be lost, so I ran along the line and pushed my men down the bank, ordering them to go to work pulling out the passengers and setting fire to the cars.

I noticed while my men rushed toward the train, the conductor was jumping from a passenger car, waving his lantern, shouting, "All right gentlemen, the train is yours."

It did not take long to pull out the passengers. While all of this was going on, I stood on the bank, leaning on a cane, giving directions to the men. John Puryear of the Command reported that a car was filled with Germans, and they would not get out. I ordered him to set fire to the car and burn the Germans, if they did not come out. As it happened, they were immigrants going west to homestead and did not understand a word of English. There were a lot of the New York Herald newspapers on board for General Sheridan's army to read. These were circulated throughout the train and used as fuel for the fire. Once the train was torched with fire, now took in the situation and came tumbling, out of the flames.

[...]e were helping the passengers to climb the steep [...]of my pickets, Cab Maddux, came dashing up and [...]that the Yankees were coming. I immediately gave orders [...]o mount quickly and form while another man was sent to find out if the report was true. He soon returned and said the report was false. The men dismounted and returned to work. I was very angry with Cab for almost creating a stampede. I told him that I had a good mind to have him shot, but I did not. Cab claimed that he created the report because the men were gathering the spoils and he did not think it was fair for him to be away picketing for their benefit. That still did not satisfy my anger against him.

A great many ludicrous incidents occurred. A passenger claimed immunity for himself because he was the member of an aristocratic church in Baltimore. One lady ran up to me and exclaimed, "Oh, my father is a Mason!"

"I can't help it, but you shall not be harmed," said I.

Once this lady and many of the other ladies traveling on the train realized they would not be harmed, and were reassured of their personal safety, their spirits revived, and they enjoyed the adventure. As a matter of fact, while the train was being destroyed by my men, I conversed freely with the passengers. When asked by one passenger the reason for the raid on the train, I replied, "General Stevenson will not guard the railroad, and I am determined to make him perform his duty."

While we were in the process of destroying the train, two of my men, Charlie Dear and West Aldridge came up to me, shouting, "Greenbacks, greenbacks." They reported that they had captured two U. S. Paymasters, Majors Ruggles and Moore, and their satchels of greenbacks. I immediately sent them out by a small party under Charlie Grogan. They were to meet us over the Blue Ridge at our rendezvous in Loudoun County.

Whether my men got anything in the shape of pocketbooks, watches, or other valuable articles, I never inquired. I was too busy attending to the destruction of the train to see whether they did. The soldiers on the train were taken as prisoners. Quite a collection of prisoners was got together for the homeward march; tender good-byes were spoken, much more tender on the part of my men than the forsaken civilians, and with sparks flaring into the black sky and the prisoners hanging their dejected heads, the little column vanished as silently as it had come, fading into the autumn night. Some of the men turned once more to glance at the burning train and the civilians clustered around the burning cars.

Among the Yankee prisoners was a German lieutenant, who had recently received his commission and was on his way to join General Sheridan's army. I rode with him for several miles, striking up a conversation. After we were pretty well acquainted with each other, I said, "We have done you no harm. Why did you come over here to fight us?"

"Oh, I have only come to learn de art of war," said the German lieutenant.

I then left him and rode to the head of the column, because the enemy was near, and there was the prospect of a fight. It was not long before the German officer came trotting up to join me. I scarcely recognized him. One of my men had exchanged his old clothes with him for his new uniform. The German officer voiced a complaint. I asked him if he had not told me that he came to Virginia to learn the art of war.

"Yes, but whoever heard of such treatment of prisoners," said the German lieutenant.

"Very well, this is your first lesson. Those are our tactics," said I. Now it must not be thought that the habit of appropriating the enemy's goods was peculiar to my men. Because through all of the ages it has been the custom of war.

Before we reached the Shenandoah River, a citizen told us that Captain Blazer was roving around the neighborhood looking for us. He commanded a picked corps, armed with Spencer seven-shot carbines that had been assigned by General Sheridan, the duty of looking for me. My men had an easy time of capturing the train, and, although they were not indifferent to greenbacks, their mettle was up when they heard that "Old Blaze," as they called him was about. They were eager for a fight. It was not long before we struck Captain Blazer's trail and saw his campfires where he had spent the night. I could no longer restrain the men. They rushed into the camp, but he was gone. But this only postponed his fate for a few weeks, when Captain Dolly Richards met him in battle and wiped him out. I will later write of Old Blaze in my narrative.

We crossed the Shenandoah River and the Blue Ridge Mountain before noon and found Charlie Grogan's party with the greenbacks waiting for us at the appointed place in Loudoun County. At Ebenezer's Chapel near Bloomfield, the men were ordered to dismount and fall in line. I appointed three men, Charlie Hall, Richard Montjoy, and Fount Beattie to open the satchels and count the money. Once counted, I ordered the money to be divided equally among the men and officers. They each received two thousand dollars. My Command was organized under an act of the Confederate Congress to raise partisan corps; it applied the principle of maritime prize law to land war. Of course, the motive of the act was to stimulate enterprise. The men wanted me to take my part of the money. I refused. No sort of solicitations on their part could induce me to take a share. I responded to my men's pleas that I was fighting for glory, not spoils. I did not even allow my men to send any of the captured greenbacks to Pauline. My men did, however, purchase me a fine horse, Croquette, that I had admired and some red velvet slippers to wear until my sprained ankle was healed. These gifts, I did accept.

The burning of the train in the midst of General Sheridan's troops and the capture of his paymasters created a sensation. The railroad people thought that General Sheridan had not given adequate protection to their road.

The captured paymasters and other prisoners were sent south to prison. The paymasters were unjustly charged with being in collusion with me, but their capture was simply an ordinary incident of war. As the government held them responsible for the loss of the funds, they had to apply to the United States Congress for relief. After the war, one of the paymasters, Major Edwin L. Moore came to see me to get a certificate that my report to General Lee of one hundred and sixty-eight thousand dollars was based on erroneous information and was sent off before I had received the report of the commissioners appointed to count and distribute the money. The captured sum of money was actually one hundred and seventy-three thousand dollars.

Yankee troops were rushed from many points to guard the Baltimore and Ohio Railroad and the Chesapeake and Ohio Canal. My objective had been accomplished.

Chapter Twenty-Four

Retaliation II

In 1886, the *Official Records of the Union and Confederate Armies* were published. The Official Records gave us great access to reports and correspondences written by officers of both armies during the war. In the Official Records there was a report dated, August 17, 1864. I read the report from General Sheridan to General Grant:

"*Mosby had annoyed me and captured a few wagons. We hanged one and shot six of his men yesterday.*"

This had been the unfurling of the black flag against my Command. My convictions were right. I had wanted General Sheridan's soldiers to know that if they desired to fight under the black flag, I would meet them. It had greatly angered me that war could be so uncivilized.

A few days after I returned to the Command after being wounded, many Yankee prisoners had been captured, but the Command had taken no revenge against them for the brutal executions of my men at Front Royal. They were waiting on me. I determined to demand and enforce every belligerent right to which the soldiers of a great military power were entitled by the laws of war. But I resolved to do it in the most humane manner and in a calm, judicial spirit. It was not an act of revenge but a judicial sentence to save not only the lives of my own men but the lives of the enemy. It had that effect. I regret that fate thrust such a duty upon me. I do not regret that I faced and performed it. I never did anything that my conscience more thoroughly approved. The following correspondence I sent to General Lee by my brother, Willie, speaks for itself:

"General, I desire to bring through you to the notice of the government the brutal conduct of the enemy manifested towards the citizens of this district since their occupation of the Manassas road. When they first advanced up the road, we smashed up one of their trains, killing and wounding a large number. In retaliation they arrested a large number of citizens living along the line, and have been in the habit of sending an installment of them on each train. As my Command has done nothing contrary to the usages of war, it seems to me that some attempt at least ought to be made to prevent a repetition of such barbarities. During my absence from my Command the enemy captured six of my men near Front Royal. These were immediately hanged by order and in the presence of General Custer. They also hung another lately in Rappahannock. It is my purpose to hang an equal number of Custer's men whenever I capture them."

General Lee responded to my correspondence:

"I have directed Colonel Mosby, through his adjutant, to hang an equal number of Custer's men in retaliation for those executed by him."

The world has never known that I reported it to General Lee and that he and Secretary Seddon not only approved it but ordered me to do it. I did not tell any of the men from my Command that I had received the order from General Lee.

On Sunday, November 6, the Command was assembled at Rectortown. Captain Dolly Richards had returned from the Shenandoah Valley the previous day with fourteen Yankee prisoners, their horses and equipment. With these prisoners that Captain Richards brought in, it made a total of twenty-seven, all belonging to General Custer's cavalry. Now that I had a number of General Custer's men, I decided that seven of them should be taken and executed, in retaliation for the six men of my Command hung or shot at Front Royal after the fight with General Merritt's division, and for another

Private A. C. Willis, Company C, who was hung by Colonel William Powell at Gaines Cross Road, on October 13.

I will now tell you the circumstances in the latter case about A. C. Willis. When the Yankee raiding parties were passing through our area, they sent a spy ahead to learn where fine cattle and horses were to be found, and their hiding places when the raiders were about. This man passed himself off on the farmers as a Confederate soldier, who had escaped from a Yankee prison. Some men discovered his true character and making a search for him, found him at the residence of Mr. Chancellor. After questioning him and satisfying themselves as to who and what he was, they took him out and shot him. It was thought by Colonel Powell that these men were from my Command, but they were not. In retaliation for this, Colonel Powell's men captured Willis at a blacksmith's shop near Gaines Cross Roads. Willis was taken to the colonel's headquarters where he was questioned and informed that he would be executed. This is the account by an eyewitness of Willis' death:

"After capturing him they selected a spot where stood a tall, slender white-oak sapling. Man after man ascended to the top, until their weight bore it to the ground, where they held it firm while they pinioned his arms behind him and placed a halter around his neck. Then making the halter fast to the extreme end of the sapling, at a given signal they simultaneously relinquished their hold, when he could be seen swinging back and forth, until the sapling had spent its force, his lifeless body dangling in the branches close to its trunk."

Colonel Powell not only burned the Chancellor house, barn and all out buildings, but also allowed his men to leave a placard on Willis' breast with the following inscription: "A. C. Willis, a member of Company C, Mosby's Command, hanged by the neck in retaliation for the murder of a U. S. soldier by Messrs, Chancellor, and Myers."

Around noon, the twenty-seven prisoners from General Custer's command were taken under heavy guard from a schoolhouse where they had been confined and drawn up in single line. The Yankees appeared comfortable and cheerful, expressing their surprise at receiving such kind treatment at the hands of my men. Among them were two officers, one being Captain Brewster, commissary of substance, General Custer's command, and the other was a lieutenant of artillery. But soon the tranquility of the scene was rudely and painfully disturbed. As my brother, Willie, read the order, reciting the sad facts that led up to it, and declaring the dreadful climax that faced us, his solemn tones were more than once interrupted by emotion. The poor Yankees had been putting the best face they could upon the prospect of a long imprisonment, and were chatting and jesting with some heart. I will leave the reader of this narrative to imagine the awful change that passed along the devoted line as they realized the importance of my brother's words. When told by Willie that they would be executed, one Yankee cavalryman replied, " I understand the reason for this. It is in retaliation for the hangings at Front Royal, and I do not condemn you for it. But I desire to make this statement: though I now belong to General Custer's command, yet I did not belong to it when that deed was perpetrated. I do not think, in justice, that I ought to be punished for the actions of that officer before I had any connection with him."

My own men, too, were scarcely less affected. The prisoners had been in their company for a day or two, and, as was always the case after the first embarrassment of capture had passed, quite pleasant relations had been established. My men had ridden with them, laughed and talked, and divided our rations and tobacco with them; and indeed between some of them and my men quite a feeling of comradeship existed. The precipitation of the present state of affairs was a shock to my men. I watched as the eyes of more than one man from my Command were filled with tears. I recalled, Harry

Hatcher, the bravest of the brave, wept like a child when the order was read by my brother.

I appointed Edward Thomson to superintend the sad affair. I withdrew from this painful scene. I recalled saying to him that this duty must be performed for the protection of my men from the ruthless Custer and Powell.

Twenty-seven pieces of paper, seven of which were numbered and the remainder blank were put in a hat. Three of my men took the hat, shook it up and then one of them held the hat above his head while each prisoner was required to draw one slip of paper. The numbered pieces meant death by hanging, the blanks Richmond and Libby prison.

As the Yankees took a piece of paper from the hat there were various emotions depicted on the countenances of each man, who put out his hand in the hat. Firmness with closed lips and un-quailing eye; stolid indifferences; and fear with ashen cheek and trembling hand, were all there for each one. As each hand was taken from the hat, expression of joy and relief would brighten the countenance, or a groan of anguish or a cry of despair would burst from their lips.

The condemned men were at once set apart and closely guarded. The two officers had drawn blanks, but not a drummer boy by the name of, James Daly. A few minutes after the drawing was over, my sergeant major, Guy Broadwater, informed me that the drummer boy had drawn a numbered piece of paper to be hung. I ordered another drawing to take the place of the drummer boy. In truth, he ought never to have been subjected to the lottery in the first place.

Once again the prisoners were drawn up in a single line, but now only one numbered slip was in the hat. One of the two officers, Brewster escaped, but not the other. His face grew pale and for a moment his voice quivered. He said, "And must I be hanged?"

The condemned Yankee officer, Lieutenant Disosway asked for the opportunity to write a farewell letter to his wife and that it and his watch and ring should be sent through the lines to her. He was given the assurance they should be sent at the first opportunity.

I ordered Edward Thomson and his detail of men to take the prisoners to the Valley Turnpike, as near to General Sheridan's headquarters as possible and execute them.

Edward Thomson led his men and the condemned Yankee prisoners up to Ashby's Gap, where they stopped for supper and to procure some rope from the residents. The prisoners were placed in single file, tied with the rope, while one of Thomson's men rode in front with one end of the rope tied to his saddle, while a second rode behind holding the other end. In this way, it was difficult for the prisoners to escape.

There was one incident that took place at Ashby's Gap, after Edward Thomson led the condemned Yankee prisoners away to carry out the execution. Captain Montjoy and Company D were returning from a scout in the Shenandoah Valley with more prisoners from General Custer's cavalry. In the course of conversation between the parties, the Yankee officer recognized a Masonic emblem upon the person of Captain Montjoy, and gave him the signal of distress of that fraternity. Captain Montjoy responded, and took the responsibility of substituting one of his own captives in the place of his Mason brother, whom he brought on back with him. This action by Captain Montjoy met with the approval from some of my Command, but not with me. I severely reprimanded Captain Montjoy for interfering with the decree of fate, declaring to him that my Command was not a Masonic lodge. This was done for the sake of discipline.

When Edward Thomson and his men reached the Valley Turnpike, it was dark and rainy. One of the prisoners had already escaped, and fearful of meeting with further mishap such as meeting a Yankee patrol, it was decided to carry out the sentence. About one-half mile west of Berryville, in a wooded area, Thomson's men executed the condemned

Yankee prisoners. Before the last Yankee prisoner was executed, he asked for time to pray. Thomson ordered his men not to shoot until he gave the word, and then told the Yankee to pray as long as he wished. The prisoner by some means untied his hands and suddenly struck Thomson, who stood in front of him, a blow which knocked him down; then jumping over his prostrate body, he darted off into the woods and was lost to sight. It was an easy matter, I guess, to escape in the darkness for the Yankee was not recaptured. My men pinned a note to the clothing of one of the Yankees that was executed. It read: These men have been hung in retaliation for an equal number of Colonel Mosby's men hung by order of General Custer at Front Royal. Measure for measure.

* * * *

After the condemned Yankee prisoners had been sent off for execution, I asked Lieutenant Grogan to carry a letter to General Sheridan, notifying him of the hanging of these men.

"Oh, no, Colonel; I don't want to get a rope around my neck," said Grogan.

I immediately turned to John Russell, who always took a plain matter-of-fact view of things, and who never stopped to consider the risk when an order was given to him. He was entrusted with the delivery of the following letter to General Sheridan:

"General: Sometime in the month of September, during my absence from my Command, six of my men, who had been captured by your force, were hung and shot in the streets of Front Royal, by the order and in the immediate presence of Brigadier-General Custer. Since then another (captured by a Colonel Powell on a plundering expedition into Rappahannock) shared a similar fate. A label affixed to the coat of one of the murdered men declared that 'this would be the fate of Mosby and all his men.'

Since the murder of my men, not less than seven hundred prisoners, including many officers of high rank, captured from your army by this Command, have been forward to Richmond, but the execution of my purpose of retaliation was deferred in order, as far as possible, to confine its operation to the men of Custer and Powell. Accordingly, on the 6th instant, seven of your men were by my order executed on the Valley pike, your highway of travel.

Hereafter any prisoners falling into my hands will be treated with the kindness due their condition, unless some new act of barbarity shall compel me reluctantly to adopt a line of policy repugnant to humanity."

After handing the letter to John Russell, I asked him if he knew what he was up against. He replied, "Yes colonel. I know it is going to be hell to get through Custer's men at Millwood, but I can't think of those boys and men up there in the gap being hung simply because I am afraid of making the attempt,"

I told John Russell that I would keep the Command on the eastside of the Shenandoah River until he got back or until I received word that he had been shot or hung. I gave him the sealed letter to General Sheridan, and about one hundred letters written by the condemned Yankee prisoners to their loved ones. There was nothing else to say.

This is John Russell's narrative of his efforts to deliver the letters and his meeting with General Sheridan.

It was about 2:00 o'clock and I had eight miles to go before I could expect to see Yankee troops.

I got on my horse and slipped out of Paris with as little fuss as I could, for I did not want anyone except the colonel to know where I was going. I had no difficulty down the mountain, and I crossed the Shenandoah River at Berry's Ferry without interference.

When I got to Millwood, three miles west of the river, I went to old Mr. Clark, who kept a store at Millwood, to find out if the Yankee lines had been changed, and he told me that they were about four miles to the west of Millwood, and that General Custer, whose command was holding that part of the Yankee lines, had his headquarters about a mile behind the lines. Mr. Clark thought I was out on a scout, for I had frequently been by Millwood when trying to get information for the colonel.

When I asked Mr. Clark what he thought my chances were of getting into Winchester under a flag of truce to carry a letter to General Sheridan from Colonel Mosby, he seemed scared to death.

Mr. Clark told me that I was a fool. And that Custer's men knew there were no Confederate cavalry anywhere near there except Mosby's men, and that they would shoot me on sight. He advised me to go back to Paris. I asked him if Judge Page of Pagebrook was at home, and he told me that he was. I made up my mind to go on and have a talk with the judge.

When I told the judge that I was going to try to get through to Winchester, the old gentleman also told me that he thought I was a fool. I kind of commenced to believe that myself. The judge told me the nearest Yankee picket was on the back road about a mile and a half from Pagebrook. I bade him good-bye and rode out the back gate into the road to Winchester.

After I had gone about a mile and a half, I came out of the woods and saw some Yankee troops on the hill to the right of the road. I immediately commenced waving a white handkerchief which I had tied to a stick. The soldiers did not seem to see the handkerchief, for they came riding down the hill in a trot, firing their carbines at me. I waved the handkerchief as high as I could and tried to dodge the balls that came zipping around me. They did not seem to pay attention to me. There were a dozen or more of them and they were still shooting. I turned my horse and galloped out of sight in the woods. It was about sundown. They came only a little way and stopped shooting. I think they feared a trap.

I went back to Pagebrook, saw the judge and told him just what had happened. He again told me that I was a fool, and that I had better go back to Mosby and tell him that the Yankees had fired on a flag of truce. I felt that he was right. I was a fool. But still, I had promised the colonel to get that letter to General Sheridan or be killed doing it.

I asked the judge if I could stay the night at Pagebrook and he said no. I then asked if I could sleep in the barn, and he told me he would rather I went somewhere else. He was afraid the Yankees would come, find me there and burn his house. I did not blame the old gentleman at all. I told him that maybe I would take a chance on the barn, but he need not know I was there. I went to sleep in the feed room, after having made up my mind to try again in the morning.

I was up before sunup, fed my horse and rode out to the back road again. After I got to the clearing, I saw a picket up the road and commenced waving my white handkerchief again. He shouted to me to halt. He was one hundred yards away. I halted and he commenced to call, "Officer of the guard! Officer of the guard." I kept on waving the white handkerchief and presently an officer and several men rode up to the picket.

This officer shouted to me to advance, and the men covered me with their carbines as I did so. I continued to wave the white handkerchief and when I got a few yards from them the officer told me to halt and asked me what I wanted. I told him I had a letter from Colonel Mosby to General Sheridan and wanted to go through to Winchester to deliver it, but he said as I belonged to Mosby's command he had orders to shoot on sight.

I told him that Mosby had one hundred prisoners who were going to be hanged unless I got through to Sheridan, or if he shot me, and I advised him not to do it. He sent one of his men away, and after fifteen minutes a colonel came galloping up with his staff and escort.

The colonel asked me what I wanted. I told him what I had told the other officer. He said that I had better give him the letter from Colonel Mosby, as well as the other letters. I intended to obey my orders if I possibly could. I told him I had orders to deliver the letters to General Philip H. Sheridan and that, while he could kill me and take them away from me, he would only get them in that way. The colonel after thinking a while, said he would take a chance of taking me to General Custer.

About a mile from that place we turned into a lawn where I was told to dismount. As I was getting off of my horse a young man with long yellow hair hanging down on his shoulders, came out of the house and, after saluting the colonel told him what had happened. When the colonel stated that I was one of Mosby's men, and before he said anything about the letters, this young man, who I knew by description to be Custer, shouted, "I will hang the ---- to the first limb in the woods!" The colonel went on telling him about the one hundred prisoners about to be hanged and then he cooled down.

He told them to take me inside, which they did, and then said to me: "Give me those letters."

I told him that he had force enough to take them away from me, but I had orders to deliver the letters to General Sheridan and I intended to do so unless he took them. He then went across the hall and called several officers and shut the door. What they talked about, I don't know, but while they were away the colonel and several officers came up to me and asked me about the men who were to be hanged. I told them I did not know anything about it except that I thought the colonel intended hanging them in retaliation for our men that they hanged at Front Royal and elsewhere.

After a while, Custer came out and told me he ought to have me hung, but he would send me to Winchester. I told him to suit himself. I also suggested that if I did not get back to Paris, he could depend on it that one hundred of his men would be swung up. He went away swearing and mumbling. I was soon blindfolded, put on my horse, and with a number of men surrounding me, was started out onto the road again.

About midday we got to Winchester and halted at the house on the corner of Loudoun and Piccadilly Street. They told me to get down. I was led inside and the bandages taken off my eyes. There was a small, nice looking officer in the room. He told me that he was the provost marshal and that I should give him the letters. I told him that I had letters for General Sheridan and that I would do so unless they were taken away from me by force. He thought for a moment and then said that I was right to obey my orders and that he would send me to General Sheridan's headquarters. I was taken by two soldiers as guard to General Sheridan's headquarters at the Lloyd Logan house. They never took my side arms, but my horse was taken away and cared for.

At General Sheridan's headquarters, I was taken into a long room like a parlor, with a number of officers and men at the far end, and told to sit down. I don't know how long I waited but after a while a group of officers rode up in front of the house and dismounted. They came up on the porch, led by a handsome officer, who passed down to the end of the room and sat at a desk. I was told by one of my guards that the officer was Adjutant General Russell. He had the same name as my own. Adjutant Russell spoke with one of the guards and I was then directed to come to his desk. He received me very courteously, stated that he understood that our names were the same, and after some further talk asked me to give him the letters to General Sheridan, as he was adjutant general and empowered to undertake such business.

I told him that I would like to do as he suggested, but that I had orders to deliver the letters to General Sheridan in person. He laughed and said that I was perfectly right in obeying orders, and that if I waited a few minutes, possibly about half an hour, General Sheridan would be in. I told him that I was sent there to wait, and wait as long as necessary.

In about fifteen minutes General Sheridan came in, or, at least, I knew it was General Sheridan, for he was a short, thickset man in a general's uniform. He walked like a cavalryman. He walked back to the end of the hall with General Russell following him. In a few minutes, General Russell came out and told my guards to take me to the general.

I entered the room and found General Sheridan sitting at a table. He told the guards to go out and close the door. He asked me what I wanted. I told him that I had a letter from Colonel Mosby as well as about one hundred letters from some Federal prisoners who were under sentence to be hanged. I handed him the letters and told him that I had been ordered to put them in his hands, and I had done so, in spite of efforts of the officer near Pagebrook, General Custer at his headquarters, the provost marshal at Winchester, and General Russell, to get me to give them up to them.

He smiled and said that no man could fail in his duty if he obeyed his orders. He asked me to sit down while he read the letter from Colonel Mosby.

When he was through reading, he looked over the letters from the prisoners and then asked me whether I did not think it was cruel and inhuman to hang these men? I told him I certainly did, but that this execution, as well as others that had taken place on our side, was in retaliation for the same work on the part of his men and that General Custer had started the whole wretched business by executing the men in Front Royal for ambushing the train.

He asked me whether I did not think it a breach of civilized warfare for our men to have fired on the train in the first place. I told him that I did think so but for the fact that it had been under a misapprehension and that the men engaged in the ambush had no idea the train contained anything but sutler and supply wagons; that these men were simply trying to get a chance to get some of the supplies contained in the wagons by stampeding the wagon guard.

"Just like Mosby. Always looking for a chance to get at the eatables," said General Sheridan, laughing.

He asked me how I was able to get to Winchester. I told him fully; also about being fired on so briskly when I was waving a flag of truce. At this General Sheridan became very grave and stated that there was no excuse for such conduct. He said that he would see that nothing like that happened again and complimented me on keeping on with my mission when I had every excuse for going back. I told him I wanted to go back, but could not get the faces of the prisoners out of my mind.

He got up, struck out his hand to me and complimented me on doing what I had done and the way I felt about it. He said I was to go to the Taylor House, where I would be given a room and fed, and to wait there till he sent for me, as he would have to communicate with General Grant before he could answer the letter received from Colonel Mosby. He bid me good-bye, shook hands again, called in a guard as well as one of his aides, and told the latter that I was to be put up at the Taylor House and, turning to me, said, "Of course, with the understanding that you will give me your word not to leave Winchester without my permission." I gave it.

About 11:00 o'clock the next day, I was sent for by General Sheridan. The general had a letter addressed to Colonel Mosby and sealed. He said he wanted me to deliver it. He said that he would send an escort of cavalry with me as far as Millwood in order to protect me from annoyance by the Federal troops, for feelings against Mosby and his men were running high at that time. He asked me if I could guarantee that the escort would not be attacked when Millwood was reached. I could not guarantee the escort against a sudden attack if the two parties met on the road and before I could stop our men. He said that was true enough. I told him that if he would send a small escort to Berryville I would guarantee that they would meet none of our men going around in that way and that we would miss any Federal troops, as General Chapman of the Federal army was at Kennon's Shop with his brigade and we would not run into them, for they were three miles north of Berryville. General Sheridan smiled and asked me how I knew where General Chapman was, but I smiled and said nothing.

After agreeing to my proposal, he bid me good-bye and it was not long before I was back at Paris with the answer to the colonel's letter. The escort treated me like a prince all the way and we had quite a time of it, for they had more than one bottle of champagne and put three in my saddle-pockets. I had a chance to stay all night at my home near Berryville, which was really the reason why I suggested that route instead of the one to Millwood direct.

I don't know what the letter from General Sheridan contained any more than I knew the wording of the first one from Colonel Mosby, but I do know that the one hundred prisoners were not hanged and from that time hangings on account of the Front Royal incident and incidents growing out of it were stopped.

* * * *

John Russell was my trusted scout and one of the best men to serve in my Command. He endured much to get my letter to General Sheridan. Because of his good work, General Sheridan acknowledged the justice of the deed by ordering my men to be treated with the humanities of war. I acquit General Sheridan of all responsibility for the deed at Front Royal. I doubt whether he ever heard of it before he got my letter. As for General Custer, he never denied it. Contemporary evidence is against General Custer. I wonder if he also denied burning dwelling houses around Berryville.

I have never been called in question for this act of executing the Yankee prisoners, although I assumed all responsibility for it. I never took refuge under General Lee or Secretary Seddon's names. To have done so would have appeared like an apology for doing what was right. There is no act of my life that I review with more satisfaction. Again, my retaliation was a merciful act. It saved the lives of our men and the lives of the Yankees. If not, the war would have degenerated into a massacre.

Lieutenant John Russell
Source: *Courtesy of Stars & Bars*

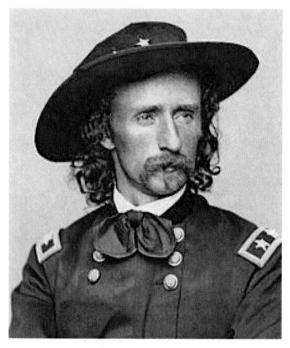

General George Custer
Source: *Library Of Congress*

CHAPTER TWENTY-FIVE

Old Blaze

In common with all Northern and Southern people, General Sheridan called us guerrillas. Although I have never adopted it, I have never resented as an insult the term guerilla when applied to me. General Sheridan says that my battalion was "the most redoubtable" partisan body that he met. I certainly take no exception to that. The highest compliment ever paid to the efficiency of my Command is the statement, in General Sheridan's memoirs, that while his army largely outnumbered General Early's, yet their line of battle strength was about equal on account of the detachments he was compelled to make to guard the border and his line of communication from partisan attacks. Ours was the only force behind him.

As I said earlier in my narrative, I would write about Old Blaze. Now is the time. In the fall of 1864, Captain Richard Blazer had received a special contract from General Sheridan to take me and my men, dead or alive, and wipe us out. Captain Blazer was a brave man from western Virginia, who had gone into the Northern army, and had so distinguished himself that he was especially chosen for the task of driving away or destroying my Command. Captain Blazer's men were an independent command, taking their name from their leader. They numbered one hundred men from Ohio and western Virginia, equipped with seven-shot Spencer rifles, and especially picked to deal with bushwhackers.

In many ways, Captain Blazer operated much like my Command. He desired to move swiftly, be on the move by daylight and camp at night. He hoped that by being friendly with the local citizens that they might not be so kind as to inform us of his movements. Captain Blazer certainly proved to be a thorn in my side.

My Command's first fight against Captain Blazer and his men took place on September 4, at Myers's Ford, just southeast of Charlestown. Seventy-five men from Company A under Lieutenant Nelson were in camp along the Shenandoah River at Myers's Ford. Lieutenant Nelson had pickets along the river, but none protecting his rear toward the Blue Ridge Mountains. Captain Blazer's men used the mountains and unexpectedly attacked Lieutenant Nelson. Lieutenant Nelson's men were dismounted and their horses were unsaddled. Lieutenant Nelson and Sergeant Johnson tried to rally them. In his efforts to do so, Lieutenant Nelson was able to get twenty-five of his men mounted. They bravely charged Captain Blazer's men. Lieutenant Nelson was shot in the leg. He fell back, and as he did, his men followed. Some of the other men under Lieutenant Nelson's command, who could not mount their horses quickly enough, started toward a gap in the fence, with Captain Blazer's men closely behind them. Thirteen of my men were killed and six wounded in the fight.

I was not at the fight. I had been off on another raid near Harpers Ferry. When I was told of the fight at Myers's Ford between Lieutenant Nelson's men and Captain Blazer's command, I was greatly displeased, especially after learning that my men had fled in compete disorder.

My men had been skirmishing with Captain Blazer's command for the past several months. It was evident that my men and Old Blaze's could not occupy the same section of country. One or the other must go. Which one was a question to be settled only by a decisive battle. It came about when Captain Montjoy was routed by Captain Blazer's men near

Berryville. I was sick with a cold, so I ordered Captain Dolly Richards, who was one of the most aggressive officers in my Command, to take companies A and B and wipe Blazer out and go through him.

Companies A and B under Captain Dolly Richards of my Command crossed the Blue Ridge Mountain and the Shenandoah River in a terrible rain storm, and camped for the night without fire or shelter at Castleman's woods, a few miles northeast of Berryville. Captain Richards learned that Old Blaze had notice of his approach.

Each command recognized that the decisive hour had come, and was none the less eager for the fray. But each also appreciated the advantage of getting the bulge on the other, as Harry Hatcher called it. The bulge is causing the enemy to flee in panic by a swift and unexpected attack.

Each command maneuvered for position. Captain Richards and his men rode in ravines, under river bluffs, while hostile scouts frequently caught sight of each other from neighboring hills.

Around daylight of November 18, two of Captain Richards' scouts, Charley McDonough and John Puryear were returning from a scout in the area of Kabletown. As they rode up a hill, they found themselves within a short distance of several other soldiers dressed in Confederate uniforms. As they approached, McDonough and Puryear took it for granted that they were some scouts, but did not recognize them. Charley was wanted with a price on his head by the Yankee authorities for bushwhacking. He was very cautious of making new acquaintances. He rode away, leaving Puryear to await the two strangers. As it turned out, the two strangers were what we called, Jessie Scouts. Jessie Scouts were Yankees that disguised themselves by wearing Confederate uniforms to deceive us. Puryear was fooled. The two Jessie Scouts made him their prisoner. Charley returned to Dolly Richards and reported what had happened.

John Puryear was taken to Lieutenant Cole of Captain Blazer's command. Lieutenant Cole questioned Puryear as to the whereabouts of my Command. Puryear refused to give him information. Lieutenant Cole threatened Puryear with instant death if he did not give him information. Puryear would not do so, therefore, Lieutenant Cole proceeded to carry out his threat. The Yankees placed a rope around the neck of Puryear, and suspended him from a tree until nearly unconscious, and then lowered him again and asked questions. Puryear refused to answer any questions concerning my Command. This method of getting information was used a second and third time. Puryear still refused to answer Lieutenant Cole's questions. The brutal torture ended.

With the information from Charley McDonough, Captain Richards found an opportunity to strike Old Blaze and wipe him out for once and all. Captain Richards told his men:

"Blazer is now camped near Kabletown; as soon as you come in sight of his pickets, draw your pistols and move off at a gallop, but don't fire a shot or raise a yell until you hear the shooting in front. Don't shoot until you get close to them, among them. They've got Puryear and four other prisoners and you may kill some of them."

Captain Richards and his men moved quickly along and soon came in sight of the blue smoke curling up in the woods near Kabletown. When the woods were reached, the Command moved on at a gallop and dashed into the Yankees' camp, but found it deserted. The fires were still burning, a huge pile of corn in the center of the camp, and a bundle of newspapers lying unopened nearby, showed that the enemy had left but a short time before Captain Richards' arrival. Scouts were sent out and soon returned, bringing the word that Old Blaze had passed on but a few moments previous to our coming, and was moving toward the Shenandoah River.

Captain Richards moved his men down the river road at a quick pace. As Captain Richards and his men moved along the road, a couple of Yankee cavalrymen were observed dashing across a field from one piece of woods to another. The whole Yankee column, moving slowly soon came in the sight of Captain Richards' scouts near Myerstown.

Captain Richards and his men soon reached a narrow strip of woods, not more than one hundred yards wide, which borders the road on the south and runs parallel with a considerable distance. Just behind the woods was an open field, which sloped rather abruptly from the woods into a deep valley and rises again toward the south, in full view of the road at this time of the year. Along the top of this hill, on the southern boundary of the field, ran an old rail fence. From this fence to the road the distance was perhaps three hundred yards.

After passing through these woods, Captain Richards left a few men scattered here and there as scouts. Just beyond them to the south, under the brow of the hill, Company B was drawn up in line of battle, facing the road, so disposed that the enemy would not see them until one or the other should reach the hilltop. Still farther to the south, drawn in the vale, Company A was halted in line of march.

Captain Blazer and his men arrived. Private David Carlisle, who I understand had been imbibing a little dashed into the woods and after looking at the enemy, he galloped back, while firing a shot at them. This alerted Captain Blazer and his men of our presence. They dismounted and began to take down a fence along a ridge at the south end of the field. Captain Richards thought by Captain Blazer's actions that he intended to fight at a long range, which would give them every advantage with their guns.

Captain Blazer moved his men through the gap in the fence that his men had created. When this happened, Captain Richards ordered Lieutenant Hatcher to pull down a section of fence in their rear. Company A was ordered to move off as if retreating. The ruse had the desired effect. Captain Blazer thought the bulge was on because his men began to charge. After noticing the maneuver by Company A, Company B charged and hit the left flank of Old Blaze's men. Captain Blazer's men were of true metal. They stood the surprise and shock like heroes. The two lines closed up, and for more than a minute stood horse to horse, emptying their revolvers into each other's faces. At this point murderous work was done on both sides. The Yankees began to give away. Not even a halt was made. Captain Richards' men carried the enemy in hopeless, reckless rout back through the woods into the road.

When Company B charged Old Blaze's men, Lieutenant Hatcher turned Company A around and swept over the intervening space at full speed and dashed with the fury of a tornado into the right flank of the Yankee column. At first, Old Blaze's men used their seven-shot rifles until Captain Richards' men were too close and then the Yankees used their revolvers. Old Blaze's men fought desperately, but our men pressed on, broke them and finally drove them from the field.

Old Blaze stood his ground until he saw that the day was hopelessly lost and his veterans had fallen thick around him. Then and only then did he betake himself to flight.

More than a mile up the road, Old Blaze was overtaken in his flight by a burly young man, Private Syd Ferguson. Pursuer and pursued had emptied their revolvers. Old Blaze paid no heed to the youth's call on him to halt until Ferguson finally, running beside him, knocked him prone to the road with the butt of his revolver. Old Blaze upon his capture said, "Boys, you have whipped us fairly. All I ask is that you treat us well."

During the chase, Lieutenant Cole was captured by Private John Alexander. According to Alexander, John Puryear rode up after being released from captivity with a pair of revolvers drawn. Puryear was about to shoot

Lieutenant Cole when Alexander shouted, "Don't shoot him; he has surrendered."

"The rascal tried to hang me this morning," said Puryear.

Alexander asked Lieutenant Cole if these charges were true. Lieutenant Cole hesitated, no response, then the crack of a pistol and he fell dead. Alexander said Lieutenant Cole had been bleeding profusely from a wound to the breast, which he had received in the fight. He added, "As I moved away he rolled his dying eyes toward me with a look I shall never forget."

In the fight at Myerstown, Old Blaze's loss was twenty-one killed, a large number wounded, many mortally, and twenty-two prisoners captured. Fifty horses and their equipment were also captured. As for Old Blaze, he was sent off to Libby Prison in Richmond. His command ceased to exist. Old Blaze had been wiped out!

Captain Richard Blazer
Source: *West Virginia in the Civil War*

Chapter Twenty-Six

Fiery Trails

After an attack against the Manassas Gap Railroad on October 14, 1864, our four pieces of artillery were sheltered on Little Cobbler Mountain. One of my men from the artillery company was captured. His name was John Lunceford. He was captured by the Thirteenth New York Cavalry. After being questioned by the Yankees, they surprised my men and captured all of our guns. So with no guns for the artillery company, it was time to reorganize. According to Order 261, from the Adjutant and Inspectors Office in Richmond, the artillery company was formally disbanded. On Monday, November 28, the Command assembled at Salem where the artillery company was reorganized into Company G. Tom Richards, Dolly's brother, was elected as captain of the new company. John Murphy, who had tried to form his own partisan company over on the Northern Neck of Virginia and failed, instead joined my Command. He was promoted to first lieutenant. Garland Smith was promoted to second lieutenant and John Puryear third lieutenant. I had told John Puryear that I would make him a lieutenant for his gallantry. But, I jokingly added that I did not want him to command any of my men.

Alfred Glascock was promoted to captain of Company D, to replace Captain Richard Montjoy. Captain Montjoy was killed on November 27, while fighting the Yankees near Goresville in Loudoun County. Captain Montjoy was a great loss to my Command. He died too early for liberty and his country's Cause, but not too early for his own fame. To his comrades in arms, he had bequeathed an immortal example of daring and valor, and to his country, a name that will brighten the pages of history.

By December 1864, the war had practically ceased between the contending armies in the Shenandoah Valley. The greater portion of General Early's forces had been transferred to the lines around Petersburg, while General Sheridan had taken up his winter quarters at Winchester. My own Command, which had been operating against General Sheridan's communications, never went into winter quarters, but kept up a desultory warfare on outpost, supply trains, and detachments. Although the Southern army had disappeared from General Sheridan's front, we kept his soldiers busily employed to guard against surprises as when General Early's army had confronted them. Unable to exterminate us by arms, General Sheridan resorted to applying the torch, attempting to drive us from the district in which we operated by destroying everything that could support man or horse. Instead of quelling, his efforts only stimulated the fury of my men. It made no difference if it was snow, sleet, and the howling storms through the long watches of the winter nights, General Sheridan's men had to wait for a sleepless enemy to capture or kill them.

General Sheridan wanted to eliminate us by waging war against the local citizens in hopes they would turn against us. That didn't happen. In writing my narrative, I discovered a message in the *Official Records of the Union and Confederate Armies* from General Sheridan to General Halleck announcing his intentions. The telegram was written on November 26, 1864, and stated his intentions against the citizens of Loudoun and Fauquier Counties. It reads as follows:

"I will soon commence work on Mosby. Heretofore I made no attempt to break him up, as I would have employed ten men to his one, and for the reason that I have made a

scapegoat of him for the destruction of private rights. Now there is going to be an intense hatred of him in that portion of the valley which is nearly desert. I will commence on Loudoun County, and let them know there is a God in Israel. Mosby has annoyed me considerably; but the people are beginning to see that he does not injure me a great deal, but causes a loss to them all that they have spent their lives accumulating. Those people who live in the vicinity of Harpers Ferry are the most villainous in this valley, and have not been hurt much. If the railroad is interfered with, I will make some of them poor. Those who live at home in peace and plenty want the duello part of this war to go on; but when they have to bear the burden by loss of property and comforts, they will cry for peace."

General Sheridan wrote in his own memoirs, published in 1888, that he directed General Merritt and two brigades of cavalry to march into the Loudoun Valley and operate against my Command. This is what he wrote about the Yankees' destruction of private property:

"Merritt was to take care to clear the country of forage subsistence, so as to prevent the guerrillas from being harbored there in the future, their destruction or capture being well-nigh impossible, on account of their intimate knowledge of the mountain region. Merritt carried out his instructions with his usual sagacity and thoroughness, sweeping widely over each side of his general line of march with flankers, who burned the grain and brought in large herds of cattle, hogs, and sheep, which were issued to the troops."

The Yankees' raid on the civilians was devastating. All of us witnessed flames bursting from haystacks, barns, and stables. Then as the fires began to blaze lazily, the night wind stirred up the dying embers of the result of some poor farmer's toil, the bright flames would shoot up for a few moments, illuminating the scene. When we thought the enemy was finished with their work of destruction, we soon determined that it was really just commencing. Soon again, the curling smoke was rising in dense volumes, streaming heavenward. As the fires became more numerous, the heavy mass of smoke spread out and settled over the valley like a thick fog. The fog obscured the view so that at one time, while riding along, a few men of my Command could distinctly hear the voices of their enemies in conversation, although they could not see them.

From Monday afternoon until Friday morning, the Yankee cavalry's area of operations was through the beautiful Loudoun Valley and a portion of Fauquier County, burning and laying waste to everything. They robbed the people of everything they could destroy or carry off. They carried off horses, cows, cattle, sheep, hogs; killing poultry, insulting women, and pillaging houses. They burned all mills and factories, as well as hay, wheat, corn, straw, and forage. Barns and stables, whether full or empty were burned.

The citizens represent the Yankee raiders as being the most inhuman, barbarous, hardened wretches which had ever passed through that country. The wails, tears, and entreaties of women were answered only with a savage oath and scornful laugh.

My men did, however, manage to save a great deal of livestock for the farmers by driving it off to places of safety. They ran the livestock to places that had already been burned, and their kept them concealed as much as possible.

Whenever an opportunity was offered, squads of my men rushed into the Yankee raiders, shooting, wounding and killing some. The Command as a whole, I decided not to assemble to offer resistance. There was not much that we could do to stop the atrocities by the Yankee raiders.

* * * *

On the day that General Merritt and his Yankee raiders withdrew back across the Blue Ridge Mountains to the

Shenandoah Valley, I departed to have a conference with General Robert E. Lee about my plans for future operations. I turned command over to Captain William Chapman, and taking one of my men, Boyd Smith, I went to the army's headquarters in Petersburg, Virginia. When I arrived at Richmond and got off the train, I recognized Doctor Aristides Monteiro, an old college mate, who I had not seen in thirteen years. At the time, he was a surgeon with General Wises' brigade. After meeting Doctor Monteiro, I informed him that I was on my way to General Lee at his headquarters, and that I wanted to return to my Command with as little delay as possible. I asked him to join my Command, which he agreed to do. I agreed to go with him to make all of the arrangements for his assignment to my Command. I wanted Doctor Monteiro because Doctor Dunn of my Command was too fond of fighting instead of curing. I wanted someone who took more pride in curing than killing. Doctor Monteiro remained with me as my Command's surgeon throughout the duration of the war.

While with General Lee, I discussed dividing my Command in half since I had seven organized companies. I wanted to send one half to the Northern Neck of Virginia, which is that area east of Fredericksburg and the Rappahannock River to the south and the Potomac River to the north. The Northern Neck of Virginia had not been devastated by the war such as Northern Virginia. I would give the other half of the Command to Dolly Richards in Northern Virginia. I would retain compete command over my men on the Northern Neck as well as in Northern Virginia. I also believed that sending some of the men from my Command to the Northern Neck of Virginia would ease the difficulties on the civilians who lived in Loudoun and Fauquier Counties. They had suffered greatly, but had remained loyal to the Southern Cause. To carry out my plan, I wanted to obtain promotions for two of my captains,

William Chapman and Dolly Richards. Both of these men had gallantly distinguished themselves in battle.

After spending a few hours with General Lee, he informed me that he did not have the authority to organize my Command into two battalions. He suggested that the matter be discussed with Secretary of War James Seddon. On December 6, I wrote Secretary Seddon:

"I beg leave to recommend, in order to secure greater efficiency in my Command, that it be divided into two battalions, each to be commanded by a major. The scope of duties devolving upon me being of a much wider extent than an officers of the same rank in the regular service, but small time is allowed me to attend to details of organization and discipline. I am confident that the arrangements I propose would give me much more time both for planning and executing enterprises against the enemy."

I returned to my men with good news. William Chapman was to be promoted to lieutenant-colonel and given command of one half of my Command to go to the Northern Neck, while Dolly Richards was to be promoted to the rank of major. I was promoted to colonel.

* * * *

On the day after my return from Richmond, December 21, I had gone to the house of Joe Blackwell, a farmer in upper Fauquier County, to attend the wedding of my ordnance sergeant, Jake Lavender. A report came that a body of the enemy's cavalry was advancing on the road to Salem, a few miles away. Not caring to interrupt the wedding festivities, I rode off with one man, Private Tom Love, to scout. We were riding across the field of the Glen Welby farm when we saw two Yankee cavalrymen approaching. Soon a number of others appeared and they began firing at us. I knew then that these were the flankers of the main body of the enemy out of sight over the hill. Tom Love and I galloped away a few hundred yards where we halted on a hill. The Yankees did not pursue us. We watched as the whole column in blue moved on the road to Rectortown. When they arrived, we noticed that they kindled fires and seemed to be camping for the night.

It was about dusk. A cold, drizzling rain was falling and freezing, the road was covered with sleet, and icicles hung in clusters from the trees. After satisfying myself that the Yankee cavalrymen had prepared to spend the night there, I sent word to Lieutenant-Colonel Chapman and Major Richards to get their men ready to attack the Yankees' camp the next morning. Tom Love and I started off in another direction to notify some of the other officers and collecting the men.

Within a mile of Rectortown, we were passing the house of Ludwell Lake. Lake was famous for always setting a good table. The lights were shining through the windows. It tempted me, as I was cold and hungry, to stop where I knew we would be welcomed. I proposed to Tom Love that we should dismount and get warm and get something to eat. Love wanted to stay out at the gate and keep watch while I was eating supper. No, I insisted, it wouldn't do me any good if he were out here in the cold. I assured him there was no danger; get down.

The family was at supper, and we were soon seated at the table enjoying some good coffee, hot rolls, and spareribs. Among those there was a Mrs. Skinner, whose husband was then a prisoner at Point Lookout, Maryland.

We were enjoying our supper and Mrs. Skinner's account of her trip to Point Lookout, when suddenly we heard the tramp of horses around the house. One door of the dining room opened toward the backyard. On opening it, I discovered several Yankee cavalrymen. Hastily shutting the door, I turned to the other one, but just then a number of Yankee officers and soldiers walked into the room.

I was better dressed that evening than I ever was during the war. Before going to Richmond, I had gotten a complete suit from head to foot across the Potomac River. I had a drab hat with an ostrich plume, with gold cord and star; a heavy, black beaver-cloth overcoat and cape lined with English scarlet cloth, and a gray cloak, also lined with scarlet. My overcoat and cape were lying in the corner. I wore a gray sack coat with two stars on the collar to indicate my rank, gray trousers with yellow cord down the seam and long cavalry boots.

After the Yankee officers entered the room, I placed my hands on my coat collar to conceal my stars, and a few words passed between us. The situation seemed desperate, but I had made up my mind to take all chances for getting away. I knew that if they discovered my rank, to say nothing of my name, they would guard me more carefully than if I were simply a private or a lieutenant.

Firing by the Yankee cavalrymen began in the backyard. One of the bullets passed through the window and struck me in the stomach. When I look back on that time, it was a miracle how the shot could have missed everyone else in the room and hit me, but it did. My self-possession in concealing the stars on my collar saved me from being carried off as a prisoner, dead or alive. The Yankee officers had not detected the stratagem until I exclaimed that I was shot. The bullet that struck me created only a stinging sensation, and I was not in the least shocked. My exclamation was not because I felt hurt, but to get up a panic in order that I might escape. It had the desire effect. Old man Lake and his daughter waltzed around the room, the Yankee cavalrymen on the outside kept up their fire, and this created a stampede of the officers in the room with me. In the confusion to get out of the way, the supper table was knocked over and the tallow lights put out. I was left in the room with Love, Lake, and his daughter.

I saw that this was my opportunity. There were nine hundred and ninety-nine chances out of a thousand against me, but I took the single chance and won. By this time the terrible wound was having its effect; I was bleeding profusely and getting faint. There was a door which opened into an adjoining bedroom, and I determined to play the part of a dying man. I walked into the room, pulled off my coat, on which the insignia of my rank, tucked it under the bureau so that no one could see it, and then lay down with my head toward the bureau. After several minutes the panic subsided. The Yankee officers returned to the scene. The room in which I lay was dark, and it was some minutes before the soldiers collected their senses sufficiently to strike a light.

During all this time, I lay on the floor with the blood gushing from my wound. In those few minutes it seemed to me that I lived my whole life over again; my mind traveled away from the scenes of death and carnage, in which I had been an actor for four years, to the peaceful home and the wife and children I had left behind.

I overheard the soldiers ask Mrs. Skinner who I was. I was well acquainted with her. Her brother was in my Command. I listened with fear and trembling for her answer. She declared that I was a stranger. That she had never seen me before. That I was not one of Mosby's men, and she did not know my name. A Negro belonging to Ludwell Lake was introduced. He failed to recognize me. When asked about my identity, he said that I was a stranger in the neighborhood. His testimony removed all doubt. Mrs. Skinner and the Negro saved my life.

At last, a candle had been lighted. My enemies came into the room, and the first thing they did was ask me my name. I gave a fictitious one. I said that I was Lieutenant Johnson. They wanted to know which command I belonged to. I did not tell them the right one. I answered that I belonged to the Sixth Virginia Cavalry. I wanted to conceal my identity, as I knew the feelings of the North against me and the great anxiety to either kill or capture me. I had on a flannel shirt which was now soaked with blood. The soldiers opened my clothes and looked at my wound, while I apparently gasped for breath. A doctor examined the wound and said that it was mortal, that I was shot through the heart. He located the heart rather low down, and even in that supreme moment I felt tempted to laugh at his ignorance of human anatomy. I only affected a few words and affected to be dying. They left the room, hurriedly, after stripping me of my boots and trousers, evidently supposing that a dead man would have no use for them. The only sensible man among them was an Irishman, who said, "He is worth several dead men yet."

As they were about to leave the house, one of the Yankee officers said to Lake, "Have him decently buried; he seems to be a brave soldier."

Fortunately they never saw my coat. They passed out under the impression that I was ready for the grave. I lay perfectly still for some five or ten minutes. It seemed to me many hours, but at last, as I felt assured that the enemy had gone, I rose from the pool of blood in which I was lying and walked into the room where Lake and his daughter were sitting by the fire. They were as much astonished to see me as if I had risen from the tomb. They too had thought me dead.

There was a big log blazing, and the room was warm. We examined the wound, but we could not tell whether the bullet had passed straight into the body, or after penetrating, had passed around it. My own belief was that the wound was mortal; the bullet was in me; that the intestines had been cut. Mrs. Skinner gave me some coffee, but I was too sick to drink it.

I later learned that Tom Love and several of my men were prisoners. They were shown my hat and overcoat and asked if they knew the person who had worn them. All denied any knowledge of me. The Yankees returned to camp, little dreaming who it was that had been a prisoner in their hands.

As soon as Lake recovered from the shock of seeing me alive, he went out and got a couple of Negro boys to yoke a pair of young-half-broken oxen to haul me away to a place of safety, for we feared that the enemy would find out who I was and return. I was rolled up in quilts and blankets and put into an ox-cart. It was an awful night of a howling storm of snow, rain, and sleet. I was lying on my back in the cart. We had to go two miles to the house of a neighbor, over a frozen road cut into deep ruts. When we reached there, I was almost perfectly stiff with cold, and my hair was a clotted mass of ice. The family had not gone to bed and one of my men, George Slater, was at the house. A courier was sent to the wedding party to carry the news to my brother, my other men, and before daybreak a great many of the men and two surgeons were with me. George Slater had been with General Stuart when he was shot a few months before. I called to him. I said, "George, look at my wound, I think I am shot just like General Stuart was."

George pulled up my shirt and told me that he thought the bullet had run around my body. This turned out to be the case because it had lodged in my left side. Early in the morning, the ball was extracted from my body.

It was a lucky shot for me. It was the means of my escape from imprisonment.

A few days afterward, tidings came down to the Yankees' camp down at Fairfax that I was the one wounded at Lake's house. A force of Yankee cavalry was sent to search for me, but although I was still in the neighborhood, they did not find me. I was informed later that when the Yankee cavalry returned to Mr. Lake's house, they diligently searched the house and premises. They raved. The ladies of the house were taken and interrogated as to where that wounded man was and told that if they did not tell, their house would be burned down. The only reply the Yankees received was "Burn on, we do not know where he is."

The enemy, satisfying themselves that I was not on Mr. Lake's property, fell into line and marched away. The Yankee cavalry continued to look for me, but I was moved from one home to another. By doing this, not only the Yankees were ignorant of where I was, but even my own men did not know.

About a week after I was severely wounded, I was taken to my father's house in Lynchburg. Doctor Monteiro had not reached my Command before I was brought away, so he came to my father's house to see me. Doctor Monteiro was a great wit and had only been with me for a few minutes when he got me to laughing, though in considerable pain. This produced a hemorrhage from my wound, and it took all his surgical skill to repair the damage his talk had done.

In the proceeding days that Doctor Monteiro was with me, I was able to give him a graphic and interesting account of my adventures since our parting in Richmond. I told about the night I was wounded, that I was carrying important papers and dispatches in the pocket of my overcoat, and if found by the Yankees, the papers would have betrayed me.

Five days after being wounded, the *Richmond Times Dispatch* and the *New York Herald* reported that I was "dead and buried." The *New York Herald* published my obituary "like Morgan, Anderson and other guerrillas of like character, Mosby has met with a dog's death." But then many of the newspapers had to correct themselves by writing "Mosby is not yet dead. He may possibly recover."

CHAPTER TWENTY-SEVEN

The Final Days

Before leaving my father's homestead in February, 1865, my mother grieved. She knew the day had come and the hour had passed that saw her dearest one leave once more the household group to go back to battle for his country. It was one of the saddest events of her life. But she knew that God was with us in the Army as well as around the peaceful and secure fireside.

Before returning to my Command, I went to Richmond. While there, I was honored by the Virginia House of Delegates as a military hero and given an honored seat by the Confederate House of Representatives. Next, I paid a visit to Governor William Smith. I sat for a portrait with a French artist and discussed with him some of my Command's previous operations. I had every mark of respect and attention shown to me while in Richmond.

I recall the last time that I saw General Lee. He was not only kind, but affectionate, and asked me to dinner with him, though he said he hadn't much to eat. There was a leg of mutton on the table; he remarked that some of his staff officers must have stolen it. After dinner, he spoke freely about his feelings on the campaign of 1862 against Richmond. When I bade him a good-bye after our interview, I had no idea that it was my final parting with him as my commander.

But the days of the Southern Confederacy were fading. Though the war was waged as earnestly, and the Southern people were true to their cause, as at any time since the commencement, still one could see that there was a longing for peace. About this time, rumors were in circulation of peace negotiations. A conference to that end was held at Fortress Monroe. Representing the Southern Confederacy were Vice President Alexander Stephens, and the honorable R. M. T. Hunter. They met with Abe Lincoln. I recall that after returning to my Command, Private Marshall Crawford told me that my men had been informed of the news of the peace conference by Bush Underwood while scouting in Fairfax. The intelligence had cast a gloom not only over the officers and men of my Command, but over the whole of "Mosby's Confederacy." Although the farmers and soldiers were living on half allowance, gold at one hundred dollars, and the citizens refusing to take Confederate money, they had not relaxed their efforts in the least degree. The officers and men had unanimously resolved that if the Confederacy went down, the present generation and those that came after them should not say that they did not discharge their duty.

After I returned to the Command, I was received by my brave followers with the wildest demonstrations of vociferous joy. My well-tried veterans gathered around me with noisy manifestations of affectionate regard. The officers were gathered and plans were instantly perfected to organize the many volunteers that were constantly flocking to my Command into new companies and rapidly filling the wasted ranks of the old. Meanwhile, Companies C, E, F, and G had already gone to the Northern Neck of Virginia under Lieutenant-Colonel William Chapman in accordance with my previous orders. Companies A, B, and D under Major Dolly Richards had remained in Northern Virginia. And it was with him that I stayed.

* * * *

The great Burning Raid made by the Yankees was the destruction of our stores and provender. As will be readily understood, our horses had to be kept in tip-top condition. To secure supplies was a prime necessity.

Near the center of Loudoun County was a rich section farmed by Quakers. Their farms even in war time had been successful. They were non-combatants, and were with few exceptions loyal to the United States Government. Their barns and storehouses were full, and these provisions for our necessities I could not hesitate to appropriate. A detachment of one hundred and fifty of my men was sent up into this Egypt to impress wagons and haul the grain away to our homes in southern Loudoun and Fauquier.

It did the Quaker women and men good to see my men enjoy their pies and jams; and I am sure that the eyes of the demure maidens flashed quite naturally as they served apples, nearly as rosy as their cheeks to my men, who did not fail to give some expression of their appreciation. But while all on the surface was so lovely, we knew that these same folks were in close touch with the Yankee forces across the Potomac River, and that the grapevine telegraph kept their friends constantly advised of the situation. We knew, too, that their devotion to peace would not deter them from any kind of cooperation with us. That our said friendship with them would secure the quiet rest of prison life. So every morning the men would rendezvous at Hamilton, or as it was also called, Harmony. If the reports of our scouts and pickets were favorable, they were dispersed to pursue the duties of their new vocation. But one morning that did not happen; the expected was about to happen.

It was on March 20, 1865, Private John Chew and several other scouts entered the town of Hillsborough. Chew and the other scouts were notified by a lady that the Yankees were at the other end of the town. When Chew and the others scouts were noticed, the Yankees chased them for several miles and then returned to their camp at Hillsborough. The Yankee force appeared to consist of a considerable wagon train escorted by cavalry. The cavalry was made up of the Twelfth Pennsylvania and the Loudoun Rangers. The Loudoun Rangers were Quakers from the Potomac River region of Loudoun County, who were loyal to the Union. The Yankees were under the command of Colonel Marcus Reno. They were sent to drive us out of Loudoun County.

The next day, the Yankees appeared to be moving toward Purcellville. With this news, the men fell into a flutter. The thing looked so inviting. I was cautious. Instead, I moved the Command off to the village of Lincoln, near Purcellville. Scouts were sent out to take observations of the moving Yankee column.

Sure enough, my scouts found the wagon train moving quietly down the road toward Hamilton with its cavalry escort. The Yankee cavalry opened a long range fire on my scouts and then chased them a short distance back toward Lincoln. But on this scout, my men discovered that the wagons were like Trojan horses, loaded with Yankee infantry. When my scouts reported this to me, I sent them back and ordered them to stay on the Yankee wagon train's flank and keep me advised of their movements.

Now I want to give you an idea of the terrain that was in this area where the fight took place. The road out of Hamilton takes a very eccentric course toward Lincoln. Leaving the turnpike about the middle of the former village, it runs southeasterly, passing open lots and farmhouses and then through woods, for about one half mile; then turns abruptly westward past William Tavenner's field for about two hundred yards, when it turns at a right angle over a hill and passing another body of woods, breaks away southwesterly toward Lincoln. Hills and dales and abrupt turns mark the whole course. The body of woods last mentioned drops away from the road into a little dell; and into this my scouts were moving.

My scouts were near the outskirts of Lincoln, some distance north of the Tavenner's homestead when the Yankee infantry deployed into the open field south of the town. These things were reported to me.

I planned an ambush by posting Captain Glascock, with Company D and a portion of Company A, in a piece of woods to the left of the road to Silcott Springs. Six well-mounted men were ordered by me to ride forward and attack the enemy's advance and then fall back past the woods in which Captain Glascock's men were concealed. This was to be accomplished in order to draw out the cavalry from the infantry. The ruse succeeded. The whole Yankee cavalry force started in pursuit of the six men, who fled wildly, as though surprised and terror-stricken.

On came the Yankee cavalry, shouting and yelling. Their advance swept before us. While they approached, I gave orders for my men to fall back a little further from the road, so as to keep out of sight as much as possible. Some of my men did not understand the movement and it caused some confusion. The Yankee cavalry had slowed their pace. Captain Glascock realized that the opportunity might be lost, so he ordered the men forward.

I was sitting on my horse in the Tavenner's yard when Captain Glascock and his men came trotting out of the woods. Once out of the woods, Captain Glascock gave the order to charge. My men broke into a gallop and hurled themselves upon the flank and front of the astonished foe. The Yankee cavalry stood their ground and fought for a few minutes, then gave way and fled back toward Hamilton pursued by Captain Glascock and his men, who rained bullets among them.

Not far from the woods the road entered a narrow lane, with a high, steep bank on each side. Into this lane the panic-stricken Yankees jammed themselves. The Yankees and their horses pressed so tightly together that some time elapsed before they could get forward.

I had followed and was now on the top of an embankment waving my men on, who with loud cheers followed up the chase. When the retreating Yankees reached a piece of woods close to Hamilton, they attempted a rally, and briefly there was a hand-to-hand fight between them and my men. Here was where we suffered some slight loss of men. Again the Yankee cavalry resumed their flight.

On the left of the woods, where the Yankee cavalry made their brief stand, their infantry was posted behind an orange hedge. When my men approached, they rose up and fired into them. If it would not have been for their fire, our pursuit would have continued, and but few of the cavalry would have escaped. The fight had been sharp and desperate.

While this part of the fighting was taking place, I left the embankment and galloped along the Yankees' flank up to the woods. I soon ordered the men to fall back because of the Yankee infantry's musketry.

Nine of the Yankees were killed and a number wounded, some mortally. Thirteen were captured along with fifteen horses. My loss was two killed and four wounded.

After drawing off my men, we halted in a field in full view of the Yankees. My men cheered, waved their hats, and used every means to draw the cavalry away from the infantry. Some men ventured too close and the Yankees again began firing. One of my men, Private Joe Griffin was wounded. His horse was killed. As he tried to seek shelter in the woods, he was captured.

That evening, pickets were placed near and around the town to watch the movements of the Yankees, but they went into camp. It rained that evening and throughout the night. Over the next few days, we skirmished with the Yankees, but by Thursday, March 30, the fighting had ended. The Command once again proceeded to the Quaker settlements in Loudoun, and the business of pressing corn continued.

Lt. Col. William Chapman
Source: Author's Collection

Major Adolphus "Dolly" Richards
Source: *Author's Collection*

Chapter Twenty-Eight

Is It True

In March of 1865, Generals Lee and Grant still faced each other at Petersburg, Virginia. General Sherman and his Yankee army were driving up through the Carolinas against General Joseph Johnston's army. It was during this time that I received a message from General Lee's assistant adjutant-general, Walter Taylor. I was instructed by General Lee to collect my Command and watch the country in front of Gordonsville to the Blue Ridge and the Shenandoah Valley. My Command was the only force now in that section and General Lee relied on me to watch and protect the country. This put me in command of all our forces in Northern Virginia. After receiving General Lee's order, I sent for Lieutenant-Colonel Chapman's men from the Northern Neck of Virginia to rejoin the Command.

On April 5, I assembled fifty men at the North Fork Church, south of Purcellville in Loudoun County to form Company H. I had the men drawn up in line facing me and said, "Men, I nominate George Baylor of Jefferson County, captain of this Company. All in favor of Baylor, say aye."

I received a feeble response from the men. I did not call for the nays. I then said, "George Baylor is unanimously chosen captain."

I personally knew George Baylor. He had served in the war since its commencement. He was a lieutenant with the Twelfth Virginia Cavalry until he resigned his commission. One time while on detached service, he captured a company of Yankee cavalry and performed other exploits which is why I chose him for my Command. And he was also very familiar with our region of operations in Jefferson County. Edward Thomson, who had been in charge of the detail of men chosen for the executions near Berryville, was promoted to first lieutenant. James Wiltshire was promoted to second lieutenant and Frank Carter third lieutenant. After the elections, the men were dismissed with the understanding that they would be assembled the next day at Snickersville for operations.

The next day fifty-two of them assembled at Snickersville and were led by Captain Baylor into the Shenandoah Valley. I had ordered Captain Baylor and his men to find Captain Keyes and his Loudoun Virginia Rangers.

On the way toward Charlestown, Captain Baylor and his Company learned the Loudoun Rangers were camped at Keyes Switch along the Shenandoah River. Near Keyes Switch, a Yankee infantry regiment was camped with pickets stretching down to the Shenandoah River. It was necessary for Captain Baylor and his men to pass by the picket post in order to capture the Rangers. My men, dressed in blue overcoats, passed without molestation, keeping perfectly in rank, making no effort to capture or disturb the pickets. The Yankee pickets were very polite, gave the usual military salute of presenting arms. The men of Captain Baylor's Company were impressed. After passing safely past the Yankee picket post, Captain Baylor's men rode quietly to within fifty yards of the Rangers' camp. After seeing them in their cavalry tents, horses tied to stakes, and engaged in various diversions, Captain Baylor ordered a charge. A few seemed disposed to fight, but most were surprised and surrendered. A few shots soon quieted the more bold. Some ran for the bushes and made good their escape, but the greater part were made prisoners. The loss of the enemy was two killed, four wounded, and sixty-five prisoners. Captain Baylor also captured eighty-one horses and their equipment.

Captain Baylor loss was one wounded, Frank Helm of Warrenton. Captain Baylor and his men gathered up the prisoners, horses, and equipment. They fired the tents and wagons, all in full view of the Yankee infantry, while sounding the long roll on their drums to fall in line. The river was crossed at Keyes's Ford, and pursuit was not attempted by the enemy.

* * * *

Heavy firing was heard on the other side of the Potomac River in Maryland. After dark, reports arrived that the heavy firing was in honor of the fall of Richmond. No credit was attached to it by my men, but there was a great deal of speculation about it. We retired that night to awake in the morning and find out that it was a fearful reality. I recall the day so well. That morning, I was laughing and speaking with Captain Baylor and his prisoners. Doctor Aristides Monteiro was sitting on a log reading the *Baltimore America* newspaper. He called me and asked "Is it true?"

Doctor Monteiro was pointing to a double-lead column that told of the fall of Richmond and the surrender of General Lee's army on the 9th. I gazed at the fatal lines that foretold the death of our country. Tears gathered in my eyes. Officers gathered around us. Men, who were hardened veterans that had faced death, now dropped their heads in profound grief. Their sigh and moist eyes interpreted their deep feelings better than language could express it. I was dumb with grief. The rest of my men gathered around me. I had the paper in one hand and General Wetzel's report in the other. I said to them that our poor country has fallen a prey to the conqueror. The noblest Cause ever defended by the sword is lost. The noble dead that sleep in their shallow though honored graves are far more fortunate than the survivors. I thought I had sounded the profoundest depth of human feeling, but this is the bitterest hour of my life. I was much concerned about the news. I was so greatly despaired. My men and I did not want to give up the Cause. Later that day, in a conversation with Sergeant John Corbin and Marshall Crawford, I told them that there was nothing else for me to do but to fight on.

April 14 was a beautiful spring day. One of the most remarkable official military papers ever written by one officer to another was received by me from General Winfield Scott Hancock. General Hancock had taken General Sheridan's position and was now the commanding officer of the Middle Department in Winchester. His letter, written by his chief of staff, General C. H. Morgan said:

"I am directed by Major-General Hancock to enclose to you copies of letters which passed between Generals Lee and Grant on the occasion of the surrender of the Army of Northern Virginia. Major-General Hancock is authorized to receive the surrender of the forces under your command on the same conditions offered to General Lee, and will send an officer of equal rank with yourself to meet you at any point and time you may designate convenient to the lines for the purpose of arranging details, should you conclude to be governed by the example of General Lee."

While at Glen Welby, Colonel Carter's home, this place like others had treated us very hospitably during the war. I recalled that during these last days of the Southern Confederacy, I visited Waveland, the home of the Washington family, quite often. It was a place of light and life, of music, laughter, beauty and bliss. Whenever I was sad or disheartened by misfortunes of my Command or country; whenever I was depressed in spirit or any disaster cast its shadow of gloom across my pathway of duty, I would invariably visit the delightful Waveland and have these dark forebodings of sad thoughts laughed out of me by the bright and cheerful magic of that charmed circle of lovely young ladies.

I sent Channing Smith and a couple of other men to Richmond to seek out General Lee's advice on the matter. While waiting for General Lee's answer, I began a reply to General Hancock's letter, but with much uncertainty to its results. I sent General Hancock the following answer to his letter:

"I am in receipt of a letter from your Chief of Staff General Morgan, enclosing copies of correspondence between Generals Grant and Lee, informing me that you would appoint an officer of equal rank with myself to arrange details for the surrender of the forces under my command. As yet I have no notice through any other source of the facts concerning the surrender of the Army of Northern Virginia, nor, in my opinion, has the emergency yet arisen which would justify the surrender of my Command. With no disposition, however, to cause the useless effusion of blood or to inflict upon a war-worn population any unnecessary distress, I am ready to agree to the suspension of hostilities for a short time, in order to communicate with my own authorities or until I can obtain sufficient intelligence to determine my future actions. Should you accede to this proposition, I am ready to meet any person you may designate to arrange the terms of the armistice."

I sent the letter to General Hancock by Lieutenant-Colonel William Chapman, Captain Frankland, Doctor Monteiro, and my brother, Willie. In 1890, Doctor Monteiro published his war experiences and his journey to see General Hancock. This is what he wrote:

We crossed the Shenandoah River at Berry's Ferry and reached within four miles of Winchester at ten in the evening where shelter for the night was obtained from a hospitable stranger. The proprietor of the farm was absent, but his kind lady, with that hospitality so characteristic of the good people of the Shenandoah Valley, prepared supper and made us feel comfortable. When the farmer returned from Winchester and entered the house, he said, "Bad news. The

President of the United States has been assassinated, and Colonel Mosby is charged with the horrible crime."

We were not prepared to encounter this unexpected calamity. Without the power of foresight, we knew enough of furious hate to divine the probable result of this unprovoked and egregious crime.

After a restless night, we proceeded to Winchester. We soon came into sight of the pickets from the Twelfth Pennsylvania Cavalry. After preparing a flag of truce by tying a white handkerchief to a stick, I carried the emblem forward. The others had all refused to do so. I was challenged and asked, "What command, Major?"

"Mosby's"

A loud and prolonged shout went up along their entire line. One bronzed and weather-beaten old veteran stepped quickly to the front and reached out his hand. With honest face and sincere tears, he said, "Thank God! The war is over. I know the end has come when Mosby's men surrender."

The Yankee made me forget my own grief and mortification. We were met by the Yankees without insult or bombastic spirit, but instead with the hand of friendship.

We were taken to General Reno's headquarters until two officers from General Hancock's headquarters arrived to escort Lieutenant-Colonel Chapman and myself to an interview with General Hancock. Captain Frankland and Willie Mosby were left behind.

A rumor had generally circulated throughout the Yankee army that Colonel Mosby was on a visit to General Hancock, and the entire army turned out to see him. The road to Winchester was rendered almost impassable by the mass of soldiers gathering through curiosity to see the guerrilla chief. General Hancock occupied a large brick house on the north side of Main Street in Winchester. With some difficulty Lieutenant-Colonel Chapman and I made our way through the dense crowd of soldiers in blue uniforms.

Lieutenant-Colonel Chapman and I were given an interview with General Hancock to deliver Colonel Mosby's response. General Hancock carefully perused the communication for a brief period of time. He was wrapped in profound thought. The response was just in time to save our people from great loss and suffering. General Hancock had given an order only a few hours previous to Lieutenant-Colonel Chapman's and my arrival, for ten thousand men to go into the counties of Loudoun and Fauquier as the last terrible resort, for the purpose of destroying every house that continued to give shelter to Mosby and his men. The general manifested much feeling for the people of these two counties. He assured us that the cruel order would be immediately countermanded.

Now returning to my narrative, Chief of Staff C. H. Morgan, wrote a letter on behalf of General Hancock to be delivered by Lieutenant-Colonel Chapman to me. It read as follows:

"*Colonel, Major-General Hancock directs me to acknowledge the receipt of your communication by the hand of Lieutenant-Colonel Chapman, of the 15th instant, in reply of mine of the 11th. The General does not think it necessary to designate an officer to meet you to arrange an armistice, as you suggest.*

Understanding, however, your motives in hesitating to surrender your command without definite intelligence from your former superiors, the General is very willing to allow a reasonable time for you to acquire the information you desire. It is not practicable for you to communicate with General Lee, as he is no longer in authority.

With such evidence, as will undoubtedly satisfy you that further resistance on the part of your command can result in no good to the cause in which you have been engaged.

In full view of these facts, the General will not operate against your command until Tuesday next, at 12M., provided there are no hostilities from your command. This agreement to be understood to include the Department of Washington and the Potomac River line. It is possible some difficulty may arise from the operation of guerilla parties not of your command, but the General hopes you can control the matter. On Tuesday at noon the General will send an officer of equal rank with yourself to Millwood to meet you and ascertain your determination, and if you conclude to surrender your command to arrange details. Lieutenant-Colonel Chapman will be able to give all the information you desire as to the probable terms.

If you consent to the above arrangements, please notify Brigadier-General Chapman, at Berryville, as soon as practicable."

After Lieutenant-Colonel William Chapman returned from General Hancock's headquarters, I assembled the men at Salem on April 17, to inform them that a truce was in effect, and that its terms were to be respected. Meanwhile, Channing Smith had just returned from Richmond with General Lee's reply to my question for instructions as to what I should do now that the Army of Northern Virginia had surrendered. General Lee's reply was that he was under parole, and could not, for that reason, give his advice. He said to Channing, "Go home, all of you boys who fought with me, and help to build up the shattered fortunes of our dear old state."

Although, I had received General Lee's advice, General Joseph Johnston's army in the Carolinas had not surrendered, I knew the sands in the hour-glass of the doomed Confederacy were fast fading, but decided that it was not time to surrender. Therefore, I decided to disband. It was my duty to permit the officers and men to return to their respective homes to await further orders.

* * * *

On April 18, at ten in the morning, I directed all my officers and a few of my most trustworthy scouts to rendezvous at Paris. Twenty well-mounted and well-equipped men were waiting for me when I arrived.

We forded the Shenandoah River and arrived at Millwood, thirty minutes ahead of schedule. General Chapman and several Yankee officers were already there waiting for us. General Chapman expressed much regret that the time allowed us by the terms of our truce was so limited; that he had some doubt that we could accomplish our purpose and arrange the final terms of surrender before the hour of twelve. He was acting on orders from General Hancock and had no option in the matter. But, General Chapman did take the liberty of arranging another truce for twenty-four hours. I accepted.

The next morning, we arrived at Millwood at the same time as the previous day. General Chapman and fifteen Yankee officers were waiting on us. The meeting went on peaceful and civil until General Chapman and I came to the most interesting and important phase, the surrender of my Command. While I was informing General Chapman that I would not surrender my Command, Private John Hern came bursting into the room where the meeting was being held, shouting, "Colonel, the damn Yankees have got you in a trap: there is a thousand of them hid in the woods right here. Let's fight 'em, Colonel. We can whip 'em."

I rose to my feet and placed my hand on my revolver. I kept my eyes on the Yankee officers and informed them that if the truce no longer protected us, we were at your mercy; but we shall protect ourselves. If at this critical moment some hot-headed Partisan had made any move towards trouble, or a hammer of a six-shooter had clicked in cocking, that room would have developed a catastrophe. If I would have given the word, not one Yankee officer in the room would have lived a minute. But nothing happened. When finished, I departed from the meeting, followed by twenty of my officers unmolested. We mounted our horses and rode away toward the Shenandoah River.

The next day, Friday, April 21, at Salem, I assembled my Command for the last time. In a field just west of the village, eight companies, about two hundred men formed ranks. What was to be done had to be so to save the country from destruction. General Hancock had forty thousand men at Winchester.

I rode along the line and inspected the men of my Command one final time. It was warrior honoring warrior. While I passed every man, I knew as I looked into his eyes that he must calmly consider the fact that he must sever forever the cords which had so long bound our destinies in one common Cause. It needed not the hand of a painter, or poet to picture our emotions; they shone forth from every countenance and spoke from every eye. The crisis had come; the trials of the war were severe, but this cup contained the concentrated bitterness of all our trials.

I halted my horse between Lieutenant-Colonel William Chapman and Major Dolly Richards. I had penned my address to my men earlier that morning at Glen Welby. When writing I had some of the feelings of Boabdil when he took his last look at the Alhambra. My brother Willie read:

"Soldier! I have summoned you together for the last time. The vision we have cherished of a free and independent country, has vanished, and the country, is now the spoil of a conqueror. I disband your organization in preference to surrendering it to our enemies. I am now no longer your commander. After association of more than two eventful years, I part from you with just pride, in the frame of your achievements, and grateful recollections of your generous kindness to myself.

And now at this moment of bidding you a final adieu accept the assurance of my unchanging confidence and regard. Farewell."

Each of those present was so occupied with his personal grief and regrets that the full effect of the occasion did not present itself. Singly and in groups, the participants in this saddest of farewells, gave way to their feelings in a manner that requires no description. Strong men, who had laughed in the face of the gravest dangers and smiled at the pains of grievous wounds, walked apart and wept. I, myself had wept. It had been hard to suppress the tears. I was standing beside a fence along side the road, holding my hat in my hand, receiving the clutch of friendly hands, and bestowing brave words on the men with whom I had fought for the lost Cause. The wild excitement of the past two years, the crash of pistols and carbines, the yell of victory, and the fever of battle were all ended.

I told the men that they could do whatever they chose; that if they went to General Hancock they could get their paroles and be protected in their homes. I did not intend to surrender, but go South, possibly to join with General Johnston's army.

* * *

On April 22, Lieutenant-Colonel William Chapman gathered all of the men who wished to be paroled and rode to Winchester. Among them were some of my most gallant and fateful men, Walter Frankland, Alfred Glascock, and Sam Chapman.

A two thousand dollar reward was offered for my capture by General Hancock because I did not surrender. Therefore, I rode South with a small group of men to the suburbs of Richmond. I sent John Munson and Coley Jordan into the city to discover the situation. When I did not hear from Munson and Jordan, I sent Ben Palmer into the city. He returned with a copy of a Richmond newspaper which contained an account of General Johnston's surrender to General Sherman. While waiting on Munson and Jordan to return, Ben and I took dinner with a farmer. The farmer was curious who I was. When he asked me my name, I told him. The farmer said, "Colonel, where is your Command?"

"There it stands! That is all that is left of it," said I, pointing to Ben Palmer.

John Munson had returned and wanted to raid some Yankees and steal their horses. I told Munson that it was too late. It would be murder and highway robbery now. We are soldiers and not highwaymen.

Afterward, I gave each of the men of my Command who followed me to Richmond an affectionate farewell. I rode away to my father's home in Lynchburg, where I was paroled in June 1865. Life cannot afford a more bitter cup than the one I drained at Salem, nor any higher reward of ambition than that I received as Commander of the Forty-Third Battalion Virginia Cavalry. **Mosby: The War Years**, had ended.

F. Beattie, L. Hutchison, J. Mosby, G Turberville
Manassas, Virginia, July 20, 1914

Source: Courtesy of Bernie Becker

MOSBY REFERENCES

CHAPTER ONE

1) "Who Was Mosby?" Mosby Heritage Association. Middleburg, Virginia.
2) John S. Mosby Genealogy. Womack Genealogy Network.
3) Gray Ghost: The Life of Colonel John Singleton Mosby. James Ramage. University Press of Kentucky. Pages 1, 9, 11, 16, 19-21.
4) Mosby's Memoirs. Colonel John S. Mosby. J. S. Sanders & Company. Pages 1, 7-8.
5) Reminiscences of a Mosby Guerrilla. John Munson. Hathi Library. Page 2.
6) The Life and Times of John Singleton Mosby. Kevin Siepel. Bison. Pages 4-6, 18.
7) War Reminiscences and Stuart's Cavalry Campaigns. John S. Mosby. Dodd, Mead & Co. Pages 5-6

CHAPTER TWO

1) Gray Ghost: The Life of Colonel John Singleton Mosby. James Ramage. University Press of Kentucky. Pages 33-34, 37.
2) Bold Dragoon. Emory M. Thomas. Vintage Civil War Library. Pages 50-52, 69.
3) Mosby's Memoirs. Colonel John S. Mosby. J. S. Sanders & Company. Pages 30-32.
4) History of the 1st Virginia Cavalry. Robert Driver. H. E. Howard Publishing. Page 9.
5) Mosby. Charles R. Thorne. Charles R. Thorne Publishing. Page 4.
6) Jeb Stuart to Flora Stuart. July 30, 1857.
7) Berkeley County and Martinsburg in the Civil War. B.C. Jaycee-ettes. Page 4.
8) Blue and Gray Magazine. Volume XXII, Issue 4. Battle of Falling Waters. Page 16.
9) OR Series I, Volume I, No.11. Colonel T. J. Jackson. Page 186.
10) Mosby Myth: A Confederate Hero in Life and Legend. Paul Ashdown-Edward Caudill. Scholarly Resources. Page 17.

11) War Years with Jeb Stuart. Lt-Col. W. W. Blackford. Charles Scribner Pub. Page 16.
12) Mosby Myth: A Confederate Hero in Life and Legend. Ashdown-Caudill. Scholarly Resources. Page 23.
13) War Reminiscences and Stuart's Cavalry Campaigns. John S. Mosby. Dodd, Mead & Co. Pages 7, 9, 11.

CHAPTER THREE

1) History of the 1st Virginia Cavalry. Robert Driver. H. E. Howard Publishing. Pages 3, 11-12.
2) Mosby's Memoirs. Colonel John S. Mosby. J. S. Sanders & Company. Pages 47, 48, 52.
3) Bold Dragoon. Emory M. Thomas. Vintage Civil War Library. Pages 76-77.
4) Confederate Military History. Volume III. Chapter VI.
5) First Battle of Bull Run. William Davis. LSU Press. Pages 133, 144.
6) OR Series I Volume II No.11. Colonel T. J. Jackson. Pages 185-186.
7) OR Series I Volume II No. I. Brigadier-General Irvin McDowell. Pages 303-305.
8) OR Series I Volume II No.64. General P. G. T. Beauregard Pages 440-441.
9) OR Series I Volume II No.81. General Joseph Johnston. Pages 470-477.
10) OR Series I Volume II No.82. Brigadier-General Thomas Jackson. Page 481.
11) OR Series I Volume II No.83. Colonel J. E. B. Stuart. Pages 482-485.
12) Battle & Leaders. General P. G. T. Beauregard (First Battle of Bull Run) Page 213.
13) The Edge of Mosby's Sword. Gordon B. Bonan. Southern Illinois Press. Page 4.

CHAPTER FOUR

1) Gray Ghost: The Life of Colonel John Singleton Mosby. James Ramage. University Press of Kentucky. Pages 38, 42.
2) Mosby's Memoirs. Colonel John S. Mosby. J. S. Sanders & Company. Pages 86-87, 100-101.
3) History of the 1st Virginia Cavalry. Robert Driver. H. E. Howard Publishing. Pages 20, 23, 29.
4) McClellan's Own Story. General George B. McClellan. DSI. Pages 61, 66-67.
5) I Rode With Jeb Stuart. Major H. B. McClellan. DeCapo. Pages 41-42.
6) OR Series I Volume II No. 3. Colonel Isaac Stevens. Pages 169-172.
7) OR Series I Volume II No.17. General Jeb Stuart. Pages 183-184.
8) War Reminiscences and Stuart's Cavalry Campaigns. John S. Mosby Dodd, Mead & Co. Pages 16-17, 20-21.
9) Abingdon Virginian. Volume 4. June 27, 1862.

Chapter Five

1) John Mosby to Pauline Mosby. March 1, 1862.
2) Mosby's Memoirs. Colonel John S. Mosby. J. S. Sanders & Company. Pages 105-107.
3) History of the 1st Virginia Cavalry. Robert Driver. H. E. Howard Publishing. Pages 30-31.
4) Mosby Heritage Foundation. Middleburg, Virginia.
5) Mosby. Charles R. Thorne. Charles R. Thorne Publishing. Page 4.
6) John Mosby to Pauline Mosby. April 25, 1862.
7) Bold Dragoon. Emory M. Thomas. Vintage Civil War Library. Pages 105-106.
8) Mosby Myth: A Confederate Hero in Life and Legend. Ashdown-Caudill. Scholarly Resources. Page 23.
9) War Years with Jeb Stuart. Lt. Col. W. W. Blackford. Charles Scribner Publishing. Page 61.
10) Gray Ghost: The Life of Colonel John Singleton Mosby. James Ramage. University Press of Kentucky. Page 45.
11) I Rode With Jeb Stuart. Major H. B. McClellan. DeCapo. Page 50.
12) OR Series I Volume XI/1 No.1. General George B McClellan. Pages 5-7, 749.
13) OR Series I Volume XI/1 No.15. General Joseph Johnston. Pages 275-76.
14) OR Series I Volume XI/1 No.60. General James Longstreet. Pages 564-569.
15) OR Series I Volume XI/1 No.101. General Joseph Johnston. Pages 933-35.
16) Battles & Leaders. Castle. "Opposing Forces at Seven Pines." Page 219.
17) To The Gates of Richmond. Stephen W. Sears. Houghton Mifflin. Page 145.
18) From Mosby's Command. Horace Mewborn. Butternut & Blue. Page 114.

Chapter Six

1) History of the 1st Virginia Cavalry. Robert Driver. H. E. Howard Publishing. Pages 35-36.
2) Gray Ghost: The Life of Colonel John Singleton Mosby. James Ramage. University Press of Kentucky. Pages 46, 47.
3) Mosby's Memoirs. Colonel John S. Mosby. J. S. Sanders & Company. Pages 110-115.
4) Bold Dragoon. Emory M. Thomas. Vintage Civil War Library. Pages 111, 115.
5) I Rode With Jeb Stuart. Major H. B. McClellan. DeCapo. Pages 54-56, 61.
6) OR Series I Volume XI/1. General Robert E. Lee. Page 1004.
7) Mosby's Fighting Parson. Peter Brown. Willow Bend Books. Pages 10-11.
8) Southern Historical Society Papers. Richmond Times, May 22, 1898. John Mosby.
9) John Mosby to Pauline Mosby. June 16, 1862.
10) OR Series I Volume XI/1 No.9. Captain William Royall, 5th U. S. Cavalry. Pages 1020-21.
11) OR Series I Volume XI/1 No.6. Colonel Richard Rush, 6th Pennsylvania Cavalry. Page 1017.

12) OR Series I Volume XI/1 No.21. General Jeb Stuart. Pages 1036-41.
13) Mosby and His Men. J. Marshall Crawford. G. W. Carleton & Company 1867. Page 53.
14) War Reminiscences and Stuart's Cavalry Campaigns. John S. Mosby. Dodd, Mead & Co. Pages 231, 234-235.
15) Rebel Chronicles. Steve French. New Horizon Publishing. Pages 12, 34.

Chapter Seven

1) OR Series I Volume XI/2 No.1. General George B McClellan. Pages 1254-55, 68-69.
2) OR Series I Volume XI/2 No.93. General Fitz John Porter. Pages 224-228.
3) OR Series I Volume XI/2 No.227. General Thomas Jackson. Pages 553.
4) OR Series I Volume XI/2 No.201. General Robert E. Lee. Pages 490-493, 496-498.
5) OR Series I Volume XI/2 No.207. General Jeb Stuart. Page 521.
6) Mosby's Memoirs. Colonel John S. Mosby. J. S. Sanders & Company. Pages 124-127, 129-132, 135.
7) Mosby. Charles R. Thorne. Charles R. Thorne Publishing. Page 5.
8) Francis Marion. Wikipedia Online Dictionary.
9) Gray Ghost: The Life of Colonel John Singleton Mosby. James Ramage. University Press of Kentucky. Page 51.
10) Mosby Myth: A Confederate Hero in Life and Legend. Ashdown-Caudill. Scholarly Resources. Pages 29-30.
11) John Mosby to Pauline Mosby. July 23, 1862.
12) John Mosby to Pauline Mosby. August 6, 1862.
13) OR Series I Volume XI/2 No.207. General Jeb Stuart. Page 119.
14) Battles & Leaders. Castle. Major-General Fitz John Porter. Pages 330-31.
15) Mosby and His Men. J. Marshall Crawford. G. W. Carleton & Company 1867. Pages 55, 59.
16) War Reminiscences and Stuart's Cavalry Campaigns. John S. Mosby Dodd, Mead & Co. Pages 239, 243, 246-248.
17) History of the 4th Virginia Cavalry. Kenneth Stiles. H. E. Howard, Inc. Page 142.
18) From Mosby's Command. Horace Mewborn. Butternut & Blue. Page 119.

Chapter Eight

1) Mosby's Memoirs. Colonel John S. Mosby. J. S. Sanders & Company. Pages 135-137, 143-145.
2) Bold Dragoon. Emory M. Thomas. Vintage Civil War Library. Pages 139, 143-144, 147.
3) Battle of Cedar Mountain. Wikipedia Online Dictionary.
4) War Years with Jeb Stuart. Lt. Col. W. W. Blackford. Charles Scribner Publishing. Pages 93, 99-102, 128-129, 133-134, 146-147.
5) I Rode With Jeb Stuart. Major H. B. McClellan. DeCapo. Pages 94-95.
6) OR Series I Volume XII/2 No.26. General Robert E. Lee. Page 178.

7) OR Series I Volume XII/2 No.28. General Thomas (Stonewall) Jackson. Pages 181-184.
8) OR Series I Volume XII/2 No.127. General Robert E. Lee. Page 555.
9) OR Series I Volume XII/2 No.193. General Jeb Stuart. Pages 725-726, 729-731, 736-738.
10) Southern Historical Society Papers. Rockbridge News, December 1895.
11) Escape Across The Potomac. CW Whitehair. Infinity Publishing. Pages 166, 171, 179.
12) OR Series I Volume XII/2 No. 26. General Jeb Stuart. Pages 818-819.
13) OR Series I XIX/1 No.197. General Julius White. Page 523.
14) OR Series I XIX/1 No.264. General Thomas Jackson. Pages 954-955.
15) OR Series I XIX/1 No.202. Return of Casualties.
16) OR Series I XIX/1 No.210. General William Pendleton. Pages 830-832.
17) OR Series I XIX/1 No.84. General Fitz John Porter. Pages 339-341.

Chapter Nine

1) Gray Ghost: The Life of Colonel John Singleton Mosby. James Ramage. University Press of Kentucky. Page 56.
2) John Mosby to Pauline Mosby. November 24, 1862.
3) War Reminiscences and Stuart's Cavalry Campaigns. John S. Mosby. Dodd, Mead & Co. Pages 27-31.
4) OR Series I XXI No.264. General Robert E. Lee. Pages 547-548.
5) OR Series I XXI No.17. General Jeb Stuart. Pages 731-732.
6) A Southern Spy In Northern Virginia. Charles Mauro. History Press. Pages 64-66.
7) Partisan Life With John S. Mosby. John Scott. Harper & Brothers Publishing. Pages 20-21, 24.
8) Bold Dragoon. Emory M. Thomas. Vintage Civil War Library. Pages 196-197.
9) History of the 1st Virginia Cavalry. Robert Driver. H. E. Howard Publishing. Page 52.
10) Mosby's Memoirs. Colonel John S. Mosby. J. S. Sanders & Company. Page 150.
11) Blue and Gray Magazine. Vol. XVII, Issue 4. "Mosby's Confederacy." Page 8.
12) OR Series I XIX/1 No.1. Major Charles Taggart. Pages 65-66.

Chapter Ten

1) Partisan Life With John S. Mosby. John Scott. Harper & Brothers Publishing. Page 35.
2) Mosby's Men. John Alexander. Neale Publishing. Pages 15, 24-26, 29, 31.
3) Reminiscences Of A Mosby Guerrilla. John Munson. Moffat, Yard And Company. Pages 7-8, 21, 36-37.
4) 43rd Battalion Virginia Cavalry Mosby's Command. Keen & Mewborn. H. E. Howard. Pages 14-15.

5) War Reminiscences and Stuart's Cavalry Campaigns. John S. Mosby. Dodd, Mead & Co. Pages 43-45.
6) Mosby's Rangers. Jeffery Wert. Touchstone Books. Pages 73, 75, 117, 119.
7) Mosby's Rangers: Forty-Third Battalion Virginia Cavalry. James J. Williamson. Ralph B. Kenyon Publishing. Pages 18, 23, 26-27.
8) U. S. Grant's Personal Memoirs. General Ulysses S. Grant. Modern Library. Pages 381-382.

Chapter Eleven

1) Mosby's Rangers: Forty-Third Battalion Virginia Cavalry. James J. Williamson. Ralph B. Kenyon Publishing. Page 15.
2) Mosby's Rangers. Jeffery Wert. Touchstone Books. Pages 40, 44.
3) Partisan Life With John S. Mosby. John Scott. Harper & Brothers Publishing. Pages 25, 27.
4) War Reminiscences and Stuart's Cavalry Campaigns. John S. Mosby. Dodd, Mead & Co. Pages 39-41, 45.
5) Partisan Life With John S. Mosby. John Scott. Harper & Brothers Publishing. Pages 25-26.
6) Blue and Gray Magazine. Vol. XVII, Issue 4. "Mosby's Confederacy." Page 9.
7) Mosby's Memoirs. Colonel John S. Mosby. J. S. Sanders & Company. Pages 151, 157-160, 167-168.
8) A Southern Spy In Northern Virginia. Charles Mauro. History Press. Pages 96, 98-100.
9) OR Series I XXV/1 No.1. Colonel Percy Wyndham. Page 5.
10) OR Series I XXV/1 No.2. John S. Mosby. Pages 41-42.
11) OR Series I XXV/1 Lt. Col. Robert Johnstone. Pages 41-42.
12) OR Series I XXV/1 No.1. Major Charles Taggart. Page 55.
13) OR Series I XXV/1 No.2. John S. Mosby. Pages 65-66.
14) 43rd Battalion Virginia Cavalry Mosby's Command. Keen & Mewborn. H. E. Howard. Pages 26-27.
15) Washington Sunday Star. John S. Mosby. October 8, 1911.

Chapter Twelve

1) Mosby's Memoirs. Colonel John S. Mosby. J. S. Sanders & Company. Pages 171-183.
2) 43rd Battalion Virginia Cavalry Mosby's Command. Keen & Mewborn. H. E. Howard. Pages 32-33, 35-36.
3) Blue and Gray Magazine. XVII, Issue 4. "Mosby's Confederacy." Horace Mewborn. Pages 14-15.
4) Richmond Dispatch. May 6, 1894. James J. Williamson.
5) Partisan Life With John S. Mosby. John Scott. Harper & Brothers Publishing. Pages 43-45, 51.
6) Mosby's Rangers: Forty-Third Battalion Virginia Cavalry. James J. Williamson. Ralph B. Kenyon Publishing. Pages 35-40, 46.

7) Sunday Evening Star. October 8, 1911.
8) Richmond Daily Dispatch. Vol. XXIX, No.61. March 12, 1863.
9) OR Series I XXV/1. Captain John S. Mosby. Pages 1121-1122.
10) OR Series I XXV/1 No.1. L. L. O'Connor. Provost Marshal, Fairfax C. H. Page 43.
11) OR Series I XXV/1 No.2. Captain W. H. Hall. Page 43.
12) OR Series I XXV/1 No.3. General Fitz Lee. Page 44.
13) Gray Ghost: The Life of Colonel John Singleton Mosby. James Ramage. University Press of Kentucky. Page 70.
14) Mosby and His Men. J. Marshall Crawford. G. W. Carleton & Company. Page 71.
15) The Philadelphia Inquirer. March 10, 1863.

CHAPTER THIRTEEN

1) 43rd Battalion Virginia Cavalry Mosby's Command. Keen & Mewborn. H. E. Howard. Pages 39-40, 44.
2) Mosby's Rangers. Jeffery Wert. Touchstone Books. Pages 49, 52.
3) Mosby's Memoirs. Colonel John S. Mosby. J. S. Sanders & Company. Pages 185, 194.
4) Religious Herald. Samuel Chapman. January 9, 1902, January 16, 1902.
5) Mosby's Fighting Parson. Peter Brown. Willow Publishing. Pages 83, 112.
6) The Edge of Mosby's Sword. Gordon Brown. Southern Illinois Press. Pages 66, 71.
7) Civil War Times. Volume XLIII, No. 6. "Mosby's Rangers April Fools' Surprise." Pages 28-29.
8) Gray Ghost: The Life of Colonel John Singleton Mosby. James Ramage. University Press of Kentucky. Page 80.
9) Mosby's Rangers: Forty-Third Battalion Virginia Cavalry. James J. Williamson. Ralph B. Kenyon Publishing. Page 52.
10) Reminiscences Of A Mosby Guerrilla. John Munson. Moffat, Yard And Company. Pages 55, 57-58, 63.
11) Partisan Life With John S. Mosby. John Scott. Harper & Brothers Publishing. Pages 65, 67.
12) John Mosby to Sam Chapman. June 4, 1900.
13) War Reminiscences and Stuart's Cavalry Campaigns. John S. Mosby. Dodd, Mead & Co. Pages 99, 101, 103-110.
14) OR Series I XXV/1 No.3. Captain John S. Mosby. Pages 72-73.
15) OR Series I XXV/1 No.1. General Julius Stahel. Pages 77-78.
16) OR Series I XXV/1 No.2. General Robert E. Lee. Page 79.
17) OR Series I XXV/1 No.1. Major Charles Taggart. Pages 65-66.
18) OR Series I XXV/2. Confederate Correspondence #4. General Robert E. Lee. Page 679.
19) OR Series I XXV/2. Confederate Correspondence #4. Stuart to Mosby. Pages 857-858.

Chapter Fourteen

1) War Reminiscences and Stuart's Cavalry Campaigns. John S. Mosby. Dodd, Mead & Co. Pages 118, 120, 123, 126, 130, 133-135, 139, 142-143, 147-151.
2) 43rd Battalion Virginia Cavalry Mosby's Command. Keen & Mewborn. H. E. Howard. Pages 51, 54.
3) Partisan Life With John S. Mosby. John Scott. Harper & Brothers Publishing. Pages 84-86, 95.
4) Blue and Gray. Volume XIX, Issue 1. Horace Mewborn. Pages 7-10.
5) Mosby's Fighting Parson. Peter Brown. Willow Publishing. Pages 116-117.
6) Reminiscences Of A Mosby Guerrilla. John Munson. Moffat, Yard And Company. Page 68.
7) Mosby's Rangers: Forty-Third Battalion Virginia Cavalry. James J. Williamson. Ralph B. Kenyon Publishing. Pages 63, 65.
8) From Mosby's Command. Horace Mewborn. Butternut and Blue. Pages 99-100.
9) Mosby and His Men. J. Marshall Crawford. G. W. Carleton & Company 1867. Page 79.
10) OR Series I XXV/1 No.1. General Julius Stahel. Pages 1117-1118.
11) OR Series I XXV/1 No.2. Colonel William D. Mann. Page 1118.
12) OR Series I XXV/1 No.3. Major Benjamin Chamberlain. Pages 1106-1107.
13) OR Series I XXV/1 No.2. General George Stoneman. Pages 1067-1068.
14) OR Series I XXV/1 No.1. General Julius Stahel. 1104-1105.
15) Confederate Correspondence #6. Stuart to Lee. Page 750.
16) Mosby's Memoirs. Colonel John S. Mosby. J. S. Sanders & Company. Pages 197-198.

Chapter Fifteen

1) Mosby's Rangers: Forty-Third Battalion Virginia Cavalry. James J. Williamson. Ralph B. Kenyon Publishing. Pages 71, 80, 441.
2) Gray Ghost: The Life of Colonel John Singleton Mosby. James Ramage. University Press of Kentucky. Page 89.
3) Blue and Gray. Volume XXVII, Issue 4. "Mosby's Confederacy." Horace Mewborn. Pages 17, 19, 20.
4) War Reminiscences and Stuart's Cavalry Campaigns. John S. Mosby. Dodd, Mead & Co. Pages 158, 163, 172-173, 180.
5) Mosby's Rangers. Jeffery Wert. Touchstone Books. Pages 89, 91.
6) From Mosby's Command. Horace Mewborn. Butternut and Blue. Pages 143-146.
7) Stuart's Cavalry in the Gettysburg Campaign. John S. Mosby. Moffat Yard & Company. Pages 63, 78-80.
8) Partisan Life With John S. Mosby. John Scott. Harper & Brothers Publishing. Pages 105-106, 108.
9) A Southern Spy In Northern Virginia. Charles Mauro. History Press. Page 83.
10) OR Series I XXVII/2 No.336. General Alfred Pleasanton. Page 908.
11) OR Series I XXVII/2 No.579. Colonel Thomas Munford. Pages 747-748.
12) OR Series I XXVII/2 No.565. General Jeb Stuart. Pages 688-693.

13) OR Series I XXVII/2. Union Correspondence #5. General Joseph Hooker. Pages 44, 53.
14) OR Series I XXVII/2. Confederate Correspondence #1. Lee to Stuart. Page 913.
15) OR Series I XXVII/2. Confederate Correspondence #1. Longstreet to Stuart. Page 913.
16) OR Series I XXVII/2. Confederate Correspondence #1. Lee to Stuart. Page 923.
17) OR Series I XXVII/2. Confederate Correspondence #1. Stuart to Robertson. 927-928.
18) Battles and Leaders. Colonel John S. Mosby. Castle. Pages 251-252.
19) Battles and Leaders. General B. Robertson. Castle. Page 253.
20) SHSP. Volume XXIII. Colonel John Mosby. Richmond Times. Feb. 2, 1896.
21) Wearing Gray. John Esten Cooke. E. B. Treat Publishing. Page 124.
22) Mosby's Memoirs. Colonel John S. Mosby. J. S. Sanders & Company. Page 217.

Chapter Sixteen

1) Mosby's Rangers: Forty-Third Battalion Virginia Cavalry. James J. Williamson. Ralph B. Kenyon Publishing. Pages 87-88, 90, 102, 105, 110-11.
2) 43rd Battalion Virginia Cavalry Mosby's Command. Keen & Mewborn. H. E. Howard. Pages 78, 84-85.
3) Mosby's Rangers. Jeffery Wert. Touchstone Books. Page 104.
4) Washington Star. August 29, 1863.
5) The Edge of Mosby's Sword. Gordon Bonan. Southern Illinois Press. Pages 90, 92.
6) Mosby's Fighting Parson. Peter Brown. Willow Publishing. Pages 132-133.
7) Gray Ghost: The Life of Colonel John Singleton Mosby. James Ramage. University Press of Kentucky. Pages 117-118, 122, 221-222.
8) Mosby's Memoirs. Colonel John S. Mosby. J. S. Sanders & Company. Pages 259, 261, 264.
9) Partisan Life With John S. Mosby. John Scott. Harper & Brothers Publishing. Pages 80, 198, 141.
10) A Southern Spy In Northern Virginia. Charles Mauro. History Press. Pages 84, 107.
11) Valley News Echo. Vol.4, No.8. August 1863. Page 4.
12) Valley News Echo. Vol.4, No.10. October 1863. Page 4.
13) Valley News Echo. Vol.4, No.11. November 1863. Page1.
14) OR Series I XXIX/1 No.1. Colonel Charles Lowell. Pages 68-69.
15) OR Series I XXIX/1 No.1. Colonel Thomas C. Devin. Pages 94-95.
16) OR Series I XXIX/1 Report of Maj. John S. Mosby. Pages 80-81.
17) OR Series I XXIX/1 Report of Maj. John S. Mosby. Pages 552, 492, 495.
18) OR Series I XXIX/1 Colonel Charles Lowell. Pages 652, 658, 992.
19) OR Series I XXIX/2. Union Correspondence #3. General C. Schurz. Page 68.

Chapter Seventeen

1) Partisan Life With John S. Mosby. John Scott. Harper & Brothers Publishing. Pages 177, 179-180, 182.
2) Mosby's Rangers: Forty-Third Battalion Virginia Cavalry. James J. Williamson. Ralph B. Kenyon Publishing. Pages 119, 125-127, 131.
3) Mosby's Memoirs. Colonel John S. Mosby. J. S. Sanders & Company. Pages 267-269.
4) Blue and Gray. Volume XVII, Issue 6. "Mosby in the Shenandoah Valley." Horace Mewborn. Pages 11-12.
5) Mosby and His Men. J. Marshall Crawford. G. W. Carleton & Company 1867. Pages 140, 144, 150.
6) Richmond Enquirer. June 11, 1864.
7) Blue and Gray. Volume XVII, Issue 4. "Mosby's Confederacy." Horace Mewborn. Page 38.
8) 43rd Battalion Virginia Cavalry Mosby's Command. Keen & Mewborn. H. E. Howard. Page 100.
9) Gray Ghost: The Life of Colonel John Singleton Mosby. James Ramage. University Press of Kentucky. Page 128.
10) The Edge of Mosby's Sword. Gordon Bonan. Southern Illinois Press. Pages 98-99.
11) OR Series I XXXIII, No.4. Major John Mosby. Page 15.
12) OR Series I XXXIII, No.1. General Jeremiah Sullivan. Page 17.
13) OR Series I XXXIII, No.2. Major Henry Cole. Pages 17-18.
14) OR Series I XXXIII, No.2. Report of Major John S. Mosby. Page 9.
15) "Battle in the Snow." Adams County Star and Sentinel. November 11, 1881.
16) Mosby's Fighting Parson. Peter A. Brown. Willow Publishing. Page 142.
17) Richmond Daily Dispatch. January 18, 1864.

Chapter Eighteen

1) Partisan Life With John S. Mosby. John Scott. Harper & Brothers Publishing. Pages 179, 182, 185, 200-201, 206.
2) 43rd Battalion Virginia Cavalry Mosby's Command. Keen & Mewborn. H. E. Howard. Pages 105-106, 114, 346.
3) Mosby and His Men. J. Marshall Crawford. G. W. Carleton & Company 1867. Page 172.
4) Mosby's Rangers: Forty-Third Battalion Virginia Cavalry. James J. Williamson. Ralph Kenyon Publishing. Pages 142-143.
5) Reminiscences Of A Mosby Guerrilla. John Munson. Moffat, Yard And Company. Pages 84-86.
6) Blue and Gray Magazine. XVII, Issue 6. "Mosby in the Shenandoah Valley" Horace Mewborn. Page 13.
7) The Edge of Mosby's Sword. Gordon Bonan. Southern Illinois Press. Page 105.
8) Richmond Dispatch. May 10, 1896. James J. Williamson.
9) Richmond Dispatch. March 1, 1864.
10) OR Series I XXXIII, No.1. General Robert Taylor. Page 159.

11) OR Series I XXXIII, No.2. Colonel John Mosby. Pages 159-160.

Chapter Nineteen

1) Mosby's Rangers: Forty-Third Battalion Virginia Cavalry. James J. Williamson. Ralph B. Kenyon Publishing. Pages 179-180.
2) 43rd Battalion Virginia Cavalry Mosby's Command. Keen & Mewborn. H. E. Howard. Pages 118, 132.
3) Mosby and His Men. J. Marshall Crawford. G. W. Carleton & Company 1867. Page 208.
4) Partisan Life With John S. Mosby. John Scott. Harper & Brothers Publishing. Pages 231-232, 236, 238.
5) OR Series I, Volume XXXVII/1. Colonel Robert S. Rogers. Page 73.
6) OR Series I, Volume XXXVII/1. General Franz Sigel. Page 357.
7) OR Series I, Volume XXXVII/1. Union Correspondence #5. General U. S. Grant. Page 492.
8) OR Series I, Volume XXXVII/1. No.2. General Max Weber. Page 357.
9) OR Series I, Volume XXXVII/1. Union Correspondence #13. Colonel L. B. Pierce. 693.
10) OR Series I, Volume XXXVII/1. Union Correspondence #13. Lt. Col. C. H. Gatch. 694.
11) OR Series I, Volume XXXVII/1. Union Correspondence #13. J. W. Garrett. 693.
12) OR Series I, Volume XXXVII/1. Union Correspondence #13. General Max Weber. Pages 693-695.
13) Valley News Echo. Volume V, No. VI. June 1864.
14) Valley News Echo. Volume V, No. V. May 1864.
15) Stuart's Cavalry in the Gettysburg Campaign. John S. Mosby. Moffat, Yard & Company. Preface.
16) Southern Historical Society Papers. Rockbridge County News. November 28, 1895.
17) Wearing of the Gray. John Esteen Cooke. E. B. Treat& Company. Pages 125-126.

Chapter Twenty

1) Mosby's Men. John Alexander. Neale Publishing Company. Pages 89-90, 92.
2) Partisan Life With John S. Mosby. John Scott. Harper & Brothers Publishing. Pages 238-241, 246.
3) Mosby Memoirs. John S. Mosby. J. S. Sanders & Company. Page 278.
4) 43rd Battalion Virginia Cavalry Mosby's Command. Keen & Mewborn. H. E. Howard. Pages 137, 140, 145.
5) Mosby's Rangers: Forty-Third Battalion Virginia Cavalry. James J. Williamson. Ralph B. Kenyon Publishing. Pages 184-187.
6) Blue and Gray. Vol. XXVII, Issue 4. "Mosby' Confederacy." Horace Mewborn. Pages 41-42.
7) John Mosby to William Chapman. January 22, 1911.

8) OR Series, Volume XXXVII/1, No.1. Colonel Charles Lowell. Pages 358-360.
9) OR Series, Volume XXXVII/1, No.2. Colonel Henry Lazelle. Pages 360-361.
10) OR Series, Volume XXXVII/1. Union Correspondences #3. General E. B. Tyler. Page 72.
11) OR Series, Volume XXXVII/1. Union Correspondences #3. J. W. Garrett. Page 65.
12) Journal of Amanda Virginia Edmonds. Amanda Virginia Edmonds. July 7, 1864.

CHAPTER TWENTY-ONE

1) Harpers Ferry Under Fire. Dennis E. Frye. Donning Company. Pages 162-163.
2) Mosby Memoirs. John S. Mosby. J. S. Sanders & Company. Page 283.
3) Mosby's Rangers: Forty-Third Battalion Virginia Cavalry. James J. Williamson. Ralph B. Kenyon Publishing. Pages 208-209, 231.
4) Reminiscences Of A Mosby Guerrilla. John Munson. Moffat, Yard And Company. Pages 103-105, 108-110.
5) 43rd Battalion Virginia Cavalry Mosby's Command. Keen & Mewborn. H. E. Howard. Page 157.
6) Mosby and His Men. J. Marshall Crawford. G. W. Carleton & Company 1867. Page 241.
7) Journal of Amanda Virginia Edmonds. Amanda Virginia Edmonds. August 14, 1864.
8) Richmond Times. John S. Mosby. March 31, 1895.
9) Richmond Inquirer. September 1, 1864.
10) Valley News Echo. Volume 5, No.7. July 1864.
11) Valley News Echo. Volume 5, No.8. August 1864.
12) Richmond Daily Dispatch. August 13, 1864.
13) Richmond Daily Dispatch. August 16, 1864.
14) The Philadelphia Inquirer. August 13, 1864.
15) The Philadelphia Inquirer. August 18, 1864.
16) Mosby's Fighting Parson. Peter A. Brown. Willow Publishing. Page 248.
17) OR Series, Volume XXXVII/2. Union Correspondences #18. J. W. Garrett. Page 440.
18) OR Series, Volume XXXVII/2. Union Correspondences #21. Gen Couch. Pages 515-516.
19) OR Series, Volume XLIII/1. Union Correspondences #2. Gen. Grant. Pages 710, 721.
20) OR Series, Volume XXXVII/2. Union Correspondence #15. A. A. G. Halpine. Pages 367-368.
21) OR Series, Volume XLIII/1. Union Correspondences. Col. Chipman. Page 792.
22) OR Series, Volume XLIII/1, No.1. General Philip Sheridan. Page 19.
23) OR Series, Volume XLIII/1, No.3. A. A. G Peabody to General Kenly. Page 628.
24) OR Series, Volume XLIII/1, No.5. Col. John S. Mosby. Pages 633-634.

25) OR Series, Volume XLIII/1, No.4. General Robert E. Lee. Page 633.
26) A History of Jefferson County West Virginia. M. K. Bushong. Heritage Books. Pages 172-173.
27) OR Series, Volume XXXVII/1, No.80. General Robert E. Lee. Page 346.
28) OR Series, Volume XXXVII/1, No.79. General Jubal Early. Page 5.

CHAPTER TWENTY-TWO

1) Mosby Memoirs. John S. Mosby. J. S. Sanders & Company. Pages 286, 298, 301-302.
2) Mosby's Rangers: Forty-Third Battalion Virginia Cavalry. James J. Williamson. Ralph B. Kenyon Publishing. Pages 213, 215, 222, 233.
3) Mosby's Fighting Parson. Peter A. Brown. Willow Publishing. Pages 209-210, 226-228.
4) Partisan Life With John S. Mosby. John Scott. Harper & Brothers Publishing. Pages 280-282, 304, 317-320.
5) 43rd Battalion Virginia Cavalry Mosby's Command. Keen & Mewborn. H. E. Howard. Pages 162-163, 172.
6) Reminiscences Of A Mosby Guerrilla. John Munson. Moffat, Yard And Company. Page 147.
7) Blue and Gray. Volume 17, Issue 6. "Mosby In The Shenandoah Valley." Page 40.
8) The Edge of Mosby's Sword. Gordon Bonan. Southern Illinois Press. Pages 124-125.
9) New York Times. August 25, 1864.
10) The Richmond Enquirer. September 1, 1864.
11) New York Times. August 19, 1864.
12) Valley News Echo. Volume 5, No. 8. August 1864.
13) Richmond Times. September 3, 1899.
14) Richmond Daily Dispatch. September 23, 1864.
15) Mosby and His Men. J. Marshall Crawford. G. W. Carleton & Company 1867. Page 258.
16) Southern Historical Society Papers. Volume 24. Richmond Daily Dispatch. March 1, 1864.
17) OR Series I, Volume XLIII/1. Union Correspondence #5. General Grant. Page 811.
18) OR Series I, Volume XLIII/1. Union Correspondence #7. Lt. Col. A. J. Forsyth. Page 831.
19) OR Series I, Volume XLIII/1. Union Correspondence #7. A. A. G. Taylor. Page 832.
20) OR Series I, Volume XLIII/1, No.2. Colonel Henry Gansevoort. Pages 617-618.
21) OR Series I, Volume XLIII/1, No.5. Lt. Col. John Mosby. Page 634.
22) OR Series I, Volume XLIII/1, No.5. General Robert E. Lee. Page 635.
23) OR Series I, Volume XLIII/1, No.172. General Lee to Secretary Seddon. Page 553.
24) OR Series I, Volume XLIII/1, No.135. General Wesley Merritt. Page 441.

25) OR Series I, Volume XLIII/1. Union Correspondence. General Sheridan. Page 822.
26) Under Custer's Command. James Henry Avery. Potomac. Pages 109-110.

CHAPTER TWENTY-THREE

1) Mosby Memoirs. John S. Mosby. J. S. Sanders & Company. Pages 312, 304, 306-308, 312-321, 326, 331.
2) Partisan Life With John S. Mosby. John Scott. Harper & Brothers Publishing. Pages 322, 324-325, 327, 336.
3) Mosby's Rangers: Forty-Third Battalion Virginia Cavalry. James J. Williamson. Ralph B. Kenyon Publishing. Pages 251, 254, 257-258, 263.
4) 43rd Battalion Virginia Cavalry Mosby's Command. Keen & Mewborn. H. E. Howard. Pages 189-190.
5) Mosby's Men. John Alexander. Neale Publishing Company. Pages 106, 108, 115.
6) Reminiscences Of A Mosby Guerrilla. John Munson. Moffat, Yard And Company. Pages 223, 225.
7) Mosby. Charles Thorne. Charles Thorne Publishing. Page 22.
8) Journal of Amanda Virginia Edmonds. Amanda Virginia Edmonds. October 6, 1864.
9) OR Series I, Volume XLIII/1. Union Correspondence #11. General Halleck. Pages 272- 273.
10) OR Series I, Volume XLIII/1. Union Correspondence #11. General Halleck. Page 267.
11) OR Series I, Volume XLIII/1. Union Correspondence #11. General Grant. Page 258.
12) OR Series I, Volume XLIII/1. Union Correspondence #14. General Halleck. Page348.
13) OR Series I, Volume XLIII/1. Union Correspondence #14. General Augur. Pages 334-335.
14) OR Series I, Volume XLIII/1. Union Correspondence #14. General Sheridan. Page 339.
15) OR Series I, Volume XLIII/1. Union Correspondence #15. General W. H. Seward. Page 360.
16) OR Series I, Volume XLIII/1. Union Correspondence #15. General Stevenson. Pages 368-369.
17) OR Series I, Volume XLIII/1. Union Correspondence #15. Secretary Stanton. Page 381.
18) OR Series I, Volume XLIII/1, No.4. General Robert E. Lee. Page 633.
19) OR Series I, Volume XLIII/1. Confederate Correspondence #3. General Lee. Page 920.
20) Philadelphia Inquirer. October 1864.
21) Valley News Echo. Volume 5, No.10. October 1864.
22) Richmond Daily Dispatch. October 10, 1864.
23) Richmond Daily Dispatch. October 18, 1864.

CHAPTER TWENTY-FOUR

1) Partisan Life With John S. Mosby. John Scott. Harper & Brothers Publishing. Pages 358-359.
2) Mosby's Men. John Alexander. Neale Publishing Company. Pages 142-144, 146-147.
3) Mosby's Rangers: Forty-Third Battalion Virginia Cavalry. James J. Williamson. Ralph B. Kenyon Publishing. Pages 288, 290, 294-295.
4) Mosby and His Men. J. Marshall Crawford. G. W. Carleton & Company 1867. Page 288.
5) Richmond Times. September 3, 1899.
6) John Mosby to Sam Chapman. August 26, 1899.
7) Blue and Gray. Volume 17, Issue 6. "Mosby In The Shenandoah Valley." Pages 44, 46.
8) OR Series I, Volume XLIII/1. Confederate Correspondence #3. Colonel John Mosby. Page 920.
9) OR Series I, Volume XLIII/1. Confederate Correspondence #3. Colonel Mosby. Pages 909-910.
10) OR Series I, Volume XLIII/1. Confederate Correspondence #3. General Lee. Page 910.
11) OR Series I, Volume XLIII/1. Confederate Correspondence #3. Secretary Seddon. Page 910.
12) OR Series I, Volume XLIII/1. Union Correspondence #6. General Sheridan. Page 822.
13) Southern Historical Society Papers. Volume XXVII. Richmond Times.12/8/1899.
14) The Official Records of The Union and Confederate Armies. Washington Government Printing Office. 1880.
15) Valley News Echo. Volume 5, No. 11. November 1864.

CHAPTER TWENTY-FIVE

1) Southern Historical Society Papers. Volume XXVII. John S. Mosby.
2) Personal Memoirs P. H. Sheridan. General P. H. Sheridan. Jenkins and McCowan. Page 99.
3) Civil War Times. Volume XIX, No. 7. Jeffery Wert. Pages 12, 18.
4) Mosby's Rangers. Jeffery Wert. Touchstone. Page 203.
5) Mosby's Fighting Parson. Peter A. Brown. Willow Publishing. Page 219.
6) The Life Of Colonel John S. Mosby. James A. Ramage. University of Kentucky Press. Pages 224-225.
7) Mosby's Men. John Alexander. Neale Publishing Company. Pages 120, 122-124, 126, 128.
8) Mosby's Rangers: Forty-Third Battalion Virginia Cavalry. James J. Williamson. Ralph B. Kenyon Publishing. Pages 302, 304-305.
9) OR Series I, Volume XLIII/1. Union Correspondence #2. General Sheridan. Pages 27-28.
10) OR Series I, Volume XLIII/1. Union Correspondence #26. Lt. Col. J. W. Forsyth. Page 648.

11) OR Series I, Volume XLIII/1. Union Correspondence #26. A. A. G. S. F. Adams. Page 648.
12) OR Series I, Volume XLIII/1, No.1. Captain Richard Blazer. Pages 615-616.
13) Journal of Amanda Virginia Edmonds. Amanda Virginia Edmonds. November 28, 1864.

Chapter Twenty-Six

1) 43rd Battalion Virginia Cavalry Mosby's Command. Keen & Mewborn. H. E. Howard. Pages 200, 226, 231, 350.
2) Personal Memoirs P. H. Sheridan. General P. H. Sheridan. Jenkins and McCowan. Pages 99-100.
3) Mosby's Rangers: Forty-Third Battalion Virginia Cavalry. James J. Williamson. Ralph B. Kenyon Publishing. Pages 322-323, 327.
4) The Life Of Colonel John S. Mosby. James A. Ramage. University of Kentucky Press. Page 236.
5) The Edge of Mosby's Sword. Gordon Bonan. Southern Illinois Press. Page 144.
6) War Reminiscences by the Surgeon of Mosby's Command. Aristides Monteiro. C. W. Williams Printer. Pages 13-14.
7) Mosby and His Men. J. Marshall Crawford. G. W. Carleton & Company 1867. Page 328.
8) Blue and Gray. Volume 17, Issue 4. "Mosby's Confederacy." Horace Mewborn. Page 45.
9) Mosby Memoirs. John S. Mosby. J. S. Sanders & Company. Pages 334-346.
10) Richmond Daily Dispatch. December 27, 1864.
11) Richmond Daily Dispatch. December 29, 1864.
12) Richmond Enquirer. December 24, 1864.
13) OR Series, Volume XLIII/1. Confederate Correspondence #4. Lt. Col. John S. Mosby. Page 937.
14) OR Series I, Volume XLIII/1. Union Correspondence #34. Col Gamble. Pages 831-832.
15) OR Series I, Volume XLIII/1. Union Correspondence #34. Ass. Adj. Gen. J. Taylor. Page 832.
16) OR Series I, Volume XLIII/1. Union Correspondence #34. Col H. Wells. Page 834.
17) OR Series I, Volume XLIII/1. Union Correspondence #34. Gen. John Stevenson. Page 838.
18) OR Series I, Volume XLIII/1. Union Correspondence #34. Gen. John Stevenson to Stanton Page 838.
19) OR Series I, Volume XLIII/1. Union Correspondence #34. Gen. Sheridan. Pages 838-839.
20) OR Series I, Volume XLIII/1. Union Correspondence #34. Maj. D. Frazar. Pages 843-844.
21) OR Series I, Volume XLIII/1. Union Correspondence #28. Gen. Sheridan. Pages 679-680.
22) OR Series I, Volume XLIII/1. Union Correspondence #29. Lt. E. Myers, ADC. Page 719.

23) OR Series I, Volume XLIII/1. Union Correspondence #30. Gen. Sheridan. Pages 730-731.

Chapter Twenty-Seven

1) Mosby's Rangers: Forty-Third Battalion Virginia Cavalry. James J. Williamson. Ralph B. Kenyon Publishing. Pages 340, 355-360.
2) Mosby Memoirs. John S. Mosby. J. S. Sanders & Company. Page 354, 375-376.
3) Partisan Life With John S. Mosby. John Scott. Harper & Brothers Publishing. Page 457.
4) 43rd Battalion Virginia Cavalry Mosby's Command. Keen & Mewborn. H. E. Howard. Page 242.
5) Mosby's Rangers. Jeffery Wert. Touchstone. Pages 273-274.
6) Mosby. Charles Thorne. Page 23.
7) Rebel Chronicles. Steve French. New Horizon Publishing. Page 232.
8) Mosby Heritage Association. "Who Was Mosby?"
9) Mosby and His Men. J. Marshall Crawford. G. W. Carleton & Company 1867. Page 331.
10) Mosby's Men. John Alexander. Neale Publishing Company. Pages 154-155.
11) Richmond Daily Dispatch. January 10, 1865.
12) Richmond Daily Dispatch. February 14, 1865.
13) OR Series I, Volume XLVI/3. Union Correspondence #4. Gen. W. Hancock. Page 82.
14) OR Series I, Volume XLVI/3. Union Correspondence #4. Colonel C. H. Morgan. Page 84.
15) OR Series I, Volume XLVI/3. Union Correspondence #4. Colonel. M. Reno. Page 85.
16) OR Series I, Volume XLVI/2. Union Correspondence #36. General John Stevenson. Page 898.
17) OR Series XLVI/1. No. 1. General W. S. Hancock. Page 526.

Chapter Twenty-Eight

1) Mosby Memoirs. John S. Mosby. J. S. Sanders & Company. Pages 356, 360-361, 371.
2) 43rd Battalion Virginia Cavalry Mosby's Command. Keen & Mewborn. H. E. Howard. Pages 259, 261, 264.
3) Bull Run To Bull Run. George Baylor. B. F. Johnson Publishing. Pages 310, 312.
4) Reminiscences Of A Mosby Guerrilla. John Munson. Moffat, Yard And Company. Pages 267-268, 271, 273.
5) Mosby and His Men. J. Marshall Crawford. G. W. Carleton & Company 1867. Pages 352-353, 365.
6) Partisan Life With John S. Mosby. John Scott. Harper & Brothers Publishing. Page 462.

7) War Reminiscences by the Surgeon of Mosby's Command. Aristides Monteiro. C. W. Williams Printer. Pages 149-150, 157-158, 174, 198, 205-206.
8) Mosby's Rangers. Jeffery Wert. Touchstone. Page 288.
9) Philadelphia Inquirer. April 10, 1865.
10) Philadelphia Inquirer. April 15, 1865.
11) Philadelphia Inquirer. April 24, 1865.
12) Journal of Amanda Virginia Edmonds. Amanda Virginia Edmonds. April 15, 1865.
13) Journal of Amanda Virginia Edmonds. Amanda Virginia Edmonds. April 17, 1865.
14) Journal of Amanda Virginia Edmonds. Amanda Virginia Edmonds. April 18, 1865.
15) OR Series I, Volume XLVI/2. Union Correspondence #28. Secretary of War Stanton. Page 683.
16) OR Series I, Volume XLVI/2. Union Correspondence #29. General C. H. Morgan. Page 714.
17) OR Series I, Volume XLVI/2. Union Correspondence #30. General Winfield Hancock. Page 725.
18) OR Series I, Volume XLVI/2. Union Correspondence #31. General C. H. Morgan. Page 750.
19) OR Series I, Volume XLVI/2. Union Correspondence #32. General Winfield Hancock. Pages 799-800.
20) OR Series I, Volume XLVI/2. Union Correspondence #34. General Winfield Hancock. Page 828.
21) OR Series I, Volume XLVI/2. Union Correspondence #34. General George Chapman. Pages 830-831.
22) OR Series I, Volume XLVI/2. Union Correspondence #34. General Winfield Hancock. Page 839.
23) OR Series I, Volume XLVI/2. Union Correspondence #34. Colonel C. H. Mitchell. Page 839.
24) OR Series I, Volume XLVI/2. Union Correspondence #35. Colonel C. H. Mitchell. Pages 869-870.
25) OR Series, Volume XLIII/1. Confederate Correspondence #4. Secretary of War John Breckinridge. Page 1389.
26) OR Series, Volume XLIII/1. Confederate Correspondence #4. Colonel John. S. Mosby. Page 1396.

Books by CW Whitehair

Sabers & Roses

Sabers & Roses takes place in Harpers Ferry. Follow the struggles and challenges of the Barker family while living on the front lines of the Civil War.

Northern Fire

Northern Fire is about the challenges and struggles of the Barker and McBride families following the Civil War.

Escape Across The Potomac

Follow the escape of 1,500 Federal cavalrymen from Harpers Ferry during the 1862 Maryland Campaign, and their capture of Confederate General James Longstreet's wagon train near Williamsport, Maryland.

Gettysburg: The Field Of Glory

Private Jonathan Russell from Loudoun County, Virginia narrates his war experiences while serving in Brigidier-General Robert Garnett's Brigade during the Gettysburg Campaign.

The Bloody Harvest

Jacob Martin is a Federal army spy involved in a world of espionage, deception, and romance. His adventures take him from Richmond, Virginia to the Battle of Antietam.

Libby Life

Libby Life is the journal of Lt. Col. Federic Fernandez Cavada. Cavada was the highest ranking Hispanic opfficer to serve in the Federal army during the Civil War. Follow his experiences from Gettysburg, Pennsylvania to confinement at Libby Prison in Richmond, Virginia.

CPSIA information can be obtained
at www.ICGtesting.com
Printed in the USA
FFOW03n0900200315
12026FF